# ON THE BASIS OF RACE

# On the Basis of Race

*How Higher Education Navigates*
*Affirmative Action Policies*

Lauren S. Foley

NEW YORK UNIVERSITY PRESS

*New York*

NEW YORK UNIVERSITY PRESS
New York
www.nyupress.org

© 2023 by New York University
All rights reserved

Library of Congress Cataloging-in-Publication Data
Names: Foley, Lauren S., author.
Title: On the basis of race : how higher education navigates affirmative action policies /
    Lauren S. Foley.
Description: New York : New York University Press, 2023. | Includes bibliographical
    references and index.
Identifiers: LCCN 2023019283 | ISBN 9781479821655 (hardcover) | ISBN 9781479821662
    (paperback) | ISBN 9781479821679 (ebook) | ISBN 9781479821686 (ebook other)
Subjects: LCSH: Affirmative action programs in education—United States. | Multicultural
    education—United States. | Higher education and state—United States. | Educational
    equalization—United States. | Discrimination in higher education—United States.
Classification: LCC LC213.52 .F65 2023 | DDC 379.2/60973—dc23/eng/20230607
LC record available at https://lccn.loc.gov/2023019283

Manufactured in the United States of America

10 9 8 7 6 5 4 3 2 1

Also available as an ebook

# CONTENTS

# AUTHOR'S NOTE

Over a decade ago, I began looking at the small number of states that ban affirmative action, asking how their universities persist in valuing racial diversity. As this book goes to press, that small number became the entire country. On June 29, 2023, the Supreme Court held that race-conscious university admissions affirmative action policies are unconstitutional and contrary to federal law in the *Students for Fair Admissions* cases brought against admissions policies at Harvard and the University of North Carolina, Chapel Hill. Going forward, the policies universities have innovated—as detailed in this book—will no doubt serve as templates for their peers nationwide in the wake of this decision. *On the Basis of Race* answers the question, "What will universities do next?"

*Students for Fair Admissions* overturns nearly fifty years of Supreme Court precedent repeatedly affirming race-conscious university admissions. In *Bakke* (1978) the Supreme Court ended the racial minority set-asides affirmative action program at the University of California, Davis, Medical School, but offered a path forward for universities practicing individualized consideration in admissions for the purpose of obtaining a diverse student body. Twenty-five years later in *Grutter* (2003) the Court affirmed that student body diversity in higher education was a compelling interest and upheld a narrowly tailored plan where race was one of many "plus factors" in a student's application. In the *Fisher* cases (2013 and 2016) the Court again affirmed that student racial diversity in the university community was a compelling interest that justified the use of race-conscious admissions policies. Breaking sharply and suddenly from its own precedent, the Supreme Court now holds that affirmative action in university admissions is not a constitutional use of race protected under the Fourteenth Amendment.

Traditional constitutional protection for public policies on the basis of race is gone. The *Students for Fair Admissions* consolidated opinion was written by Chief Justice John Roberts and joined by the five other conservative members of the Court. "The student must be treated based on his or her experience as an individual—not on the basis of race." This ban is sweeping and does not allow any justifications as a compelling interest for traditional affirmative action policies that used race as a factor in applicant admissions. However, this does not mean that race will be absent entirely from university admissions. The opinion explicitly noted that an applicant can "discuss[] how race affected his or her life, be it through discrimination, inspiration or otherwise." But the benefit to their application status cannot be from their racial identity alone. Rather, any admissions boost gained from a student's discussion of race must be tied to intangible personal characteristics, such as courage or the ability to lead. The majority opinion provides a few examples:

> A benefit to a student who overcame racial discrimination, for example, must be tied to *that student's* courage and determination. Or a benefit to a student whose heritage or culture motivated him or her to assume a leadership role or attain a particular goal must be tied to *that student's* unique ability to contribute to the university. [emphasis in original]

As discussed in this book, universities do—and will likely now expand—holistic or individualized evaluation processes to make best use of material like application essays or recommendation letters, which are now the only ways that race can enter the process.

We know that *Students for Fair Admissions* is a devastating blow for colleges and universities that prioritize student racial diversity. As discussed in the Conclusion, research on affirmative action demonstrates that race-conscious admissions policies are the most effective tool in creating a racially diverse student body. The scholarship across education, sociology, political science, and public policy is rather unequivocal on this point: banning affirmative action will result in decreased enrollment for students of color. What we do not know going forward is the extent to which this decision will further erode racial minority enrollment and success in higher education. What will be the impact of *Students for Fair Admissions* on targeted recruitment programs, scholarship awards, diversity and inclusion efforts, and student services and support on campus? If the decision is extended into these areas, it will further jeopardize the future of marginalized communities on college campuses, making it difficult for them to achieve their full potential.

For years to come, courts will be unpacking the effect of *Students for Fair Admissions*, as no doubt university policies in compliance will bring future legal challenges; for example, the use of affirmative action in military academies. In his majority opinion, Chief Justice Roberts exempted military academies from the ban on the use of race because of "potentially distinct interests." In prior affirmative action cases, the need for racial diversity and affirmative action in the military was a persuasive argument for justices to uphold the practices. In the early 2000s litigation, retired military generals filed an amicus brief asserting that they must use race-conscious recruitment and admissions at military academies in order to avoid a nearly all white officer corps. The brief played a prominent role in oral argument questioning, and sections of it were adopted in the *Grutter* opinion, which asserted that "to fulfill its mission" the military must have use of affirmative action. Perhaps Roberts's exemption in *Students for Fair Admissions* means there were five votes on the Court to let military academies continue to use affirmative action.

As the affirmative action chapter closes on university admissions, a new racial diversity chapter opens. What will be the constitutionality of resistant compliance policies? *On the Basis of Race* discusses policies with new technology, new review methods, and new state legislation in response to affirmative action bans. Universities will innovate on all of these methods, and others, to maintain their commitments to a racially diverse class. *On the Basis of Race* picks up where Justice Sotomayor's dissent in *Students for Fair Admissions* leaves off. Justice Sotomayor writes that "the pursuit of racial diversity will go on" through the use of "all available tools." Universities will comply with the holding, while resisting the decision by developing creative means to pursue racial diversity. This book explains how.

1

# Beyond the Letter of the Law

*Resistant Compliance in Racial Policy*

It was the fall of 2005, and undergraduate admissions director Chris Lucier thought the Michigan admissions office might be in for some trouble. The University of Michigan had spent the last decade in litigation over its use of affirmative action in admissions practices. In 2003, it had won at the Supreme Court. The process had been grueling for the university; it had spent millions on litigation, and all its top administrators and admissions directors had to withstand depositions. They cheered the victory in *Grutter v. Bollinger* that upheld the use of race in university admissions. Lucier and his colleagues could modify their policies and continue to use affirmative action to maintain a racially diverse student population at the University of Michigan.

Their elation, however, was short-lived. On July 8, 2003, only two weeks after losing the affirmative action challenge in *Grutter*, disappointed conservative activists took action. They had won the companion case, *Gratz v. Bollinger*, and therefore forced Michigan's Office of Undergraduate Admissions to modify the way it used race in its admissions process. But their goal was to ban affirmative action entirely. They rallied in the campus center of their most recent target and claimed the mantle of the civil rights movement. Their leader, Ward Connerly, proclaimed that universities denying white applicants "in the name of 'diversity' is a distinction without a difference in denying James Meredith access to Ole Miss because of his race."[1] Connerly stood alongside white plaintiffs in famous affirmative action cases—*Adarand Constructors v. Pena* (1995), *Gratz*, and *Grutter*—to launch the Michigan Civil Rights Initiative, a vote of the people to amend their state constitution. The decision to launch a ballot initiative paid off in 2006 when voters approved Proposal 2, amending Michigan's constitution and banning affirmative action.[2]

The ban on affirmative action was not unique to Michigan. Starting in the mid-1990s, multiple states implemented affirmative action bans, which were perceived to disadvantage certain elite state universities and benefit private peer institutions. By 2022, eight states were under complete bans on race-conscious affirmative action.[3] An appellate court banned affirmative action in Texas, Louisiana, and Mississippi in 1996, a ban that remained in effect until it was overruled by a Supreme Court decision in 2003.[4] In states with affirmative action bans, flagship state universities now had to comply with laws that did not apply to their private institutional peers.

Selective public universities perceive themselves as having the most to lose from affirmative action bans. Most public universities are not selective; they enroll students primarily from their own states. Some, however, are national universities, competing with elite private universities for the most academically high-achieving students from across the country. *Grutter* held that race-conscious polices were justified by a university's pedagogical interest in maintaining a diverse student population. After *Grutter*, universities could embrace affirmative action under the banner of diversity. States with bans backed public universities into a corner, preventing them from competing with their private institutional peers for the most highly credentialed students of color due to the prohibition on the primary strategy for enhancing racial diversity. How did administrators at these institutions respond to this challenge? How did flagship state universities continue their commitments to racial representation in the face of these putative total bans on race consciousness?

At the University of Michigan, the answer came from an unexpected place. By 2005, Lucier, admissions executive director Ted Spencer, and other high-level admissions officials—who referred to themselves as the A Team—saw the writing on the wall and feared that the ban on affirmative action would pass. They had been privately debating a solution.

At the same time that Ward Connerly and his anti–affirmative action organization were advancing the ballot initiative in Michigan, the College Board was shopping around new enrollment software. Its regional manager pitched a subscription to the lead officials at Michigan admissions, arguing that by using demographic data to analyze their applicant pool, admissions officers could bring in more full-paying students and consequently more tuition revenue. This software analyzed a complex set of demographic factors for every applicant, synthesizing what each one might be able to afford in higher education. Lucier saw something different. Technology might be the answer to maintaining racial diversity without using explicitly race-based criteria. With this software, the University of Michigan would manage to both comply with the looming affirmative action ban while also resisting the law by still prioritizing its institutional goal for a racially diverse student population.

The administrators and admissions officials at Michigan did not consider abandoning the university's commitment to racial diversity, but neither did they consider ignoring the law. In their minds, if Michigan passed a constitutional amendment, they would have no choice but to comply. What they sought was a way to do so without giving up on their goals. Their strategy was to repurpose the new enrollment software. Its targeting of socioeconomic demographic factors allowed Michigan to maintain racial diversity in its student population while complying with the letter of the law, because the software did not identify racial identity. In response to the ban, other elite universities similarly developed new policies that did not take race into account but allowed the institutions to maintain their commitments to racial diversity. These policies were created to accommodate both the law and institutional priorities, which were ostensibly opposed to one another. This book in part studies the policy innovations of the first responders to affirmative action bans, the Universities of California and Texas in 1996, and the most creative approach, the University of Michigan's use of technology.

Throughout American history, legal efforts to achieve racial equality have been met with various forms of resistance. These forms of resistance include not only the massive resistance of white supremacists who refused to comply with legal mandates for desegregation but also the ongoing efforts to implement affirmative action programs in higher education despite apparent bans in state legislation and plebiscites.[5] Separate from mass resistance are efforts to comply with the formal terms of the legal directive while refusing to comply with the evident purpose of the law. As I will explain in the chapters that follow, I call this dynamic "resistant compliance."

Resistant compliance is not a particular policy but a tool that policymakers can use. Across time, the people and the policy solutions have been dramatically different, but the method used in reaction to law is not dependent on time or ideology. Throughout American political history, complying in ways that resist has been a recurring pattern among both racially conservative and progressive social movements responding to legal mandates on race. One goal of this book is to demonstrate that contrary to the popular or conventional understanding, responses to legal mandates where race is concerned are remarkably similar, irrespective of the ideological position of the actors involved. That some actors are revered and some are reviled does not make their tools different. The same tool can build two very different projects.

A national ban on affirmative action may be on the horizon and with it the increasing use of resistant compliance. On October 31, 2022, the Supreme Court heard a challenge to race-conscious university admissions policies at Harvard and the University of North Carolina, Chapel Hill. The question of affirmative action in higher education that has now reached the court will encounter a very different bench from the last time it was reviewed in 2016. With the departures of Justices Ginsburg, Kennedy, and Breyer, the court majority that upheld race-conscious practices is no longer intact. The current nine-member court does not look favorable for university affirmative action policies. Justice Sotomayor upheld a university admissions affirmative action program in 2016, and Justice Kagan argued in favor of the practice as solicitor general.[6] However, even if Justice Jackson votes to uphold the policies, these are only three votes out of nine—far from a majority. Justices Roberts, Thomas, and Alito have all signed on to opinions that argued that the Fourteenth Amendment does not protect the practice.[7] Legal scholars and court-watcher journalists predict that the jurisprudence of the justices appointed by President Trump—Justices Gorsuch, Kavanaugh, and Barrett—may not protect affirmative action.[8] It is likely that six justices will hold that race-conscious university admissions policies violate the Constitution. If this happens, what will universities do next? To answer this question, this book looks at what universities have done in the past as a response to state bans.

## The National Landscape for Affirmative Action Bans

The commitment to racial diversity is a common mission throughout American higher education. These commitments are carried out by acknowledging and prioritizing applicants from underrepresented racial backgrounds in a university's admissions process. As of 2022, the Supreme Court permits affirmative action in higher education admissions nationally. However, eight states have state constitutions or statutes that ban the practice. Much of this book details the constitutional politics regarding the banning of affirmative action in the state under consideration. To contextualize these bans, this section details the development of the equal protection jurisprudence that currently permits the practice.

The goal of racial diversity in higher education is relatively new in American history. Throughout most of American history, universities perpetuated segregationist tactics. The historical form of admission to elite colleges and universities involved admissions preferences for—or outright bans on anyone other than—white Protestant men. Rogers Smith refers to this period as the era of ethno-nationalism and Jim Crow.[9] These discriminatory admissions policies, as Jerome Karabel shows, were used throughout American higher education.[10]

The story of the rise of affirmative action in universities is currently shifting in the literature on American politics and higher education. By the mid-twentieth century, university administrators were committed to the goal of a racially diverse student population. Scholars have traced the value of diversity in elite institutions to the beginning of the twentieth century, showing that it took hold more widely across higher education during the civil rights movement and the 1970s New Left.[11] The dominant explanation for higher education's embrace of affirmative action is that activist movements of primarily Black students demanded better representation in higher education and forced university leaders to stand up and take action.[12] New research, however, demonstrates that while on-campus movements did play a role, the story is not as simple as seems.[13]

This new research shows that race-conscious university admissions programs began to take root in the early 1960s as a response to the nonviolent civil rights movement protesting Jim Crow segregation across the South. Racially progressive college administrators were at the forefront of these changes. Michigan and UCLA were the first public universities to start race-conscious recruitment and admissions programs, both in 1964.[14] This finding not only helps us understand more precisely the arrival of the diversity imperative in higher education but also means that university policymaking was a moment of institutional change in the North as a result of civil rights protests in the South. Elite liberal arts colleges and public universities in the North and West implemented race-conscious admissions and recruitment programs as a way to expand equal opportunity on campus.

The affirmative action options for universities narrowed significantly in 1978 after the Supreme Court announced its decision in *Regents of the University of California v. Bakke*. Allan Bakke, an aspiring medical doctor, had sued the Medical School of the University of California, Davis, after his application was denied for the second time. Bakke was aided in assembling his case and finding a lawyer by Marco DeFunis, the plaintiff in a then-pending lawsuit over the University of Washington Law School's affirmative action policies.[15] Bakke, a white man, argued that the university had discriminated against him because of his race when it administered its "special admissions program."[16] In this program, a committee reviewed the applications from "economically and/or educationally disadvantaged" members of a "minority group (blacks, Chicanos, Asians, American Indians)" and reserved sixteen spots of the entering class of one hundred for students from this population.[17] Candidates for special admissions did not have to meet the same grade-point averages as the other applicants and were not evaluated against them.

The constitutional path for university affirmative action was now tenuous, as the opinions in *Bakke* were not straightforward. Four of the court's more conservative justices—Justices Stevens, Stewart, and Rehnquist and Chief Justice Burger—not only thought the University of California, Davis, Medical School's process of setting aside seats for disadvantaged racial minorities violated the law but also doubted that race could ever be a permissible consideration.[18] Four of the court's more traditionally liberal justices—Justices Brennan, Marshall, White, and Blackmun—felt that the Medical School's set-asides were a constitutional use of race and that universities could use race in admissions to remedy past discrimination.[19] This left Justice Powell's fifth vote to decide whether universities were going to have a way forward on race-conscious affirmative action.

Justice Powell's opinion left an opening for universities to continue considering race in their admissions policies. While he did not agree with the more expansive interpretation of the court's liberals, Powell still saw a justification that universities could offer in the use of race—"the goal of a heterogenous student body." He wrote:

> An otherwise qualified medical student with a particular background—whether it be ethnic, geographic, culturally advantaged or disadvantaged—may bring to a professional school of medicine experiences, outlooks, and ideas that enrich the training of its student body and better equip its graduates to render with understanding their vital service to humanity.[20]

The court's conservatives concurred in the judgment with Powell and struck the Medical School's quota program. But the Powell opinion offered a way for universities to justify explicit consideration of race: citing the interest of advancing student body diversity.

The Equal Protection Clause of the Fourteenth Amendment is generally understood to prohibit the government from differentiating people on the basis of their race. For public policies to be race conscious, then, they must be carefully designed to achieve a compelling public purpose. Justice Powell's opinion in *Bakke* had determined that a compelling purpose for affirmative action could be a university's judgment that a diverse student population enhances the educational and experiential benefits of that university's academic program.[21] Accordingly, universities quickly pivoted away from justifying race-conscious policies by reference to historical patterns of discrimination against racial minorities in the United States and began to emphasize the compelling educational interest universities have in educating students within a diverse student population.

Public universities across the country supported the diversity rationale in their amicus briefs in *Bakke*. After the decision supported the compelling interest of diversity as a justification for race-conscious practices, universities framed their policies around reciting the language and parameters of the Powell opinion.[22] This approach caused a rift between university officials and civil rights activists. Higher education administrators were aligned around complying with *Bakke* and embraced the diversity justification, but civil rights activists did not want to abandon the argument that past discrimination should also justify affirmative action practices, notwithstanding the contrary ruling of the *Bakke* court.[23] Scholars, too, critiqued the diversity rationale in favor of past discrimination arguments for affirmative action.[24]

The Powell opinion in *Bakke* left one narrow path for universities practicing affirmative action. They could look at multiple components of applicants' backgrounds in a review process and justify race consciousness as a way to achieve the goal of student body diversity. The

Supreme Court in the 1980s and 1990s did not issue another affirmative action in higher education opinion, but it signaled a wariness of policies that looked at race, regardless of the intent behind them. *Richmond v. J.A. Croson Co.* (1989) and *Adarand Constructors Inc. v. Pena* (1995), both of which addressed employment rather than education, held that affirmative action policies were subject to strict scrutiny.[25] Strict scrutiny was the most stringent and searching level of review a court could use. Judges looked skeptically at state action under strict scrutiny and rarely found the laws at issue constitutional. Invidious discrimination policies—policies meant to oppress one group of people—received strict scrutiny. *Croson* and *Adarand* seemed to confirm what *Bakke* indicated: the benign use of race would also be subject to the court's strictest, most searching form of scrutiny.

*Bakke* carved a path for universities through strict scrutiny. Elite public universities across the country oriented their policies around the language and parameters of the Powell opinion in *Bakke*, both in terms of the heterogeneous factors that could be given weight in the admissions process and in the justification that would support it—diversity as a compelling interest in higher education.[26]

Twenty-five years after *Bakke*, the Supreme Court issued two opinions on the same day that reaffirmed the core principles and holding of Powell's *Bakke* opinion.[27] *Gratz v. Bollinger* (2003) struck down the University of Michigan's points-based undergraduate admissions program as unconstitutional, and *Grutter v. Bollinger* (2003) upheld the University of Michigan Law School's holistic admissions program. Justice O'Connor supplied the critical swing vote in the University of Michigan cases, joining the court's more liberal justices to uphold the Law School's holistic admissions program in *Grutter* and siding with the court's conservatives in striking down the points-based undergraduate admissions program in *Gratz*.[28]

Affirmative action survived in *Grutter* through the University of Michigan Law School admissions plan, which qualitatively considered many factors of a student's application. The Law School's admissions process considered a student's academic credentials together with personal statements, recommendation letters, and background and life experiences, as well as underrepresented racial identities. Following Powell in *Bakke*, the *Grutter* majority appreciated that this was "a highly individualized, holistic review" that entailed "serious consideration to all the ways an applicant might contribute to a diverse educational environment."[29] Writing the majority opinion in *Grutter*, O'Connor relied extensively on the admissions methodology—called "individualized consideration"—and found that it "[bore] the hallmarks of a narrowly tailored plan."[30]

The admissions system that did not survive in *Gratz* was known as the "points system." By 1998, when the litigation began, the Michigan undergraduate admissions system assigned varying point totals for factors of an application, including alumni ties, having an outstanding essay, being an in-state student, being a student of interest to the provost, or having an underrepresented racial background. The twenty-point assignment for underrepresented racial background was the largest by a wide margin for any one factor of an application, outside academics.[31] The system was transparent and capable of being administered by all admissions readers. O'Connor used the first sentence of her concurring opinion in *Gratz* to highlight why she favored one plan and not the other; she contrasted individualized consideration with the Michigan undergraduate policy and noted that "unlike the law school admission policy . . . the procedures employed by [Michigan undergraduate admissions] do not provide for a meaningful individualized review of applicants."[32]

The *Grutter* majority also cemented the compelling interest of student body diversity as a justification for race-conscious policies. O'Connor's majority opinion in *Grutter* made it clear that the court's holding not only supported student body diversity as a compelling interest but also established that it must be present in sufficient numbers to achieve this interest.[33] However, like Powell's opinion in *Bakke*, the *Grutter* majority emphasized a broad conception of diversity that included characteristics beyond race.[34]

In certain respects, the Michigan cases did not produce a clear victory for any position on affirmative action. While university affirmative action policies survived this round of challenges, they did not emerge without some bruising. From *Grutter*, universities received holistic admissions, an imprecise, expensive tool. Additionally, individualized means are less transparent; therefore, it became more difficult to monitor how institutions arrived at these decisions.[35] Conservatives did not win the fatal race-conscious blow that they sought, and the new holistic standard would mean a harder time in the discovery process during future litigation to uncover potential wrongdoing. *Grutter* remains the standard in higher education for most of the country. However, states with bans on affirmative action limit university action and produce a constrained environment for universities to prioritize racial diversity.

## Resistant Compliance

Scholarship has documented in great detail the mass resistance of white supremacists to civil rights mandates.[36] These efforts ranged from southern governments that trumpeted their refusal to follow the law in the 1956 "Declaration of Constitutional Principles" (the so-called Southern Manifesto) to the extralegal forms of violence and intimidation carried out by the Ku Klux Klan. White supremacists repeatedly refused to comply with legal mandates that were meant to guarantee Black people access to the ballot, service on juries, and desegregation in public schools, restaurants, hotels, parks, beaches, and so on. These forms of overt hostility are not the only forms of resistance. Officials and organizations, conservative and progressive, can also maneuver quietly and out of sight to evade legal requirements. Scholarship has documented this phenomenon in universities that ignore legal mandates to end speech codes and school districts that continue to sponsor school prayer.[37]

My interest is in resistance that takes the form of compliance. Beyond refusals to follow the law, legal and political science scholars have not adequately addressed the ways some institutions and organizations create compliance policies that resist clear, unqualified legal prohibitions. Unlike mass resistance, resistant compliance involves respect for the law to the extent that the law is neither disregarded nor disobeyed. Through the same institutional or organizational response, the law is both followed and frustrated. On a spring day in 2005, Lucier, Spencer, and others at Michigan admissions purchased the new technology software because with it, they hoped, the university could maintain racial diversity while still complying with an affirmative action ban.

This book examines the dynamic of resistant compliance in part by analyzing the responses of leading public universities to affirmative action bans implemented in their states. This study illuminates part of a broader dynamic in racial politics throughout contemporary US history. The understudied story of American racial politics is legally creative. Academic institutions, like other organizations and actors, have resisted racial policies and legal mandates with which they strongly disagree while also bringing their policies into compliance with the language of the law. Finding ways to resist while complying is one mode of policymaking based on race, a strategy wielded by actors ranging from Jim Crow white supremacists to racially egalitarian progressives in the twenty-first century.

I argue that creative responses to legal directives are a recurring and defining feature of American racial politics. Institutions responding to racial legal mandates use a policymaking tool as a political response—both resisting and complying with the law as a way to protect preferred positions about racial equality. This book shows how policymakers and institutional actors practice resistant compliance and examines the mechanics of the policies they follow. Once we understand this process, we can see how resistant compliance mediates law's impact on society.

## Legal Conflict over Fundamental Norms in Racial Policymaking

This book joins the literature in American political and constitutional development in highlighting a characteristic of racial policymaking. Our

American public policy process offers multiple opportunities for parties to battle over policy adoption and implementation, including clear legal mandates, and over many different kinds of policies. Resistant compliance may not be confined to public policy battles over race, but it is particularly characteristic of contests over racial policymaking.

American civic life is defined by lawyer-dominated, adversarial politics. Throughout the American policy process, there are multiple moments in which stakeholders can contest the breadth of policy choices, including their implementation. In his famous articulation of the topic, *Adversarial Legalism*, Robert Kagan defines this system as a "method of policymaking and dispute resolution [characterized] by formal legal contestation . . . and litigant activism."[38] Kagan grapples with the shortcomings of this system, which "is an extremely inefficient and hence often unfair way of meeting the public's demand of justice and protection."[39] He devotes a conclusion to reform proposals for limiting its impact.

Our public policy process, it seems, takes for granted that it will be reviewed by the courts. Ordinary politics relies on legal process and is structured by legal language. In *Law's Allure*, Gordon Silverstein argues that beyond "traditional methods of politics—organizing, electioneering, negotiating, and bargaining," we have a "lawlike" approach to public policy, with formalized procedures and legalized language.[40] Silverstein takes us through the myriad causes and consequences of this legalized system of public policy, not the least being that it is alluring in its promise of a policy "win." Courts call to plaintiffs, offering the mirage of a decisive answer.[41]

But "litigant activism" is also responsible for social change. Charles Epp argues that lawsuits brought to enforce constitutional rights, when coupled with a proper support structure for bringing claims, disrupt unjust systems of power.[42] Megan Francis demonstrates that courts were the only resort for basic due process criminal protections in the early American civil rights movement, and Malcolm Feeley and Edward Rubin explain that judicial policymaking brought about reforms in prison conditions.[43] Litigation need not be highly visible and politically contentious—in fact, Alison Gash demonstrates that the reverse may be more effective at securing certain rights.[44] While court resolution may not be sufficient to secure social policy change, the threat of it can bring around resistant organizations.[45] Charles Epp, for instance, argues that fear of litigation has produced "legalized accountability" in local governments.[46]

Our public policy process, then, is structured around an adversarial system, with legalized language and formal procedures, where litigants feature prominently as the main actors in implementation. But the focus on lawyers misses the important ways less-traditional actors can shape and challenge implementation. Public officials in organizations targeted by law respond with policy changes that can heighten law's impact or gut its purpose.

Of course, the recognition that individuals and institutions occasionally respond to certain laws with something less than either outright resistance or full compliance is not new. Businesses try to minimize the impact of law all the time. In *Impact*, a scholarship round-up of forms of compliance, Lawrence Friedman terms these behaviors "adjustment."[47] Reactions of adjustment are still oriented to the law. Indeed, they pay close attention to its perceived limits. The goal is "to get as close to illegality as you can without falling over the cliff."[48] Adjustment can be a business tactic, employing creative accountants as a way to preserve the corporate bottom line.[49] Firms defy the law's intent and exploit ambiguity in language while the state responds by providing more specificity and closing loopholes.[50] In reverse, narrow and rigid interpretation of legal requirements can be a protest tactic. Scholars have looked at how organized groups of citizens use full compliance as a form of resistance, such as organizing mass driving at newly reduced highway speed limits to highlight their inefficiency or "work-to-rule" striking teachers giving up typically expected but voluntary service activities.[51]

Local public officials, such as school district superintendents and public university presidents, shape the implementation of social policy, especially when it comes to racial politics. Political contestation of the implementation of racial policies is a particularly deeply rooted and sustained tradition. This book asks how and to what extent egalitarian principles are realized in public policies that involve questions of racial equality and equity. It builds on a literature that establishes racial hierarchy as the fundamental point of diversion in American politics and public policy.[52] Desmond King and Rogers Smith argue that "the nation has been pervasively constituted by systems of racial hierarchy since its inception."[53] Political coalitions are formed and public policies frustrated in the service of institutional racial orders in American politics. The literature on racial policy highlights how actors have tried to resist these policy changes. Paul Frymer, for instance, documents union resistance to integration and the institutional changes to the judicial branch that unexpectedly allowed it to thwart this resistance.[54]

But resistant compliance is a distinct strategy of resistance. It involves hewing closely to what is necessary to comply without giving up organizational priorities. This phenomenon is barely acknowledged in conversations within American political development about race policy, and it has not yet been theorized. And yet resistant compliance is not only a distinct form of policymaking response, separate from mass resistance, but also a defining feature of the implementation of the American civil rights agenda. In this book, I theorize this form of policymaking as a conflict over fundamental legal norms. As policymakers have responded to racial legal mandates, it has come to constitute a significant feature of American political development.

## Ideas and Legal Impact

Resistant compliance is not a response used only by those attempting to resist racially progressive policy goals. Racial progressives also use similar responses to achieve their own radically different ends. This book integrates this known behavior into a wider theory about legal impact and resistance to fundamental norms that is not dependent on any one idea about race. To do so, it compares the mid-twentieth-century responses of segregationists to the developing mandates after *Brown* with the late-twentieth century responses of racially progressive university admissions administrators to the bans on affirmative action.

The legal language "on the basis of race" has restrained wildly divergent actors with deeply opposed practices. *Brown* mandated that school districts across the country end any legal requirements to separate schoolchildren by race. The court was succinct on this point: "Does segregation of children in public schools solely on the basis of race . . . deprive the children of the minority group of equal educational opportunities? We believe that it does."[55] Plaintiffs then brought lawsuits around the country seeking to desegregate public school districts. As chapter 2 shows, Oklahoma City in the 1960s was no exception. The school district initially made no policy change, continuing effectively to segregate schools on the basis of race. However, once the district court entered a desegregation order in *Dowell v. School Board of Oklahoma City Public Schools* (1963), the Oklahoma City Board of Education was caught between the pro-segregation political forces in the white community and the law of the United States.

Four decades later, state constitutional amendments and federal court opinions required universities to end admissions policies that acted "on the basis of race." In 1996, the Fifth Circuit applied the Fourteenth Amendment in *Hopwood v. Texas* and found that "the classification of persons on the basis of race for the purpose of diversity frustrates . . . the goals of equal protection."[56] Ballot initiative campaigns that amended state constitutions used similar language and modeled themselves on the Civil Rights Act of 1964. In 1996, the California constitution was amended to read, "The state shall not discriminate against, or grant preferential treatment to, any individual . . . on the basis of race."[57] In 2006, voters amended the Michigan constitution with the same language, banning "preferential treatment to any individual . . . on the basis of race."[58]

To be sure, there are many reasons not to equate resistance to school desegregation with resistance to affirmative action bans. Policy responses to *Brown* were motivated by white supremacist animus, the desire to *harm* and subordinate a group of people in all contexts and through all means, including violence. Affirmative action, in contrast, is a race-conscious program in higher education admissions intended to *benefit* members of racial minority groups.[59] Indeed, "colorblind" conservatives pushing nondiscrimination laws have an agenda that differs starkly from the nondiscrimination mandate in *Brown* aimed at redressing the supposed harm inflicted on white people by racially progressive policies.[60] Other scholarship has argued that the "colorblind" conservatives behind bans on affirmative action are perpetuating an ascriptive ideology and a racially hierarchical political agenda.[61]

The contestation over racial politics in American political life plays out through battles regarding citizenship and inclusion that reflect our deepest divisions over who we want to be as a people. Throughout American political life, complying in ways that resist has been a recurring pattern among both racially conservative and progressive social movements responding to legal mandates on race. Groups with antithetical ends, such as racial progressives looking to expand opportunities for people of color and racial conservatives who want to limit opportunities, encountered the same legal language banning their practices. As this book illustrates, they also used very similar means to achieve their goals. The practice of resistant compliance to racial public policies is not dependent on ideology.

## Bridging American Political Development and Law-in-Action

The core thesis of resistant compliance offers a broad theory of legal conflict in racial policymaking that serves as a bridge between American political development and the literature on law-in-action. From American political development, we know that racial hierarchy is a fundamental and persistent divide in American politics.[62] Law-in-action asks us to closely investigate how organizations perpetuate and constitute rights practices. Much of this literature studies rights practices in response to ambiguous legal mandates. I argue, however, that working around the law does not require that the law be ambiguous. In racial politics, a predominant organizational feature is a pattern of practices that comply with legal mandates that ban the organization's preferred methods of pursuing its goals. Throughout the history of civil rights in the United States, actors have devised ways to resist while complying.

The book joins other scholarship that pushes back against accounts that argue any policy change in response to law is progress, and it expands the literature to cover cases where legal ambiguity is absent. Recent work in political science and sociology focuses on the progress made after civil rights legislation and judges civil rights laws as successful when businesses and governments respond to these laws by changing their policies. Frank Dobbin, for instance, looks at the role of personnel professions in promoting their importance within the organization by making a play for increased attention to law.[63] Charles Epp argues that activists from the outside move inside an organization, promote better compliance policies, and effectively "make rights real."[64] John Skrentny explores how quickly race-conscious affirmative action policies took hold as the answer to equal opportunity legislation and "ironically" how these policies were championed by white, male Republicans and initially avoided by civil rights leaders.[65] These accounts all share the understanding that policies created in compliance with civil rights laws are evidence of progress made toward civil rights.

We cannot assume, however, that just because an organization does not openly resist a legal mandate, its compliance policies will substantively advance the legal ideals that the law purports to champion. In recent decades, the law-in-action literature has developed our understanding of how organizations limit and shape legal impact. Lauren Edelman finds that corporate civil rights policies do not advance the substance of the laws they are written to comply with. These policies give a "cosmetic" appearance of compliance that distracts judges even as numerous practices perpetuate inequality: managers ignore the policies, the fair governance on the books does not match the daily corporate experience, diversity training programs do not result in diversity.[66] Edelman argues persuasively that these corporations create legal meaning—and blunt the impact of civil rights laws—when courts and judges look to their compliance policies as the standards against which to judge compliance with civil rights laws.

We know that where the law is ambiguous, corporate incentives dictate the law's impact, whether in favor of expanding or minimizing the legal ideals. All the scholarly accounts of corporations responding to civil rights laws include cases where the law at issue was an ambiguous mandate of what was required of the targeted employers, such as the Americans with Disabilities Act, the Civil Rights Act of 1964, judicial precedent on Title VII and sexual harassment, compliance with federal affirmative action orders in contracting, and judicial precedent on police brutality.[67] But what about cases where constitutional amendments and judicial opinions directly ban a prior form of racial policy? Overwhelmingly, scholarly discussion of institutional response in these situations has been preoccupied with legal ambiguity and overt resistance.

This book breaks new ground in showing that resistant compliance does not depend on ambiguous legal language. Scholars have documented that in the face of ambiguous legal standards, corporations insert their own interests into their compliance policies.[68] But in one example from contemporary policymaking, affirmative action is the subject of clear, unambiguous legal directives. The universities in these jurisdictions did not need to ask what kind of race-conscious action, justified by what interests, the law might allow. These laws were intended to permit none. Yet clear, unqualified bans do not impact behavior in straightforward ways. Even when reformers seek and receive a judicial opinion or constitutional amendment that uses their ideal language on race, organizations still have tools with which to resist it. What the law requires is still open to influence by the organizations targeted by its mandate. We cannot assume that ambiguous legal language is what makes it possible to defy law or shirk it. A broad range of compliance responses are still possible even without ambiguity. Organizations can practice resistance via their compliance with clear legal mandates.

Resistant compliance is also practiced by organizations maneuvering to comply with law under an intense spotlight. In racial policy, compliance policies are frequently subjected to Freedom of Information Act tactics (FOIA'ed in common parlance) by social movements looking to sue and are documented by judges implementing their own court orders. These are not organizations that operate out of sight and away from litigant activism. They use resistant compliance not to avoid attention but to escape penalties when they know litigation is looming.

This book studies public actors who want to pursue practices that are out of step with the legal regime on race. *Brown* and its progeny set forth a legal requirement of nondiscrimination in school assignment, replacing the former ascriptive standard that perpetuated a "separate but equal" caste system. School districts like Oklahoma City, inured to the racism of Jim Crow, responded defiantly and recalcitrantly to the new regime. Similarly, constitutional amendments that prohibited the use of race in state policymaking were nondiscrimination legal standards, what John Skrentny has called "classical liberalism" in race policy. These anti–affirmative action bans were imposed on resistant public universities that remained attached to the old way of doing things, namely using race-conscious admissions policies, a legal standard Skrentny terms "affirmative-action liberalism."[69] The law had changed; how would these institutions respond?

In the arena of public policy and race politics, the law on the books frequently does not match what occurs in the everyday world. In *After Civil Rights*, Skrentny finds racial realism in the American workplace— while the law as written is formally neutral toward race, the workplace is race conscious with the aim of advancing what is good for business.[70] Skrentny demonstrates why race matters in the workplace when the law says it should not; employers and politicians want it to matter because they believe it will increase the effectiveness of their business or political brand. Similarly, in this book's study of resistant compliance, ideological commitments, of both the progressive and the ascriptive kind, make race matter when the law says it should not.

How do organizations operate when their goals are at odds with the governing legal regime? Here is where the business world and higher education part ways. Employers have little guidance on diversity management practices because their racial realism has rarely been challenged in court. One reason is "the difficulty and expense of litigation" over the statutory schemes regulating the use of race in employment. Skrentny's interviews with conservative litigation firms confirm this finding; in litigation, "the regulatory state will eat you alive," argues the head of the Center for Individual Rights. "That it's harder to bring these cases helps explain why there are not more of them," argues the head of the Center for Equal Opportunity.[71]

But the same is not true in all areas in which policies regarding race are implemented. Indeed, both of the organizations Skrentny cites as reluctant to litigate in the business world have been active in suing universities over affirmative action policies. The Center for Individual Rights successfully pushed "colorblind" racial conservatism on the University of Texas in its *Hopwood* challenge and also curtailed affirmative action policies at the University of Michigan in *Grutter*. Roger Clegg and the Center for Equal Opportunity were also heavily involved in the Michigan cases, providing counsel and amicus briefing support.[72]

How, then, do organizations persist in the practices they find good for business or good for education when there is a legal support structure shining a bright light on any violation? Employers in the corporate workplace and entertainment industry were too skittish to talk directly to Skrentny about the role of race in the workplace, but none felt an imminent legal threat or were crafting practices in the wake of an ongoing legal challenge. They would likely have felt differently had they been in education, where historically universities' admissions policies and school districts' integration policies are all crafted with an eye toward a recent legal challenge. As this book shows, universities in the late twentieth century and school districts in the mid-twentieth century were engaged in constitutional political contests.

Organizations practicing resistant compliance are up to date with the governing legal regime; they know it and structure their practices around it. That mid-twentieth century school districts sought ways to insulate segregation and that late-twentieth century universities acted creatively to maintain racial diversity suggests not that law is out of date but simply that it is limited in its ability to control the full measure of compliance or legal impact.

This book demonstrates that clear, unqualified legal mandates do not change the goals of targeted organizations. Across varying political ideologies, federal courts have not disabused defendants of their goals with respect to race. Voters passing constitutional amendments do not dissuade targeted organizations from their missions. When targeted by restrictive legal mandates, both champions of ascriptive racial orders and progressive racial egalitarian ideals comply with the language of the law while continuing to pursue their racial commitments.

Scholarship on American racial politics has established that segregationists frustrated civil rights mandates with a form of resistance that was excessively technical, deliberately sluggish, and crafted around being ineffective.[73] But while American political development scholarship acknowledges what Richard Valelly terms "formal legal resistance," it does not theorize its pervasiveness nor comparatively assess it across ideologies.[74] And where law-in-action scholarship recognizes what Lauren Edelman terms "cosmetic compliance," it does so assuming that legal ambiguity in the mandate's language is what allows for shirking in policymaking or creatively avoiding stringent implementation.[75] Resistant compliance is present as a response to clear legal mandates, is not dependent on ideology, and once theorized, it should be an important part of our conversations regarding how organizations may (and sometimes do) effectually limit the impact of law.

Outline of the Book

In racial policymaking, actors comply with law by abandoning newly prohibited practices and resist the law by creatively adopting new means to pursue their continued commitments. As the following chapters will detail, legal mandates that ban racial practices narrow or close off options for targeted organizations. The targets respond by pivoting their practices, not by abandoning them; a school district abandoned de jure segregation after *Brown*, and universities abandoned the practice of giving admissions preference to underrepresented racial minorities after the affirmative action bans. Actors targeted by law resist its spirit by adopting creative new policies that allow them to pursue their goals. As this book shows, their strategies include slow-walking enforcement through legal maneuvering to prolong delays and compliant policy creation with no implementation plan (chapter 2), relying on known demographic patterns to produce certain outcomes with new policies (chapter 3), expanding criteria to approximate old policy outcomes (chapter 4), and repurposing new technology (chapter 5).

The familiar story of mass resistance to *Brown* is one of judicial abdication followed by extralegal violence and terror displacing constitutional protection. Governors refused entry to students, white mobs antagonized young children, and politicians declared in the Southern Manifesto that the Supreme Court's precedent was not constitutional and did not have jurisdiction over local actions. We are familiar with the images that dominated national media, such as mobs threatening schoolchildren, like six-year-old Ruby Bridges being escorted by federal marshals, or governors blocking school entrances, like Governor George Wallace and his "Segregation Forever" speech, or protests confronting busing in the North, like the infamous image "The Soiling of Old Glory" from protests in response to court-ordered busing in Boston. Indeed, political science scholarship on the futility of courts in school change uses resistance to *Brown* as its main analytical lens.[76] But just as the familiar story oversimplifies our understanding of the historical and doctrinal implementation of the Reconstruction jurisprudence, existing scholarship oversimplifies the varieties of organizational responses to legal mandates.[77]

Resistant compliance was also a tool of political institutions in the wake of *Brown*. Local and state governments regulated primary and secondary schools with policies that had the effect of separating Black and white schoolchildren. The Supreme Court even labored to uphold these efforts, lest the racially moderate political efforts lose out to the widespread refusal to comply.[78] Across the South, school districts sought to play for time by slow-walking *Brown*, forcing the NAACP to bring individual cases to secure court orders by district. Districts did the minimum possible, claiming compliance, and forced plaintiffs to continue to keep desegregation attempts in the federal courts, such as the nineteen years of litigation that ended in *Board of Education of Oklahoma City v. Dowell* (1991). Chapter 2 examines archival material on government officials and contemporaneous media reporting to explore how the Oklahoma City Board of Education professed compliance while worked in resistance to protect racial exclusion in its responses to *Brown*. The school district created policies with no plans to implement them, exhausted appeals and legal maneuvers to prolong delays, and trumpeted superficial adjustments that did not alter the underlying policy outcomes. Here, resistant compliance was a short-term strategy, consisting of patching together compliance responses that kept the court at bay and still resisted integration.

The second empirical section of the book flips the ideology of the actors and explores how progressive university officials contested state constitutional amendments and enacted bans meant to limit race-conscious policies in university admissions. Case studies of three elite public universities unpack the relationship between complying with a ban on race-conscious practices and resisting its mandate to pursue university priorities. These chapters draw on appellate and Supreme Court cases on affirmative action, archival material on university policymaking, and extensive interviews of admissions administrators responding to late twentieth and early twenty-first-century state constitutional bans. Chapter 3 begins with a judicial ban on affirmative action, *Hopwood*, which impacted the policies at the University of Texas, Austin. At Texas, university faculty came together with Democratic state legislators to comply with the legal mandate through a race-neutral policy solution that also preserved racial diversity in university student populations across Texas. The result of their efforts, Texas House Bill 588, the so-called Top Ten Percent law, relied on the segregated nature of Texas high schools to project that admitting the top 10 percent of every high school class would capture broad racial diversity. The policy navigated its way through the state legislature aided by its beneficial impact on geographic diversity; conservative, rural Texas legislators saw opportunities here for their constituencies.

Racial policymaking is also the target of state constitutional politics. Starting in the late twentieth century, "colorblind" conservatives succeeded in ballot initiative campaigns to amend state constitutions and ban affirmative action. Chapter 4 traces the University of California's response to bans on its race-conscious admission policies. The heads of the UC system altered the admissions thresholds and created geography-specific policies with the goal of maintaining a racially diverse student population. The flagship institution, Berkeley, implemented a resource-intensive application reading process that broadened the definition of merit for admissions consideration. Across the UC system, administrative policymakers narrowly interpreted the law in their compliance and removed race from their process. They resisted the spirit of the law in their continued commitments to racial diversity and expanded categories of admissions merit that bolstered the applications of students from diverse backgrounds and underrepresented racial communities.

That the opposition is carefully monitoring policy changes does not limit an organization's ability to resist clear legal mandates. As chapter 5 details, the University of Michigan spent a decade under an affirmative action spotlight before practicing resistant compliance to the state's anti–affirmative action constitutional amendment. After winning litigation challenges to its affirmative action policies, the university's re-prieve proved short-lived when "colorblind" conservatives mobilized a state constitutional amendment three years later. FOIA'ed annually for its admissions policies and data, the university found solutions to its racial diversity commitments by repurposing technology pitched to it as a marketing tool. It kept its policies race-neutral through broad applica-tion of this technology.

The book concludes by considering the normative implications of resistant compliance for race. Conservative challenges to affirmative action have arrived at a Supreme Court that looks very different from the last one that reviewed, and upheld, university affirmative action. If these challenges succeed, universities will be able to use resistant com-pliance as a tool to meet the requirements of the law and still continue their commitments. Understanding the range of resistant compliance responses helps us contextualizes future Supreme Court action as we try to make sense of law's ability to effect social change.

This book also considers the role of universities in constitutional politics and development. These institutions are actors that shape con-stitutional meaning by engaging with new amendments and affecting their reach. As public actors, they create public policy. As sites of social movements, they agitate for new understandings of what law requires. As such, universities operate in politically meaningful ways that are ne-glected in current conversations within American political and constitu-tional development. Universities practicing resistant compliance give us a better understanding of how these actors prioritize their institutional commitments in policymaking and consequently shape the impact of the law and the meaning of the Constitution.

2

# Delaying Progress

*Resistance to Desegregation in Oklahoma City Public Schools*

It was the summer of 1962, and Oklahoma City was the closest it had ever come to desegregating its schools. Nearly ten years earlier, the Supreme Court had held in *Brown v. Board of Education* that school districts could not require students to attend one-race schools, but nothing had changed in Oklahoma City. The official segregation policy language was lifted in response to the court's decision, but school children continued to attend schools separated by race. Now, families finally had hope. The federal district court had held that the school district must create and implement a plan to desegregate.

The board of education had other ideas. It did not openly defy the court order, but neither did it change its policies to achieve the mandate of *Brown*. Instead, it charted a middle ground. It immediately began exhausting all options for appeals and then moved language around in its policies to create minimal change. It gave its school assignment plan a new name—with the same overall effect—and announced that it would hire five new Black teachers for the district. It refused to adjust boundaries, hire experts, or reassign students to achieve integration. The district, in short, practiced segregation by another name, maintaining the status quo and deferring to the "deep seated customs and feelings" of the white community.[1] The litigation over desegregation in Oklahoma City would stretch on for decades, culminating in the Supreme Court's decision *Board of Education of Oklahoma City Public Schools v. Dowell* (1991), and ultimately it would have little practical effect on the city's segregated schools.

The thirty years of the *Dowell* litigation tell both a doctrinal and a political development story. Doctrinally, for legal scholars, *Dowell* represents high court decision-making about the extent to which federal courts retain jurisdiction over desegregation orders.[2] The Oklahoma City School Board policymaking represents a capstone moment on the United States Supreme Court in *Board of Education v. Dowell* (1991). *Dowell* reached the court on the question of what role judicial supervision should play once the school district has achieved unitary status. This question is fundamental to judicial efforts to desegregate schools. It lies at the heart of many lower court cases, including a circuit court split in the 1980s that the Supreme Court decided not to hear at the time.[3] However, *Dowell* also represents a constitutional development story that has not been told in the literature. How did an institution at odds with a desegregation legal mandate continue to follow its policy preferences for twenty years before the court finally forced full compliance?

The Oklahoma City School Board complied with the legal mandate while also resisting it. The thirty-year history of desegregation attempts in Oklahoma City contains both mass resistance and resistant compliance. The school board at first made zero effort to comply with *Brown*, making small mention of abandoning legally required segregation and then continuing on with segregated business as usual. This approach did not survive judicial review. In 1963, Judge Bohanon, on the Western District of Oklahoma federal court, handed down the first of several desegregation orders to the Oklahoma City public schools. Instead of integrating schools and complying with the 1963 order, the Oklahoma City School Board practiced resistant compliance and spent the next ten years in a drawn-out litigation campaign of delay and foot-dragging over desegregation mandates. The board played for time by slow-walking implementation, avoiding compliance with legal maneuvering, and resisting the mandate of *Brown*—to free schoolchildren of the stigma of single-race education. With the time it gained, the board pursued its own priorities of neighborhood schools, voluntary transfers, and maximizing family choice. While claiming compliance, it did the minimum possible, pursued its own defiant policy goals, and forced the plaintiffs to continue litigation in the federal courts. It was not until 1972 that the district court finally desegregated the schools by taking over the school assignment policies.

This is not a story of mass resistance. Indeed, at multiple junctures in the litigation, the district court appeared satisfied with the school district's good faith in compliance. The history of desegregation litigation in Oklahoma City is a case study of both resistance and resistant compliance, and it is representative of the extended desegregation lawsuits in the late twentieth century that took place in school districts around the country.[4]

Resistance to *Brown* was more insidious than the mass resistance of the governors who blocked schoolchildren at the gate. In this chapter, the school board's policymaking is excavated from extensive examination of newspaper accounts that recorded Oklahoma City Board of Education meeting details and member explanations from 1954 through 1985. Avoiding mass protests, the superintendent and school board members bought years of delayed compliance by exhausting appeals, eroding the implementation of court orders, and producing policy statements without teeth. The litigation stretched on so long that the name of the judge—Bohanon—"be[came] a household word" over decades in Oklahoma City.[5] This chapter also draws on the orders and opinions of the Western District of Oklahoma over nearly three decades to explain how the federal court understood the school board policies in light of Oklahoma City's constitutional obligation to comply with *Brown* and desegregate its schools. In Oklahoma City, this obstructive form of resistant compliance had the effect of continuing to separate Black and white schoolchildren until the judge finally took complete control of school assignment in 1972.

The first section of the chapter argues that the lack of action on desegregation from 1955 to 1963 is best understood as resistance to a judicial mandate. After *Brown*, the district merely issued a statement that it no longer required segregation and then took zero policy action to desegregate. Next, the chapter argues that starting in 1963 with the first desegregation order, the school board pivoted to resistant compliance—complying with the constitutional mandate of *Brown* by maintaining a system free of de jure segregation while also resisting remedying the root injury of *Brown* by maintaining a system that still stigmatized schoolchildren by allowing one-race schools. The Western District of Oklahoma court chambers of Judge Bohanon issued desegregation orders to the segregated Oklahoma City school system in 1963, 1965, and 1972, not including dozens of hearings on motions, plan modifications, and procedural delays interspersed between those years. Each of the Bohanon orders was appealed by the board of education to the Tenth Circuit. Until 1973, the Oklahoma City Board of Education's compliance with the court orders amounted to resistance through judicial process, with each appeal a call for a delay and each order a request for a modification, further delay, and appeal. Organized chronologically, the chapter details the board's strategy of compliance—foot dragging, token measures, and delay—with the resistance of continued commitment to neighborhood schools and local autonomy over school policy. Lastly, the chapter discusses the aftermath of the district court's final takeover of the schools in 1972. Once the district complied with the court's school assignment plan, it was freed from under court order in 1977. By 1984, the board had reverted to its priorities for neighborhood schools and the Oklahoma City schools had resegregated. The Supreme Court upheld the return to board local control in 1991. Ultimately, the Oklahoma City Board of Education was successful in delaying integration of the city's schools for over twenty years after the Supreme Court's decision in *Brown*.

## The Ban on de Jure Segregation

Since its founding, the state of Oklahoma had required segregation in its schools. The state constitution stated, "Separate schools for white and colored children with like accommodation shall be provided by the Legislature and impartially maintained."[6] The state also had laws making it a crime to teach in or to create an integrated school.[7] In the first appearance of school desegregation litigation in Oklahoma City, the Western District of Oklahoma found both the section of the constitution and the relevant state statute unconstitutional under the Fourteenth Amendment after the Supreme Court decision in *Brown v. Board of Education* (1954).[8]

Understanding how a school district complies with a policy involves understanding what the law actually requires. In *Brown v. Board of Education*, the Supreme Court held that it was unconstitutional to require by law that students attend separate schools based on race. The court reached this conclusion because of the specific injury students suffer under a policy of "separate but equal" education for schoolchildren of different racial backgrounds. Namely, under these laws, Black schoolchildren suffer from a stigmatic injury:[9]

> To separate them from others of similar age and qualifications solely because of their race generates a feeling of inferiority as to their status in the community that may affect their hearts and minds in a way unlikely ever to be undone.[10]

By 1968, in *Green v. County School Board*, rooting out stigma was part of compliance with *Brown*.[11]

Federal courts across the country followed *Brown* and found that school districts were maintaining unconstitutionally segregated schools. Such schools were called "dual systems," and the remedy in these cases was court-ordered desegregation decrees meant to establish desegregated—"unitary"—systems. *Unitary* has not been clearly defined by the courts.[12] If the term is left vague, it is easier for defendant school districts to argue for court orders to end and return local control to the districts. If the remedy for court-ordered desegregation is to establish a system that addresses the core injury in *Brown*, then court jurisdiction should presumably extend much longer. If the remedy is nothing short of a truly integrated school system, courts have more muscle to establish orders.[13]

White backlash to *Brown* manifested in mass resistance to court orders, as scholars and news media at the time documented. The white community backlash included resistance to court-ordered busing of students; indeed, "bussing replaced 'law-and-order' as the white-backlash code word of the early seventies."[14] White families and school boards also insisted that the American tradition of local control over education should preempt court desegregation orders.

In 1974, the court in *Milliken v. Bradley* emphasized the historical tradition of local control over American education policy and schools:

> No single tradition in public education is more deeply rooted than local control over the operation of schools; local autonomy has long been thought essential both to the maintenance of community concern and support for public schools and to quality of the educational process.[15]

The majority in *Dowell* would later echo this position.[16] Unfortunately, as scholars of American political development have unearthed, traditions with long historical roots also tend to be traditions rooted in maintaining the status quo, which in the United States is a racial order based on white supremacy.[17] The goal of local control for school districts is in tension with the goal of establishing an egalitarian racial order.

Like all desegregation challenges of the mid- to late twentieth century, this tension played out in the Oklahoma City desegregation litigation. The Oklahoma City School Board, throughout the thirty years of the *Dowell* litigation, repeatedly maintained that the Constitution required less in a unitary system than the district court demanded. Therefore, the board should have control over its education policy, which included a preference against busing and for neighborhood schools. As this chapter argues, the board pursued its commitments by obstruction and delay of court orders and through slow-walking and gutting court-ordered policy changes, much to the anger and frustration of the district court. Ultimately, the Oklahoma City School Board was able to maintain its preferred commitments.[18]

## 1955–1963: Resistance to Desegregation in Oklahoma City

Nationally, many southern governments refused to comply with school desegregation in the mid-twentieth century, including refusing even to acknowledge the jurisdiction of the Supreme Court. Politicians and local governments were generally loud, defiant, and intransigent in their resistance.[19] In 1956, in the midst of mass resistance already taking place, white local officials across the South came together to sign the "Southern Manifesto."[20] The document rejected the Supreme Court's jurisdiction over school desegregation and pledged "to use all lawful means to bring about a reversal of this decision [*Brown*] which is contrary to the Constitution."[21] Some districts chose to close schools rather than desegregate.[22]

In Oklahoma, the governor did not trumpet loud defiance and a refusal to obey the Supreme Court but rather expressed a desire to maintain segregation to the legal extent possible. Governor Johnston Murray expressed that he was "heartily in accord" with the idea that white southern state attorneys general should meet to discuss

> possible legal courses of action that might be followed to preserve segregation in the public schools within the framework of the federal and state constitutions notwithstanding the court's adverse decision.[23]

Murray sought to chart a middle ground in the face of white southern defiance—not outspoken, but not an embrace of *Brown*.

The Oklahoma City School Board similarly did not support the new desegregation order in *Brown*. At an August 1955 meeting, the board members voted in favor of a resolution that was meant to satisfy the court order without actually implementing any policy change. In the resolution—"Statement Concerning Integration of Oklahoma Public Schools 1955–1956, August 1, 1955"—they appeared supportive of segregation: a "system which has been in effect for centuries and which is desired for many of our citizens."[24] They did not change any school attendance boundaries, instead saying that updates to school boundaries would no longer factor in race but would "consider natural geographical boundaries, such as major traffic streets, railroads, the river, etc."[25] They made zero student assignment changes, instead announcing a voluntary transfer policy with approval dependent on school capacity. Ultimately, the new policy had little practical effect on the balance of racial backgrounds within the Oklahoma City public schools.

The school board opposed the core argument in *Brown* and felt that white cultural preferences should prevail in student school assignment. Dr. Jack Parker argued that the hands-off, zero-implementation school board policies of the late 1950s were meant to give families the "opportunity to follow the dictates of the beliefs of the individual person" because segregation had "been in existence since statehood and attitudes have developed over a long period of time."[26] In response to the Supreme Court decision, the board doubled down on the preference of white families and took no practical action toward desegregation.

White cultural preferences, for instance, dominated the voluntary school transfer policy. The board would "practically always" approve voluntary transfer requests as long as the transferring student would be moving to a school where his or her race was in the majority.[27] This "minority-to-majority" transfer plan mostly operated to permit white students to transfer to schools that were predominantly white. The district court later found that most transfers requested by Black students were denied because of race. Functionally, this meant that in a number of schools, there was "no integration but practically complete segregation."[28] Not only did the student assignment policy do nothing to advance desegregation, but also the voluntary policy that existed was grounded in reinforcing segregation.

In its initial resistance, the board of education also limited the mandate of *Brown*, excluding school personnel from desegregation policies. Superintendent Parker testified at trial that the schools were required to be desegregated only "from the standpoint of the pupils," which meant allowing students to choose a different school to attend. Staff and teachers, like students, were not reassigned to new schools, but unlike students, they could not request voluntary transfers. Indeed, Parker testified that the board felt that integrated teaching would hurt students' education: "Nothing would be gained educationally by a desegregation of staffs and . . . the mixing of staffs could very well detract from the quality of the instructional program."[29] The result of the policy was that while Black schoolchildren could request a voluntary transfer to a different school—again, subject to board approval—if they succeeded, the teachers and staff awaiting them would almost certainly be white.

Not surprisingly, the Oklahoma City schools remained segregated. In 1961, Dr. Alfonzo L. Dowell, a local optometrist, filed suit on behalf of his son. The board of education claimed that its 1955 resolution "attained complete desegregation" in compliance with *Brown* and that no further action was required.[30] But 100 percent of students had attended segregated schools when segregation was required by law, and the board policy removing race in assignment had only dropped the number of students in segregated schools to 88 percent by 1961.[31] The total segregation of teachers also remained.

In 1963, the Western District of Oklahoma issued a ruling on *Dowell v. School Board of Oklahoma City Public Schools* and held for the first time that the Oklahoma City schools were unconstitutionally segregated in violation of *Brown v. Board of Education*. Judge Bohanon found that the "record [was] void of any tangible evidence of any other action" beyond the 1955 paper-only resolution.[32] The minority-to-majority transfer policy, the lack of any effort to desegregate when it came to school boundaries or student assignment, and the lack of any effort on teacher reassignment all indicated that the board was acting "with a desire to perpetuate a dual system."[33] The court was particularly blistering on the minority-to-majority transfer policy, calling it a policy designed to perpetuate and encourage segregation.[34] Overall, the district court found that

> The school children and personnel have in the main from all of the evidence been completely segregated as much as possible under the circumstances, rather than integrated as much as possible.[35]

While the board members did not actually stand on the schoolhouse steps and block Black children from entering, they did not need to. The district's voluntary transfer policies and historically maintained school boundaries were designed to have the same effect.

The injury to Oklahoma City school children was the same that the Supreme Court had identified in *Brown*, and the district court quoted the landmark case on the injury of stigma and the feeling of inferiority. The inferiority was amplified by denying schoolchildren integrated principals, staff, and teachers. Additionally, all schoolchildren were injured in their development of a civic, democratic education. The integration of children in mixed-race schools, the district court held, was

> indispensable if children of all ages of all races and creeds were to become inculcated with a meaningful understanding of the essentials of our democratic way of life. The benefits inherent in an education in integrated schools are essential to the proper development of children.[36]

The district court ordered that the board of education make a plan to desegregate the Oklahoma City school system in ninety days.

The injury also appeared to be one of exhaustion. Despite a remedy offering him a school transfer, the original plaintiff chose to stay at his segregated high school. The father who originally brought the suit, optometrist Dr. Alfonzo L. Dowell, had done so because he wanted his son to be able to take Latin, a class offered only at an all-white school. The district proposed to load his son with extra requirements to approve the course enrollment. While Dr. Dowell expressed joy at the decision—"I'm glad we were able to help people of all races obtain the best education possible"—his son, Robert, appeared exhausted. Now a senior in high school, Robert was interviewed by a reporter about whether he would seek to attend an integrated college after high school. "I don't think so. I've had all of that I want for a while," he replied.[37]

The Oklahoma City Board of Education and white community members reacted with hostility to the 1963 court order that required the board to create a desegregation plan. They argued that it threatened local customs and was not in the best educational interest of children. Legal counsel for the board predicted that the decision would promote hostility "because you can't ignore deep seated customs and feelings and change them overnight."[38] The Mayor's Committee on Community Relations heard testimony from a mental health professional who argued that desegregation would hold white students back in their educations.[39] The board argued that the schools were already integrated and that the court's demand for a new integration plan was untenable in the time allowed. Integration, the board argued, was the absence of de jure segregation. As one high school English teacher phrased it, "Maybe [the district court judge] feels it is just token integration. . . . The school where I teach is integrated, but there are no Negroes enrolled there."[40] On July 21, 1963, the board motioned for a new trial and gained thirty extra days in which to respond to the desegregation order.[41]

The Black community and allied organizations were thrilled with the 1963 opinion, but they were wary about the board's willingness to follow through. The Urban League of Oklahoma City issued a statement calling on the board to "immediately effectuate a plan to provide equal opportunities" instead of appealing the case.[42] The local chapter of the NAACP was skeptical, and its representative stated, "We don't have much faith in the board and very little faith in Dr. Parker. We are going to look carefully at anything they do."[43] Local community leader Dr. F. D. Moon, who would later join the board of education himself, commented that the court had ended the particularly troublesome pro-segregation transfer policy, saying, "We are very happy the infamous 'majority–minority' transfer policy, used so effectively to re-segregate schools, is outlawed."[44]

The Oklahoma City Board of Education was on notice—a federal district court had held it was resistant to desegregation and out of compliance with the constitutional mandate in *Brown*. Merely making a plan and announcing integration was not enough. The resolution of the board had to be accompanied by actual policy change, getting rid of policies that reinforced segregation—like the minority-to-majority transfer policy—and ushering in policies that promoted it. Over the next ten years, the board would shift its posture toward the courts. Instead of refusing to adopt desegregation policies outright, it would switch to a strategy of delay, foot-dragging over implementation, and erosion of court-mandated orders to continue prioritizing its preferred policies of neighborhood schools, anti-busing, and local control.

## 1965–67: Paper Compliance and Policy Statements

In the late summer of 1963, the Oklahoma City Board of Education responded to the court's order with the minimum policy change possible. It ended its odious minority-to-majority transfer plan that reinforced segregation and announced a plan to hire five new Black teachers. However, its active steps toward desegregation were structured within its own commitments—it would transfer students between schools only if they asked for the change (voluntary transfers), and it would continue to prioritize sending all students to neighborhood schools. The board announced a new school boundaries policy that did not assign students to schools based on race but drew the attendance zones for schools based on geography, thereby keeping children at neighborhood schools and essentially maintaining the previous school boundaries.[45]

Most people in the community recognized that the board's efforts would not result in meaningful change. The editors of the local newspaper, the *Daily Oklahoman*, were realistic, writing in an editorial titled "No Easy Solutions" that the existing neighborhood segregation in housing meant that without "drastic" changes in school boundaries or student assignment, merely eliminating the transfer policy and hiring more Black teachers was nothing "more than token integration."[46] However, mirroring the priorities of the board, the newspaper editors felt that *Dowell* did not require these drastic measures, despite requiring desegregation. The NAACP called the board's plan the "least effort it could make in compliance."[47]

One year later, the state of desegregation in Oklahoma City was about the same. The board's continued neighborhood school boundaries and its underutilized policy of voluntary school transfers resulted in minimal changes to desegregation. An expert panel later found that by 1965, 80 percent of Black students still attended nearly all-Black schools, and in response to the 1963 decision, "little or nothing was done" to integrate teaching staffs at schools that were one-race.[48]

The district court was losing its patience. By June of 1964, Judge Bohanon ordered a school integration study because the results of desegregation efforts were proceeding sluggishly. The board refused to employ outside experts to make recommendations on integration, so the district court asked the plaintiffs to initiate a study. The report concluded that the school district lacked any affirmative program working toward integration. Instead, the voluntary transfer program still allowed white students to flee the schools whose student bodies were overwhelmingly Black and teachers were integrated on a "token basis."[49] The completed report was filed in January 1965, and the Black plaintiff families motioned for the court to require the school district to submit a desegregation plan based on these expert recommendations.

Predictably, the board of education responded with only minimal changes to its existing policies. The board proposed to continue with geographically based neighborhood schools but to make efforts to integrate afterschool activities and require race-neutral reasons for voluntary requests for school transfers. Judge Bohanon was skeptical. At the hearing, he noted that "the public and the Negro citizens are entitled to know that this plan would be carried out in good faith" and asked the school district to hire experts on desegregation to assist them in plan recommendations.[50] The plaintiffs were thoroughly unimpressed. Dowell's lawyer, U. Simpson Tate, argued that the district's proposed plan "contributes to the maintenance of the status quo, [and] tends to perpetuate racial segregation."[51] They changed gears for the 1965 lawsuit, converting it into a class action suit and bringing in NAACP attorneys Jack Greenberg and Derrick Bell.

Not for the first time, the white community was in an uproar over potential changes to school system policies. White parents flooded board meetings with protests and warnings about more extreme desegregation measures like merging high schools or sending their children out of their neighborhoods. One parent argued at a community forum that "if colored people live in Classen's district they should have every right to attend school at Classen. Since they don't it's an artificial thing. . . . We will not let this thing wreck the education of our children."[52] The dominant sentiment among these protesting families was that the mandate in *Brown* required only that the school district not exclude neighborhood children from their neighborhood school based on race. If the neighborhood had all white families, then the school had all white children, and the district had done all that was legally required.

The board of education's policy of delay and token changes was now challenged by outside expert recommendations for the Oklahoma City schools. The district court's hearing over potential desegregation plans began on August 9, 1965. Outside experts reviewed the school board's proposal and called it "not a plan, but a policy" that lacked any sense of goals, timetables for execution, an implementation plan, or designation of responsibilities for execution.[53] The board's plans still had loopholes that allowed white students to transfer out, which the experts called an "escape route."[54] The district court agreed and held that the board was essentially just talking a good game: "Paper compliance and policy statements are insufficient to satisfy the standards of desegregation required by [*Brown II*]."[55] The Tenth Circuit would later uphold this judgment, calling the board's desegregation plan "only of a token nature."[56]

The district court's 1965 orders against the Oklahoma City School District demanded an actual plan to implement desegregation. Policy statements were not enough. The plan had to include "definable and ascertainable goals to be achieved within a definite time according to a prepared procedure and with responsibilities clearly designated."[57] In other words, the district needed to produce a statement of what was to happen, when it would happen, how it would happen, and who would be in charge of making it happen.

In addition to finding no actionable desegregation plans, the court found that the new voluntary transfer plan still had the same segregating effect. The district court's expert panel concluded that it continued to prioritize only minority-to-majority transfers and provided "an effective loophole" for white families to attend segregated schools.[58] Even though the board had adjusted the policy, the pattern of transfer approvals had the same effect as the previously invalidated minority-to-majority transfer plan from the 1963 court decision. The court found that white families were able to use the policy with the intent of avoiding a desegregated school:[59]

> Such policy tends to perpetuate a segregated system, . . . [and] deprives Negro pupils . . . of the opportunity to obtain a desegregated education.[60]

Even if the words of the policy were race neutral, it was still not desegregation if the effect of the policy's execution was to continue one-race schools.

Lastly, the court found that the district's preferred policy of neighborhood schools also reinforced segregation, not because the law required Black and white families to attend different schools but because practices outside the district's control reinforced that effect. The court took notice of resistance in white neighborhoods to Black families moving in. Additionally, it noted that realtors still discriminated when they showed houses and banks when they approved mortgages for Black families seeking to move to these areas. Therefore, it concluded that Black families had an "inability to exercise a substantial freedom of choice in determining their place of residence."[61] Because of these housing patterns, prioritizing neighborhood schools resulted in an increase in segregated schools. Since 1963, the district had built thirteen new elementary schools, nine of which were one-race schools. Only the two vocational schools with a citywide service area were integrated.[62]

The Tenth Circuit agreed on appeal: prioritizing neighborhood schools reinforced segregation. Neighborhoods were segregated because of prior laws and current practices; therefore, assigning students to schools based on rigid neighborhood school preferences "serves to maintain and extend school segregation."[63] The court noted that neighborhood schools, per se, are not unconstitutional as long as they are "impartially maintained and administered."[64] The problem with Oklahoma City was that the board of education had implemented a neighborhood school plan with a workaround that allowed white families to transfer out. Before *Brown*, plenty of students attended schools outside their neighborhoods to comply with the legal requirement that schools be segregated. After *Brown*, the Oklahoma City Board of Education's "minority-to-majority" voluntary transfer policy allowed this practice to stay in place, this time because families were choosing one-race schools over potentially integrated neighborhood schools. The district court concluded:

> Thus, it appears that the neighborhood school concept has been in the past, and continues in the present to be expendable when segregation is at stake.[65]

The Oklahoma City Board of Education's preference for neighborhood schools was a preference for one-race schools, just by another name.

The district court ordered the board to take affirmative steps toward integration, including a revamped transfer policy, new faculty assignments, and widened high school boundaries. The only "meaningful" action must be "vigorous, affirmative measures."[66] Under the new transfer policy, officials would approve requests to transfer where the student was transferring to a school where his or her race was in the minority. The new faculty assignment policy would have the goal of employing school faculty in a ratio that approximated the racial balance of the city, accomplished through both transfers of current faculty and replacements after natural turnover. Lastly, the boundaries of certain high schools should be widened to achieve a different racial balance. The orders must be implemented by 1966.[67] Removing the legal requirement of one-race schools was not enough; board policies had to actually create desegregated schools to remedy the injuries of stigma and a lack of meaningful education.

The board of education immediately appealed the decision and predicted a long delay. Coleman Hayes, attorney for the schools, argued that Judge Bohanon's order was the "artificial and forced integration of city schools" and an "unwarranted interference with the discretionary duties of the school board in operating the school system."[68] He noted that an appeal to the Tenth Circuit would both stay the decision and likely mean a year before the board would have to make any affirmative changes.[69] In January 1967, the Tenth Circuit upheld the judge's orders.[70]

## 1967–69: Slow-Walking with Legal Appeals and Implementation

The board of education used legal delay as a tactic in its resistance while complying. In April 1967, three months after losing in the Tenth Circuit, the board voted to delay further implementing the desegregation orders and instead appeal to the Supreme Court. Foster Estes, a board member, made the motion: "I'm not against integration. But, I'm against the federal government regulating our lives and telling us what we can and cannot do."[71] In June, the Supreme Court denied certiorari. In July, the board maintained that it was not resisting the court but rather seeking approval for new plans in order to develop a timeline for compliance.

Superintendent Bill Lillard defended the vote:

> Our interest is not to delay implementation of the federal court order. We aren't dragging our feet. We want to get our plan into court [for approval] as soon as possible. Then, we'll have a better idea of a timetable.[72]

After losing on appeal, the board only modified its legal delay tactics, giving the excuse that it had to make further appeals and double-check its plans with the judge.

By now, the board had added cost into its reasons for delay. At the April meeting, Estes complained that implementation of the 1965 orders would cost the city $500,000 in funds to be spent on altering school facilities to accommodate integration.[73] In its June meeting, Superintendent Lillard argued that there was no money in the budget for what was now estimated to be the $700,000 necessary to implement the desegregation orders. Therefore, he noted, integration in the upcoming 1967 school year would not be possible, and the cost would have to be a bond item or part of the 1968 school year budget.[74]

The board of education's one policy change in response to the 1965 orders illustrates its continued commitment to the status quo. In July 1967, the board initiated a voluntary majority-to-minority transfer program in which students could request to transfer to a school where their race was in the minority, if space permitted. The previous minority-to-majority transfer program—so odious to the district court—was popular among white families seeking to keep their children in all-white schools. Not surprisingly, few families were eager to voluntarily desegregate schools with their children. By the August deadline, only thirty-three students had requested a transfer.[75] Board members again stressed their desire to comply with the court but also their commitment to keeping students in their increasingly segregated neighborhoods for school. Board member Foster Estes explained after losing on appeal, "We are not against integration of the schools, we only believe that the neighborhood attendance concept is fairest to both races."[76]

The white community expressed hostility to the court orders. Throughout the fall of 1967, white parents and community members participated in panels, forums, and advisory committees in which they continually expressed frustration with the "Bohanon integration plan" that required school consolidation.[77] The sentiment was not universal, however. Some white community members in the fall of 1967 started a petition to convert the schools to open enrollment for the aid of desegregation. Petition sponsors argued that the board was resisting the 1965 orders. According to one sponsor, "We think the Oklahoma City school board is dragging its feet. We hope to show there is widespread support for full and immediate implementation."[78]

Two and a half years after the 1965 desegregation order, the board changed tactics and asked for reconsideration of the orders in light of changing circumstances. Residential segregation had continued, and the demographics of neighborhoods had shifted. The 1965 orders required changes to some school boundaries. Now, the board argued, the court should reconsider its orders because those changes would continue segregation if administered.[79] Instead, the board voted to create a biracial Committee on Equality of Educational Opportunity made up of a representative sample of community members.[80] Together with this committee, the board would recommend new school boundaries.[81]

The board coupled its request for reconsideration with the argument that it was in compliance with the 1965 orders. It stressed that it was "receptive" to the judge changing the orders "as the board proceeds toward full integration of all city schools."[82] In citing its compliance with the court's order, the board noted that under the voluntary majority-to-minority transfer plan, seventy-six students had transferred, thirty-nine schools out of ninety (instead of the prior twenty-nine) now had integrated teaching staffs, and the representation of Black teachers district-wide had gone from 12 percent to 16 percent.[83]

The commitment by the board of education to alter some school boundaries prompted a new wave of white community protests, led by some board members. Media accounts noted that the board was influenced by white families' testimony about senior students' attachment to their high school assignments, pointing out that the students had already invested emotionally in their high schools by buying class rings and club uniforms.[84] Board member Foster Estes, a leader of the white community protests, argued that there should be no further legal right to integration beyond districts' abandoning de jure segregation. At a February 18, 1968, meeting, five hundred white community members gathered in a local mortuary where Estes rallied the group, proclaiming that Black and white school children "have had the same education in Oklahoma City the past six years."[85] Estes refused to vote in favor of board compliance. "I will fight as long as there is breath in my body to vote against busing."[86]

Judge Bohanon approved the new board actions, but the agreement was short-lived. On March 4, 1968, Bohanon signed an order approving the new boundaries. But dissenting voices on the board appear to have blocked the vote. The school boundaries remained the same for the start of the 1968 school year. The intransigence of board members like Foster Estes, backed by the white community's hostility to integration orders, proved successful. The district court required board action that went against the board's interest in promoting neighborhood schools and therefore in avoiding provoking the hostility of white community members. Throughout 1969, any small movement by the board provoked backlash. The board ultimately backed off. It continued to rely on delays in the judiciary, with some help from the appellate courts.

In the spring of 1969, the board, despite contrary evidence from 1968, continued to treat voluntary desegregation efforts as sufficient to achieve desegregation. On May 30, 1969, the board approved a policy statement declining to change school boundaries and relying instead on Black families' voluntary transfers between schools to achieve desegregation.[87] Superintendent Lillard argued that changing school boundaries was "not feasible" because it would be too disruptive to students to change schools and the board "desire[d] to maintain" a position against any policy that required forcing students to be transported to a new school.[88] The plan was criticized by pro-integration organizations within the community, such as the board-appointed Committee on Equality of Educational Opportunity and the local chapter of the Urban League.[89] Pastor Norbert Kabelitz told the local newspaper that the board had "asked the blacks to go to other white schools. I'm wondering why they didn't do the reverse? The burden has always been put on the black students, and they're getting tired of it." The board's policy showed its "subtle attitudes saying we want nothing to do with any integrated schools. We seem to be moving gradually into two separate school systems again."[90]

Board members argued that moving Black schoolchildren was the only way to achieve the levels of desegregation that the court demanded. Some even argued for mandatory transfer of Black students. Board president Virgil Hill argued the focus should be on Black students because "I doubt the white community would support moving their children to all black schools."[91] Board member Melvin Rogers reiterated that this sentiment was simply practical given the circumstances: "We can gain a better percentage by taking the percentage of black students and moving them into white schools. You just have to be realistic."[92]

The court required a plan, and the May 30, 1969 plan was just that—but even the board members themselves were not convinced it would actually meet the court's requirements. At a hearing regarding the plan before Judge Bohanon in July, the best testimony the board could offer was that Superintendent Lillard was "hoping" voluntary community transfers would achieve the court's desired 70/30 white-to-Black ratio in schools.[93] He also noted, however, that zero white students had opted into the majority-to-minority transfer program thus far.[94] Board president Hill testified that a voluntary plan would fail. "It's not working today and I have serious doubts as to whether we're making much progress. . . . Nothing short of a mandatory program (will work) at this point."[95] Even its proponents did not see the policy adoption as a serious response to the court's orders. Its only function was to meet the board's need for delay.

Not surprisingly, the judge again demanded a specific, workable plan, and the plaintiffs requested more court intervention. It had now been almost four years since the 1965 desegregation court order, and the plaintiffs were asking the court for a solution. The board of education's response was more of the same; Superintendent Lillard wanted more time to study changing residential patterns, and board member Estes declared that any court-ordered adjustment of attendance zones was "tearing up the entire school system."[96] In a foreshadowing of what was to come, the plaintiff Black families asked for more court intervention. In his statement at the hearing, their attorney, John Walker, argued, "Not much has changed in actuality since 1954 except those specific things which were required by this court . . . The [school] board will do no more than the court will order it to do."[97] In 1969, the court again found that the board was dragging its feet on implementation, and it asked for new plans.

Throughout its attempts at delay, the board of education remained committed to the goal of protecting neighborhood schools, a common refrain among white families protesting the court orders. Residents of white neighborhoods were passionately opposed to the reassignment of white students to traditionally Black schools. Hundreds of white families attended community forums where parents often threatened to withhold their students from school in the hope of causing the district to lose money.[98] Board members perceived that the prevailing attitude of the (presumably white) community was "against integration by about 99 percent."[99]

Many of these white families had started to take the legal fight into their own hands, forming neighborhood associations, hiring their own lawyers, and seeking to intervene in the desegregation litigation. The board took a hands-off approach to these efforts but was happy to cite the need to hear their arguments as cause for further delay. In the fall of 1969, with only days left before school began, the Tenth Circuit vacated the district court order that would have in effect required altering attendance boundaries. The court did not discuss the merits of the district court's order, holding only that the additional intervenors had a right to be heard at a full hearing in November.[100] The superintendent greeted the decision with full respect for the new delay: "It's the responsibility of the schools to follow the order of the court."[101] The newspaper commemorated the event with a giant headline and a photo of white families protesting the orders.[102]

Motivated by the appellate court's decision, the board moved to delay even further. Its lawyers filed an appeal with the Supreme Court to move the order for a desegregation plan from November 1 to March 31, 1970.[103]

In its motion, the board continued to fight the underlying premise of the desegregation orders—that its system was segregated at all. Superintendent Lillard commented:

> We have an integrated school system now, and I think we have an obligation to make it a more integrated system in the future.[104]

The Supreme Court ultimately denied the motion, but the application for certiorari further delayed the creation of a desegregation plan. Now, four years after the desegregation orders, the 1969 school year would not include a desegregation implementation plan.

The Oklahoma City Board of Education spent the years after the 1965 desegregation order testing every possible avenue to delay implementation. Judge Bohanon's desegregation orders came down on September 7, 1965. The appeal to the Tenth Circuit, which upheld Bohanon's orders, was made almost eighteen months later. During this time, the board took no action to implement the 1965 orders. The board exhausted its appeals, which were sometimes successful as the courts recognized intervenors, causing further delay. When it was not awaiting an appeal, the board sought to extend the deadlines for implementing plans or proposed excuses, like budget restrictions, that also delayed implementation. The board argued for more time because of a lack of funds, or because of a lack of specificity, or, eventually, because too much time had passed since the original orders. It made small adjustments and proposed plans to meet deadlines that its members openly acknowledged would not desegregate the public schools. The board stressed its own compliance with the court at the same time that it delayed implementing court orders with reasons that blamed the clarity, the feasibility, and eventually the outdated nature of the court orders. Board members showed little fear of testing Judge Bohanon's patience. Eventually, however, the district court would catch up with this slow-walking compliance.

## 1970–72: Too Little, Too Late for the Board of Education's Desegregation Plan

With no further appeal options, the board had to meet a December 1969 district court deadline for a desegregation plan. In anticipation of this deadline, the board received over fifty proposals from outside individuals and organizations. Ultimately—since it had to do something—it voted to advance the "cluster plan," according to which each high school designated a subject specialty. Students would then stay in these neighborhood schools for elementary, middle, and basic high school instruction and travel for advanced subjects to an integrated high school that covered a larger swath of the city, or a "cluster" high school.[105]

While presenting the plan, the board expressed its intent to comply with it and simultaneously backed away from it in disapproval. Superintendent Lillard noted that any desegregation plan was unpopular in the community, "but we must abide by the law." Board member William Lott described the board as caught between court orders and white community hostility: "Like the story in the Bible about two masters, we got a court order and in a democracy, we've got to please the people."[106] Although the judge gave the cluster plan tentative approval, pending some modifications, and even praised the board for making any effort at all, the board waited only two days after the hearing to file a request for an extension on its amended plan.[107]

By the winter of 1970, the majority of Oklahoma City Board of Education members preferred to return to the old strategy of doing the bare minimum and pushing for more delay. The cluster plan was on the table only because the district court had forced the issue. According to board member Dr. Stanley Niles, any vote to change board policies was taken "solely to meet the demands of the district court, including threats of control by other federal agencies."[108] In addition to the cluster plan, the board voted to continue to push its voluntary majority-to-minority transfer program and support integrated afterschool activities. Additionally, toward the end of the spring, it voted to adopt a policy statement not to approve any school transfers that were made "by persons seeking to avoid school attendance with students of another race," an acknowledgement of the continued problem of white flight.[109] Not all board members were in agreement, but the dissenters were a small minority. Board member Dr. Virgil Hill told local media that he was skeptical the old policies would work. He argued in support of the cluster plan and stated that continued voluntary policies were "backward . . . a program of 'just let things take their natural course.' In other words continued racism." There was "no evidence" white families would "work cooperatively" toward integration with voluntary transfers.[110]

Even after its approval, the board of education still sought to delay and avoid its own plan. Yet on July 29, 1970, the Tenth Circuit appellate court refused to vacate the district court's orders. The district court ended its jurisdiction over the case in August 1970. It looked as though students would meaningfully integrate in the fall of 1970, for the first time since the court ordered desegregation: "There no longer will be a dual school system, but a unitary school system where schools will not be black schools or white schools but just schools."[111] Almost immediately, the board pulled back on the cluster plan, delaying its implementation for a year after receiving complaints from families. In a letter to parents, the board adopted a policy that children could stay in their previous school for the upcoming year.[112] Later that fall, the board voted to put more of the specialized courses from cluster schools back into the home base high schools, reducing the need for students to elect integrated cluster schools in order to pursue their desired courses.[113] By April 1971, Judge Bohanon had reopened the case.

The board of education had now exhausted the district court's goal of having the board create a desegregation plan on its own. The board voted to hire an outside desegregation expert after its attorney, Harry Johnson, advised that the district court would likely order it. As Johnson told them, "It's the 'in' thing to have experts," and perhaps getting out ahead of the district court would allow the board to have more control over the expert recommendation.[114] But the board was doing too little, too late. The district court had also hired an outside expert in the summer of 1971, as had the plaintiffs, with a hearing set for December. Currently, only 12 percent of students were voluntarily participating in the cluster plan.[115] Yet the board continued to prefer the plan into the fall, over the recommendations of the other experts. Board member Estes predicted that without board support, any approved plan would fail:

> It isn't right for any two men to come into a school system and tell the school system how it is to become integrated. . . . I have reason to believe it is not a working plan because it is going to be forced.[116]

But the time for control over its own desegregation plan had passed.

Delay and chipping away at court orders had bought the board of education an extra six years of prioritizing neighborhood schools, but that would end in 1972. At the December 9, 1971, hearing on the multiple integration plans, Judge Bohanon ordered the implementation of the plaintiffs' expert's plan by September 1972. Dowell and the other plaintiffs had presented the expert testimony of Dr. John Finger, from Rhode Island State University, for a desegregation approach that everyone would come to call the Finger plan.

The district court took the Oklahoma City desegregation plan into its own hands in 1972, with a result that looked dramatic when contrasted with the board's previous policies of delay and voluntary transfers. The December 1971 hearing produced a district court opinion in February 1972. In it the court ordered the school district to implement the 1972–73 "A New Plan of Unification for the Oklahoma City Public School System," which was essentially Dr. Finger's expert testimony. The Finger plan assigned Black schoolchildren in grades one through four to previously all-white schools and turned the previously all-Black elementary schools into fifth grade centers with both Black and white schoolchildren assigned to them. White children would stay in their neighborhood schools until fifth grade, and Black children would return to their neighborhood schools in fifth grade. The plan restructured middle school attendance zones to create a Black student enrollment of no more than 30 percent. These middle schools then fed into integrated high schools.[117] The district court accepted this as the only workable plan for integration among those presented, but it also maintained that it was not mandating busing. The district was also required to seek court approval for any deviations from the Finger plan.[118]

At trial, the board rejected the Finger plan and was adamant in supporting voluntary transfers and neighborhood schools. Board member Estes testified that if any other plan was adopted, "the voters will defeat the millage and we won't be able to open schools for even one day."[119] Superintendent Lillard called the Finger plan "personally offensive."[120] The board also returned to its arguments that the Oklahoma City schools had been desegregated with the 1954 policy statement. Its intent was to hew closely to (white) community sentiment against desegregation and in favor of neighborhood schools.[121]

The district court found that the board's policies had the aim of protecting neighborhood schools and not the goal of desegregation. The board's current modified cluster plan was "designed to protect the 'neighborhood schools' and to keep desegregation on a voluntary basis."[122] Even when the board was required to adopt its own plan, the cluster plan, in 1970, it still sought to inject its own preferred policy preferences. The school district "emasculate[d] the plan" approved by the last round of litigation, which moved students between schools for different subjects. The district instead kept full subject loads at schools, which "destroyed [the plan] as a tool of desegregation."[123] The board was complying with court orders by chipping away at those orders and replacing them with its own preferences.

The court sharply criticized the board of education for its years of foot dragging and delay in response to court orders. The board's policies "as historically administered . . . reflected a system of state imposed and state preserved segregation."[124] Its plans amounted to "a token effort [that] cannot even be described as a good-faith gesture."[125] The board had sought to impede judicial process. The litigation had been "frustratingly interminable . . . because of the unpardonable recalcitrance" of the district officials.[126] And now, six years after the initial order, the board had "totally defaulted in its acknowledged duty to come forward with an acceptable plan."[127] On March 26, 1976, Judge Bohanon ordered the district to pay the NAACP $170,000 in legal fees. He awarded the fees because of the board's "intransigence and bad faith . . . in seeking to preserve and protect a dual school system in defiance of constitutional imperatives for a unitary system."[128] The judge went on to call the board's actions "a deliberate course of delay, obstruction and evasion."[129]

From 1963 to 1972, the Oklahoma City Board of Education stated its compliance with the court's orders while seeking opportunities for delay and continuance of its priorities at every turn. By 1970, the court had squeezed the board into the position of consulting with experts for desegregation plans, but the plaintiffs engaged experts as well. Had the board not resisted desegregation, had it initially changed attendance boundaries and reassigned students as the cluster plan eventually recommended, perhaps the court would have dissolved jurisdiction and the board's experts would have won the day. By 1972, however, the court was wary of the board's commitment to desegregation and was willing to listen when the plaintiff's expert, Dr. John Finger, presented a dramatic plan.

Resistant compliance was a nearly decade-long way for the Oklahoma City Board of Education to pursue its policy preferences. It took almost ten years for the board's foot dragging and erosion of court orders to catch up to it. Ultimately, the Finger plan orders marked the end of the board's resistant compliance. Its elementary schools split, and fifth grade centers dominated Oklahoma City public school policies until 1985, when the board finally regained the ability to fulfill its preferred policy commitments.

### 1972–1991: The Enduring Commitment to Neighborhood Schools and Local Control

Starting when *Brown* was handed down in 1954 and all throughout the court-ordered desegregation from 1963 through 1972, the school board had been allowed to retain control of its own policies. It was ordered to create them and ordered to implement them, but control of the actual policies had remained in the hands of the board. That changed with the Finger plan, which took away the board's authority to write its own policy and stated explicitly what student assignment in Oklahoma City would look like. The board's hands were now tied. Board members were outraged when the district court took control and specified the exact method of school assignment. At the February 1972 board meeting, member Yvonne York called the Finger plan "a violation of the law. I am appalled that a federal judge would ask us to break the law."[130] Board member Dr. Herbert Knob agreed, calling the order "unjust and autocratic in the highest degree."[131] The board voted to appeal and seek a stay of the decision. Any hope was short-lived; the Tenth Circuit rejected the request on August 4, 1972.

As it began to execute the requirement of the new court-ordered school assignment policies, the board continued to reject the strategy of defying the court and mass resistance. At their August 4, 1972, meeting, board member York motioned to defy the court order and was voted down.[132] The board's vote was an unpopular stance in the white community, whose loudest voices wanted the school district to defy the courts. Two hundred angry people attended the meeting, calling on the board to refuse to desegregate schools through busing and court-ordered assignment. Throughout the meeting, audience members called out "You're yellow!" and "What are you afraid of?" to board members.[133] Some parents refused to allow their children to attend these desegregated schools. One parent at the meeting reported to the local newspaper: "The people of this city will not comply with the court order. To bus my son, gentlemen, you'll have to do it over my cold, dead body." The reporter noted that the man's son would be attending a school that was not affected by the order because it was already deemed sufficiently desegregated.[134] The Finger plan would proceed as specified by Judge Bohanon, starting in the fall of 1972.

Although it did not change its priorities, the board could no longer put forward half-hearted efforts or slow-walk the creation of new desegregation plans. The district court did not have to issue further desegregation orders or conduct trials on the school assignment policies in Oklahoma City. In August 1973, the district court rejected the board's request for attendance adjustments at two of the high schools. The court found that these adjustments were "designed to preserve these as racially identifiable schools and [are] therefore, constitutionally condemned."[135] One year later, in November 1974, the district court refused to allow the board to change the principals at two of the local schools.[136] While these motions are not inconsequential, they demonstrate how severely limited the board's control over school district policy had become. In a substantial departure from policymaking over the previous two decades, the district court was now in charge.

In 1975, the board attempted to regain control of the policies and procedures of the Oklahoma City Public Schools. In May, the board motioned for the judge to relinquish control over the school system. In its meeting, it voted to approve the statement that it was "now operating a unitary school system" and therefore moved that "the operation of the school system be returned to local control."[137] The NAACP disagreed. It called this motion "clearly premature" and requested the district court retain jurisdiction because "not all roots and branches of discrimination in the system have been eliminated."[138]

On January 18, 1977, the Oklahoma City Board of Education won the freedom it had sought for two decades. The federal district court relinquished control of the district, effectively ending its desegregation order. The court held that the Oklahoma City schools were in compliance with the Finger plan and found intent by the board to comply in the future. Judge Bohanon saw "substantial compliance" with the order.[139] After examining the request, the judge felt that terminating jurisdiction would not "result in the dismantlement of the Plan or any . . . action . . . to undermine the unitary system."[140] The board had instituted the Finger plan from 1972 to 1977, which appeared long enough to the judge to ensure compliance in the future.

The board's reaction stressed a return to its priority of local control, if not neighborhood schools. Board president Pat Potts responded to the 1977 decision with determination, calling on the board "to turn its focus from body counts to the real needs in the classroom."[141] Former board member Yvonne York was more resolute, calling on the current board immediately "to revert back to the neighborhood schools concept."[142] Superintendent Lillard restated that "the authority and responsibility to operate a school district should be with the local school board and the local citizens."[143] As usual, *neighborhood schools* and *classroom needs* were euphemisms for the same goal—school assignment plans made with the intent of pleasing predominantly white families and community preferences, not achieving integrated classrooms. For over twenty years, the board had strategized about how to pursue its priorities and prioritize neighborhood schools, even if that approach resulted in one-race schools. In the 1950s, it had resisted the law; in the 1960s it had found ways to comply while also resisting. Finally, the Oklahoma City School Board was in control of its policies.

In November 1984, the board reverted back to prioritizing neighborhood schools. At its November 19 meeting, it unveiled a new assignment plan that reassigned 36 percent of students, with the goal of reducing the numbers of students being bussed away from their neighborhood schools.[144] The new plan ended the Finger plan's reassignment of students in grades one through four and created thirteen new neighborhood schools without busing. Some Black leaders in the community, like the Urban League and state representative and former board of education member Freddye Williams, supported the plan because it eased the burden of busing on Black children. Others called the plan a return to segregation. After the board adopted its new plan on December 17, 1984, state senator E. Melvin Porter announced, "[The board] is going to be in court. There's no way in the world we can have a separate system and an equal system."[145] The local chapter of the NAACP criticized the board for adopting the plan without representation from Black communities.[146]

The board still saw itself as operating in compliance with the law. Earlier that year, when families complained again about mandated busing, the board restated its commitment to desegregation. Superintendent Donald Wright replied to the families that, although the court had relinquished control, "in no way are we free not to have a desegregation plan. We are operating now in good faith[.]"[147] However, as Superintendent Wright noted, the board had begun a study in the summer of 1984 of the busing patterns with the intent of possibly revising its plans.

In the winter of 1985, the plaintiff families sought to reopen the desegregation case at the district court. They argued that the board's new pivot away from the 1972 court-ordered Finger plan would resegregate half of the grades in the school district. Clara Luper, a petitioner and NAACP chapter official, argued, "We feel the board of education plan will resegregate public school and will turn the clock back" to the days of segregation.[148] The trial was set for April 1985.

The district court was unconvinced and refused to reopen the case. Judge Bohanon wrote for the court, finding that the board had adopted the December 1984 assignment plan for legitimate purposes, such as reducing the busing burden on Black students, increasing parent involvement, and maintaining the fifth-year centers. The new plan therefore "is not discriminatory" and was adopted without "the intent to discriminate." The court acknowledged that the racial composition might change, but that this would be a "largely unavoidable consequence."[149] Ultimately, Judge Bohanon wrote:

> The court is convinced that the board of Education is equally concerned about the health, education and well-being of both black and white students.[150]

The school district had achieved the court's purpose, and the district court was willing to give the board the benefit of the doubt.

The question of how long and under what circumstances a court can maintain control of a school district after it has achieved compliance with desegregation orders would ultimately land the Oklahoma City schools before the Supreme Court. The plaintiff families were given some hope in June 1986 when the Tenth Circuit reversed the district court opinion. The appellate court found that the 1977 declaration that the Oklahoma City schools were unitary did not on its own dissolve the 1972 court injunction that took control of student assignment and implemented the Finger plan.[151] As a result, the plaintiffs were allowed to challenge the board policy change in December 1984 as discriminatory.

The district court heard the case but remained unconvinced. In 1987, it held the Oklahoma City schools to be unitary. It officially dissolved the 1972 injunction and with it the mandate for the Finger plan.[152] The court found that the Oklahoma City school segregation resulted from "demographic change" and that when the school district was declared unitary in 1977, the court should have dissolved the 1972 injunction:

> The Oklahoma City schools were at that time, as they are today, operating as a unitary system, wholly without discrimination to blacks or other minority students, faculty or staff.[153]

Essentially, it held the segregation that persisted was not by law, but was the effect of private social decisions, and therefore it was beyond the purview of the court to step in.

The Oklahoma City Board of Education was able to prioritize neighborhood schools by practicing resistant compliance to court desegregation orders from 1963 to 1972. It took the district court stepping in and requiring a specific school assignment plan for the Oklahoma City schools to desegregate. The board initially fought the stringent court order in 1972 but ultimately agreed to implement it. The 1972 desegregation order forced public schools in Oklahoma City to be integrated for over a decade. Ultimately, however, the board members reverted to prioritizing neighborhood schools after the order was dissolved. The board, therefore, was allowed to return to its policy of neighborhood schools, despite the resegregating effects. The Tenth Circuit again reversed and vacated this decision.[154] However, after thirty years of refusing to hear appeals from the Oklahoma City schools case, the Supreme Court in 1991 upheld the district court's decision to dissolve the injunction.[155]

## Conclusion

The Supreme Court decision in *Dowell* further developed equal protection jurisprudence after *Brown*. *Dowell* articulated the standard for knowing whether a school system was in compliance with desegregation orders and therefore whether the district courts should discontinue judicial supervision and control of school board policy. The court held that lower courts should determine whether a school district had "complied in good faith with the desegregation decree" and, if so, the court should dissolve the decree if it finds the "vestiges of past discrimination had been eliminated to the extent practicable."[156] To determine whether past discrimination had ended, the district courts were to look at school district student assignment procedures and "every facet of school operations—faculty, staff, transportation, extra-curricular activities and facilities," the factors articulated in *Green v. County School Board* (1968).[157]

The decision was heavily influenced by a conservative court majority eager to get the federal courts out of the business of running local school districts. The *Dowell* majority was strongly in favor of limited judicial supervision and prioritized local control of education, so any test for dissolving desegregation orders could not be broad or sweeping. In this respect, *Dowell* was unlike the appellate court test, which "would condemn a school district, once governed by a board which intentionally discriminated, to judicial tutelage for the indefinite future."[158] *Dowell*, therefore, prioritized local control by uncoupling unitary status from the aim of *Brown*, which was ending the stigma of inferiority that resulted from segregated schools. As long as a school system was unitary, court jurisdiction would end, even if resegregation would occur or if the stigmatic injury was still present.

Three justices disagreed in dissent; if the state had required one-race schools historically, then school districts had to do something to eliminate one-race schools now. For the dissent, the injury of stigma was why the desegregation order had been mandated in the first place, so the question of whether stigma was present should be central when deciding whether the order should be dissolved. It was not enough that the school district no longer enforced segregation; "the *effects* of past discrimination remain chargeable to the school district."[159] The state historically sponsored one-race schools. The persistence of one-race schools, therefore, "perpetuates the message of racial inferiority associated with segregation."[160]

Indeed, prior Supreme Court cases required school districts to address the effects of historical segregation. The dissent cites the prior precedent holding that "school systems must redress any *effects* traceable to former *de jure* segregation."[161] "Avoiding reemergence of the harm" was part of the court's prior precedents that "insist[ed] on remedies that insure lasting integration in formerly segregated systems."[162] Removing the remedy in Oklahoma City—and therefore allowing the system to resegregate—ran contra not only to court precedents but also to the imperative to remedy the injury in *Brown*.

The majority was willing to blame segregated schools on private decisions; the dissent argued that the current housing patterns stemmed from prior racially discriminatory public policies. The majority in *Dowell* ascribed the current patterns of segregated neighborhoods to the preferences of homebuyers and therefore relieved the school district of any responsibility to integrate schools. The dissenters disagreed. They argued that dismissing segregated neighborhoods as the result of private family choices

> Pays insufficient attention to the roles of the State, local officials, and the board in creating what are now self-perpetuating patterns of residential segregation.[163]

You broke it, argued the dissenters, so you are still responsible for fixing it.

Ultimately, the result in *Dowell* was that desegregation orders could still be ended even if the injury at the root of *Brown*—that of racial stigma from forced separation—was still present and even if the schools would resegregate if the orders were ended. *Dowell*, along with other *Brown* progeny, made a pathway for continued segregation by saying that courts would not touch de facto segregation or require out-of-district busing. This result had the effect of segregating segregation from judicial oversight, with courts holding that if the problem was not caused by law, there was no constitutional violation. This meant schools could resist *Brown* by highlighting the effects of residential segregation on school composition.

*Dowell*'s impacts on a national level set a standard for district courts to follow in ending oversight of desegregation orders. The board of education at issue in *Dowell* also provided a roadmap for how to continue board priorities in the face of such orders. *Dowell* was decided in 1991, but the Oklahoma City Board of Education started its resistance to desegregation back in 1954, immediately following the *Brown* decision. Unlike more notorious white local officials across the South, the Oklahoma City Board of Education did not stand on the schoolhouse steps, close down schools, or refuse to accept the jurisdiction of the court in other ways. Its mass resistance was relatively short-lived.

Instead, the Oklahoma City Board of Education spent ten years professing to comply with the district court orders while resisting it at the same time—the hallmark of resistant compliance. It dragged out all its legal options and spent years arguing that desegregation did not imply any affirmative obligation to integrate. It made gestures toward compliance without any official action or implementation plans—"paper compliance and policy statements." It dragged its feet and then claimed it had run out of time. Most stridently, the board argued that desegregation was at odds with its core commitment to neighborhood schools, though when schools were legally required to be segregated, the school district had no problem busing students across town to maintain a segregated system.

The Oklahoma City Board of Education's resistant compliance was an attempt to comply with a ban on de jure school segregation while at the same time resisting integrating schools. The school board was a racially conservative institution, hewing to the dominant white community preference for segregation instead of the racially progressive legal mandate in *Brown*. But resistant compliance is not a fundamentally conservative tactic. Racially progressive institutions also resist legal bans while complying. Five years after *Dowell*, voters in California and the federal appellate court over Texas banned affirmative action. Universities in these states did not end their commitments to racial diversity but rather found ways to comply with these bans while continuing to promote diversity. Resistant compliance is both a conservative and a progressive project.

3

# Prioritizing Diversity

*Automatic Admissions Plan for the University of Texas*

It was the spring of 1996, and David Montejano, a faculty member at the University of Texas at Austin, was frustrated, angry, and moving quickly. The Fifth Circuit had just banned affirmative action in admissions for universities across Texas in *Hopwood v. Texas*.[1] As the director of the University of Texas Center for Mexican American Studies, he knew how crucial this admissions practice was for maintaining racial diversity in the student population. Montejano was determined to help craft a policy solution in this newly limited legal landscape. He found an ally in a state senator.

State senator Gonzalo Barrientos (D-Austin) knew what it was like to make history and understood the importance of underrepresented voices. Barrientos had risen to become the first Mexican-American state senator from Austin after growing up in a segregated community and attending a segregated elementary school.[2] He had experienced personally the effects of inequality:

> You have to live it to really know what it is about. And it is about being treated unequally. It is about not getting promotions in your work. It is about training someone else for the job you have, then getting demoted. Walk in my shoes, and see what it's all about.[3]

Barrientos was an alumnus of the University of Texas at Austin. The new ban on affirmative action struck him as an injustice, and he wanted to respond.

Barrientos and Montejano were united in their commitment to protecting racial diversity across Texas universities. They joined a team of similarly committed faculty, activists, and legislators to reach a legally compliant solution for their policy goal. Barrientos would later recall their work—and success—as one of his proudest legislative accomplishments.[4]

When the ban passed, affirmative action had been helping to achieve racial diversity at the University of Texas for some time. Since the 1960s, university administrators at Texas (and across the country) had followed policies that gave special consideration to applicants' racial backgrounds. At the end of the twentieth century, however, affirmative action bans eliminated the primary tool for creating racially diverse campuses at elite public universities and restrained their ability to maintain this diversity going forward. The story of universities' commitment and adaptation in the face of these bans makes up the rest of this book.

Within weeks of the ban on affirmative action in Texas, senator Gonzalo Barrientos was already organizing. The collection of scholars, activists, and legislators he brought together—the "brain trust"—would within a year shepherd in a public policy response. Among this group, faculty at the University of Texas zeroed in on the question of how to maintain racial diversity in their student population with new policies that, to comply with the ban, could not take race into account. Ultimately, they made use of the extensive data on de facto racial segregation in Texas public schools. If a school was almost entirely Black and Hispanic, then so would be that school's top students. Entrenched segregation in Texas could ensure racial diversity if a policy of admitting those top students applied equally to all Texas high schools. The policy solution also included room for universities to maneuver; Texas admissions personnel jumped on the chance to create school-specific policies that would still prioritize racial diversity, albeit in ways that caught a broader range of diverse students. University administrators added additional essays and contextual review to their admissions process, ensuring that students' educational background, adversity, and socioeconomic factors would weigh into admissions decisions.

This chapter begins with a discussion of the affirmative action ban that affected the state of Texas, the Fifth Circuit opinion in *Hopwood v. Texas*. Although the ban applied to all Texas universities, faculty at the University of Texas at Austin were responsible for the policy innovation that followed. Next, the chapter examines how a team of legislators and university faculty, unwilling to give up their commitments to racial diversity, innovated a new admissions policy that maximized student body racial representation in universities by leveraging preexisting patterns of segregation in state high schools. State legislators then shepherded the policy into law, with unlikely coalition allies helping them along the way. Lastly, the University of Texas implemented the new admissions policy together with changes to the application review process that allowed it to prioritize underrepresented students.

## The *Hopwood* Opinion and Banning Affirmative Action in Texas

The University of Texas at Austin had relied on Powell's opinion in *Bakke* as though it had announced set law. Recall that this 1978 Supreme Court decision provided a constitutional path for affirmative action if the review method was holistic, without the admissions process giving decisive weight to an applicant's racial background. The Texas Law School's program assigned different admissions thresholds based on race. It gave each applicant an academic rating: a number determined by an applicant's grade-point average and score on the Law School Admissions Test (LSAT). At one score, racial minorities were guaranteed admission, and at a slightly higher score, white applicants were presumptively denied admission.[5] In 1992, Cheryl Hopwood, a denied white applicant, sued.

*Hopwood* was a legal challenge by a twenty-nine-year-old aspiring lawyer, but the engine driving the case was a conservative public interest impact litigation law firm, the Center for Individual Rights (CIR). Hopwood was the "perfect plaintiff" for this case—a white woman from a lower socioeconomic background who had worked nearly full time to support herself during college yet managed an almost perfect grade-point average.[6] The Center for Individual Rights would later spearhead challenges to the University of Michigan's undergraduate and law school programs, which would ultimately be decided by the Supreme Court.[7]

The *Hopwood* plaintiffs lost the initial case in the district court and appealed to the Fifth Circuit, which reversed the lower court.[8] The appellate court ruling declined to follow Justice Powell's opinion in *Bakke*:

> There has been no indication from the Supreme Court, other than Justice Powell's lonely opinion in *Bakke*, that the state's interest in diversity constitutes a compelling justification for governmental race-based discrimination.[9]

Instead, the Fifth Circuit held that under the Equal Protection Clause of the Fourteenth Amendment, the University of Texas did not have a sufficiently compelling interest to use race as a factor in its admissions process:

> The use of race in admissions for diversity in higher education contradicts, rather than furthers, the aim of equal protection. Diversity fosters, rather than minimizes, the use of race. . . . The use of race, in and of itself, to choose students simply achieves a student body that looks different. Such a criterion is no more rational on its own terms than would be choices based upon the physical size or blood type of applicants.[10]

Despite the *Bakke* judgment, the Fifth Circuit denied in *Hopwood* that there was a compelling educational value in racially diverse student populations. Without a compelling interest, the affirmative action policy could not survive the strict review that courts apply to public policy that is race-conscious.

In concluding that the Law School was effectively operating two separate admissions tracks for white and racial minority applicants, the court

banned the use of race in university admissions. This ban went into effect across all states in the Fifth Circuit—Texas, Louisiana, and Mississippi.[11] The University of Texas appealed to the Supreme Court and was
not granted certiorari.[12] As a result, federal law on affirmative action in
university admissions was applied differently across the country, with
the majority of the states under *Bakke*—following Powell's path—and
the Fifth Circuit states now governed by *Hopwood*.

University administrators' first step was to investigate the breadth
of the new law: How widely did *Hopwood* reach? Seeking guidance on
private donation scholarships and other recruitment policies in January 1997, University of Houston president, William Hobby Jr., reached
out to Texas attorney general Dan Morales for clarification of the Fifth
Circuit decision. Three weeks later, the answer dealt another swift
blow—universities could not consider race in any capacity in their policymaking. Morales announced that the decision was not only a ban
on race-conscious admissions policies but also a ban on policies that
used race in awarding scholarships and in recruitment and retention
programs. Essentially, unless there were findings of past discrimination
on the part of the institution, "the consideration of race or ethnicity is
expressly prohibited . . . [in] all internal institutional policies, including admissions, financial aid, scholarships, fellowships, recruitment and
retention, among others."[13] Morales took to print to defend his opinion.
In a February 1997 op-ed in the *Austin American-Statesman*, he argued
that maintaining racial diversity was just a problem of creativity for admissions officials: "If our university leaders are truly committed to diversity, then our universities will be diverse."[14] *Hopwood* had corralled
the Longhorns.

The Morales opinion stunned admissions officials. Bruce Walker, director of admissions at the University of Texas at Austin, explained:

> [*Hopwood*] was bad enough. But then Attorney General Morales ex-
> tended that decision. . . . It may seem inconsequential, but it was huge. . . .
> You can't identify students to tell if they are in your applicant pool. UT

was disadvantaged relative to other schools. You then have to depend on what you know about geography. After you tinker, we're finally getting it right.[15]

David Montejano, director of the University of Texas Center for Mexican American Studies, remembered the official opinion as creating "contained chaos" amid the confusion over where to go from here.[16]

Within the chaos, administrators and faculty mobilized. The state attorney general would not provide guidance on ensuring racial diversity after the affirmative action ban, but race progressives in higher education across the state remained committed to the cause. Montejano recalls that the attorney general's opinion was the turning point for a "small working group of concerned faculty" who, together with legislators, began to collaborate on a response.[17] In the service of continued student body diversity, policymakers in Texas turned to geography.

## The Academic "Brain Trust" and the Commitment to Racial Diversity

The University of Texas at Austin administration was fiercely committed to the goal of racial diversity on the Longhorn campus. Two days after the Fifth Circuit decision, three hundred students and community members gathered on campus at a rally led by the UT president, Robert Berdahl. Here, Berdahl decried the decision, calling it "virtual resegregation."[18] Two days later, four hundred UT community members marched to the state capitol to demand an appeal.[19] President Berdahl addressed the university in an editorial published in the campus newspaper the *Daily Texan*:

A diverse student body has come to be thought of as an educational resource as important as the quality of the library, the faculty, laboratories, or any other key asset of a university. We have come a long way from the days when governors stood in the doorways blocking access to education. . . . We ought not retreat from this progress.[20]

"We are the victims in the *Hopwood* case," relayed University of Texas Law School dean Michael Sharlot.[21] Similarly, University of Texas chancellor William Cunningham responded defensively to the critique that the university system would fail to maintain racial diversity without affirmative action: "We are committed to doing everything humanly possible to have a diverse student population at the University of Texas."[22] The leaders of the University of Texas came out swiftly and strongly against *Hopwood* and the blow it struck to their educational commitment to student body racial diversity.

There was a more practical matter to contend with as well—the risk of losing out to the competition. The University of Texas at Austin is a national university, competing for the top students with universities from across the country. The Longhorns were now hobbled because the other universities were not under a ban on affirmative action. Spencer Bynes, a UT admissions official, reported:

> The very elite African American and Hispanic students are being recruited away by out-of-state schools offering them major money. In the past, I could compete because we had these minority scholarships. We don't have those anymore.[23]

Academically talented minority students who might have been aided in admission by affirmative action or might have chosen to attend UT because of race-conscious scholarships now might receive a better offer from somewhere else. Senator Barrientos was well aware of this recruiting disadvantage for the state's flagship school: "The rest of the country is using race as a factor—we're not. Our hands are tied."[24]

Senator Barrientos began by recruiting some of the top minds in educational policymaking to come up with a solution. A few months after *Hopwood*, he created a task force comprising legislators, academics, and activists to study ways to maintain diversity. The participants included scholars from the University of Texas and the University of Houston, Mexican American Legal Defense and Educational Fund (MALDEF) attorney Al Kaufmann, and legislative aides to Senator Barrientos and Texas representative Irma Rangel (D-Kingsville).[25] Ultimately, this group proposed the idea that became the new admission plan.

Segregation was endemic to Texas public high schools, which meant that researchers could estimate the racial composition of any given high school student body in Texas. David Montejano, director of the Center for Mexican American Studies at the University of Texas at Austin, led the research behind the eventual policy proposal. He started with current data on the composition of Texas high schools and proposed an automatic admission plan based on the segregation the data revealed. By looking at the current racial composition of the top students in each high school, he could estimate what top percent needed automatic admission to ensure a certain racial diversity in each entering class. He wrote:

> Generally, my estimates were based on hypothesized degrees of segregation (using the 1994 graduating class of 17,000 top 10 percenters as an example), African Americans would comprise 14.7 percent (2,500) and Mexican Americans 26.4 percent (4,500) of the top 10 percent. At 50 percent segregation, assuming for the sake of argument that "minorities" would not make the top 10 percent in integrated schools, the numbers were logically reduced by half: African Americans comprised 7.35 percent (1,250) and Mexican Americans 13.2 percent (2,250).[26]

It could not be assumed that racial minorities would be represented at the top of the class of an integrated high school in any reliable proportion. However, at a segregated high school, with its homogenous racial makeup, the top students would look like everyone else in the school.

Pervasive segregation, then, helped ensure that a race-neutral automatic admission plan would maintain racial diversity. Montejano determined that relying on segregation for an admission plan would produce a racially diverse admitted class, or at least a class that was more diverse than the current cohorts in the state's top universities.[27] The proposal, Montejano explained, "used the fact of segregation and geographic concentration of minorities at the high school level to achieve diversity at the university level."[28] Montejano argued that the plan was "simple, fair, predictable—and most importantly, it did not use race-specific criteria."[29] Years later, in an interview recalling this research, Montejano noted he had thought, "This is going to work because of the geographic concentration and segregation of Mexicanos and Blacks in the State."[30] Race-neutral public policy relied on consistent racial patterns. An admissions policy based on high school would be a way to protect racial diversity without looking at race. The automatic admissions policy became known as the Top Ten Percent plan, and later the Top Ten Percent law.

Once the policy was proposed, the next step was legislative strategy. Following the law as required by *Hopwood* was imperative. Texas representative Irma Rangel (D-Kingsville), who would ultimately guide the Top Ten Percent plan through the state legislature, trumpeted her legal background in the house debates over the proposed legislation. She cited her time as a law clerk to demonstrate her commitment to following the law:

> We have no intent whatsoever of violating any law. . . . My first job when I graduated from law school was a law clerk with a chief judge at the US district court for the western district and I know that any legislation created in this legislature is not going to supersede any federal order and we have no intent of doing that . . . we want ours to comply we do not want to violate any law.[31]

The Top Ten Percent plan was a solution precisely because its drafters saw it as compliant with the law.

Once the team had turned to strategy, it was the researchers' turn to learn. On September 6, 1996, Senator Barrientos held the Hispanic

Summit on Affirmative Action Policies, which introduced two plans for maintaining racial diversity in the wake of *Hopwood*: an automatic admission plan for the top 10 percent of each high school's graduating class and a "fifteen factor" plan.[32] After the conference, a working group was formed to design legislative strategy. Montejano recalls that "with professors and legislators sitting in a circle, the discussion often had the feel of a graduate seminar, with Rangel and Barrientos as the professors and the professors as the attentive students."[33]

Representative Rangel sent the academics back with homework. The legislators on the committee were intrigued, but they wanted more than Montejano's hypotheticals. Rangel replied to the preliminary policy report with, "This sounds very good, but I want the real numbers. Go out and do the research and come back."[34] The university researchers went back to the data, and Montejano's suspicions were confirmed. The research on the geographic and racial distribution of students confirmed his "intuitive sense" of the effects of segregation and solidified his proposal to use the top 10 percent of the high school class for the automatic cutoff.[35]

The committee had to make some assumptions where they did not have data. Their educated guesses also focused on the racial backgrounds of these student unknowns. The researchers had based the racial makeup of each high school on the data students provide when they register to take the main college entrance test, the SAT. Using SAT data for the racial distribution of a high school meant there was still a question about the four thousand students in the top 10 percent statewide who had not taken the SAT. But researchers figured that number was on their side. Montejano reported:

> Presumably, a good fraction of these were minorities which, when added to [the data they did have], might yield an automatic admissions pool that could consist of approximately 20 percent Hispanic and 10 percent Black. Again, one only had to compare these figures with the current percentages at the University of Texas at Austin to realize that a top 10 percent plan might be the best way to maintain a minimum floor for diversity.[36]

Montejano adjusted the automatic admissions thresholds and estimated to fill the gaps in his data based on student racial background. Student racial background was therefore the key variable that showed they had found the "best way" to "maintain a minimum floor for diversity." Racial diversity, in other words, shaped the way the research committee drafted its policy for legislative consideration.

With a policy crafted by the university's experts, Representative Rangel and Senator Barrientos were now in charge of formalizing the plan into law. From the professors, whom Rangel called her "brain trust," she needed ideas—the proposed plan, the data to support it, and a sounding board for questions.[37] From there, however, she wanted the legislators to shepherd the law through to completion. Their message to the academics was, "Let them handle the politics." Rangel "wanted to pursue a 'low key' approach that would not 'rile up the opposition.'"[38] Rangel was determined that the committee members would stay in their lanes.

In short, after the *Hopwood* decision, leaders in higher education across Texas came out in support of racial diversity on university campuses. University administrators, scholars, legislators, and activists immediately formed a research group to figure out how to continue this commitment in the newly changed legal landscape. Their plans were motivated by a broad concern for diversity, and specifically a concern for racial diversity now that campuses could not practice affirmative action in admissions policies. The researchers found a way to prioritize racial diversity by leveraging a policy based on preexisting de facto segregation in primary and secondary schools across the state. The research group ultimately settled on a law that granted automatic admissions to the top 10 percent of graduating high school students in the state and also guided universities on the factors they could consider for the remaining admitted students.

## Passing the Top Ten Percent Plan into Law

Though Senator Barrientos was a key player in organizing the task force that conceived of the law, in the Republican-controlled state senate, his influence was limited. Senator Teel Bivins (R-Amarillo) chaired the Senate Education Committee and therefore decided which measures in response to *Hopwood* would receive a vote in the senate. Around the time the Top Ten Percent bill was being proposed for a vote, Bivins proposed a different response. Together with Senator Royce West (R-Dallas), he introduced Senate Bill 1419, which established tiers for admission that told universities which criteria they could use to accept certain percentages of the class. The top 10 percent of a high school's graduating class was not the only factor for admission in this plan; Bivins wanted 40 percent of admitted students to come in through a combination of standardized testing, class rank, and grade-point average.[39]

Senator Bivins prioritized full compliance with the affirmative action ban and focused on removing race from any public policy. He argued that his proposed plan was a "race-neutral admission policy for our state universities [and] addresses concerns raised by the *Hopwood* decision in a race-neutral fashion."[40] He agreed that the racial diversity in Texas made maintaining racial diversity "important," but he felt that *Hopwood* mandated that any policy be race neutral.[41] Nothing race conscious would make it out of his committee.

The brain trust academics had rejected the idea of including standardized testing in the Top Ten Percent plan. With the SAT's history of privileging educational background and access, academics worried that including SAT scores in automatic admission determinations would depress the numbers of racial minorities. Watching the process, Montejano was concerned about Bivins's reformulation of admissions thresholds: "Because Mexican Americans and African Americans generally have lower SAT scores than whites, such an amendment would have effectively undermined the potential of the bill to maintain diversity."[42] In the end, however, the Republicans had majority control. SB 1419 was a "moving train," as Steve Kester, legislative aide to Senator Bivins, remarked to Democratic supporters, and it was the only policy response to *Hopwood* on the table.[43] Senator Barrientos and others ultimately gave it their support, and it passed the senate on April 10, 1997.[44]

Representative Rangel did not receive it so enthusiastically in the house. She held the power in the Texas House, and she used it to prioritize the Top Ten Percent plan. In 1997, Democrats controlled the lower chamber in Texas, which made Rangel the chair of the House Higher Education Committee, where any response to *Hopwood* would move before reaching a full vote. Rangel held the Bivins senate bill back from consideration, instead prioritizing HB 588—the Top Ten Percent admission plan. She "wanted a very simple bill [so] that the universities could understand exactly what they had to do."[45] On March 25, 1997, the Higher Education Committee sent the proposed legislation to the house floor. Debate in the house on HB 588 began on April 16 and was contentious. Republicans objected to the exclusion of the SAT and to the perceived discrimination against schools (typically wealthy and suburban) that were filled with top-performing students. They also claimed that relying so heavily on class rank would exclude Christian high schools and homeschool graduates.

Republicans argued, moreover, that the bill disadvantaged students who had not faced educational disadvantage. In addition to admitting the top 10 percent of each graduating high school class, the proposed bill authorized universities to look at various indicators of socioeconomic disadvantage or adversity. Some Republicans objected that these factors required "disadvantage diversity" from students. One member argued the bill "strikes against" students for having parents who went to college or spoke English.[46] Representative Jerry Madden (R-Richardson) argued:

> If you're white in a middle income suburban area and your mother and father went to college . . . and you're not bilingual then [a large number of] the slots in a major university are not available to you . . . this is not equitable.[47]

If admissions officers had flexibility, they would prioritize diversity of background, a factor these members felt would work against white, suburban, upper-middle-class students.

Relatedly, Republicans argued that the automatic admission plan would hurt wealthy suburban school districts. In these high schools, they argued, many academically talented students existed outside the top 10 percent of the class. The top 10 percent at a poorer performing high school was an "inequitable group" that would take spots away from students in more affluent districts, where academic merit extended well outside the top 10 percent:

> I want you to think about when you go back to your districts and you've got all these parents calling you about I can't get my child in a major university in the state of Texas if we pass this bill the reason's going to be because we've got an inequitable group taking up a significant portion [of the admitted class]. It's a sheer numbers game.[48]

Asking his colleagues how they would defend this bill back home, Representative Charles Howard (R-Sugar Land) argued that the Top Ten Percent plan went against the best interests of suburban high schools that had long enjoyed the distinction of seeing large numbers of their graduating seniors admitted to the state's top universities. Granting admission to the top 10 percent of students meant that students who had strong grade-point averages, strong standardized testing, and the advantage of a well-resourced high school education now faced steeper admissions criteria if they were not in the top 10 percent of their classes. Representative Madden claimed this was "a discriminatory bill against top performing school districts" and against "students who may not be in the top 10 percent but who are academically" still excellent.[49] These representatives saw discrimination against students who had succeeded according to the traditional indicators of success.

Republicans argued that a focus on demographics was a preference for race by another name. Representative Howard stated:

> We're going to have diversity. This is a very diverse state. We've got diversity now and we're going to have diversity in the future. What we're

talking about here is we're giving preferences and that's what the Hopwood case was all about—not to give preferences.[50]

Texas universities, Republicans contended, would have a broadly diverse student population just by virtue of admitting students predominantly from in-state high schools in a broadly diverse state. Any explicit targeting of particular demographics would violate the spirit of *Hopwood*.

Representative Rangel pushed back against claims that guiding universities with suggested admissions factors constituted discrimination against affluent students. Suggesting factors was not the same as making demographics determinative. "We don't have weights on these factors, we don't require weights on these factors," she said; rather, the bill would "give universities flexibility to choose the applicants they want."[51] Letting socioeconomic factors boost admissions decision-making was a way of leveling the playing field, not tipping it away from high-powered suburban high schools.

Ultimately, education leaders in both chambers determined the shape of the law. Republicans in the house did not come around on the Top Ten Percent plan, and the vote over the automatic admission law was partisan. It passed the house, and it became the responsibility of the respective education committees in the senate and the house to figure out a compromise. Representative Rangel held back debate in her committee over the senate version in the hope that she and Senator Bivins could work out a compromise.

Each committee leader gave credit to their counterpart in the other chamber for achieving an agreement. Senator Bivins spoke of Representative Rangel's persuasiveness with other senators:

> I was a little surprised at how easy [the senators] gave up on the 50-40-10 plan. . . . I really thought we were going to have a battle. . . . I'm not sure how she did it; the Senate just accepted her deal and took it without any changes at all, which in my opinion is rather unusual.[52]

David Montejano also suggested that Representative Rangel traded support for future measures to secure Republican votes for the Top Ten Percent plan in the senate.[53] Representative Rangel, for her part, credits Senator Bivins with supporting the house legislation. Senator Bivins brought Republican support over to the house version of the bill. Republicans "knew who their leader was, and they followed Senator Bivins. I have to give him credit."[54] Ultimately, HB 588 passed the senate on May 31, 1997.[55]

The bill was successful because the GOP perceived it as race neutral. Senator Bivins stressed that Republicans approved the legislation because "it got at a social problem in a race-neutral fashion."[56] The lone Republican vote for the Top Ten Percent plan in the house cited the race neutrality of the bill as the reason for his support. Representative Ted Kamel (R-Tyler) argued during the house debates, "This legislation is race neutral, is gender neutral, it uses the criteria that the court ruled in the Hopwood decision."[57] When pushed by colleagues to weigh in on whether the automatic admission law complied with *Hopwood*, Representative Kamel responded, "Absolutely . . . or we would be back in the courthouse."[58]

To secure the governor's signature, the public policy had to be race neutral. Terrell Smith, legislative director for governor George W. Bush, was clear on that point, making sure Representative Rangel knew in those early working group meetings that "the Governor was [interested in] whatever we do be race-neutral."[59] In a speech after *Hopwood*, Bush railed against quotas: "Texans understand that quotas pit one group of people against another. Quotas are divisive, they're not united. Quotas give people an excuse for failure, quotas give people an excuse for blaming others."[60] Governor Bush signed the Top Ten Percent plan into law on June 20, 1997.[61]

The automatic admissions law was race conscious to the people who drafted it and race neutral to the policymakers who formalized it into law. The academics in the initial "brain trust" task force drew on data on demographics and segregation to create the specifics of the law.

They wanted a *Hopwood* response that would maintain racial diversity in higher education in Texas. Running the effects of the proposed public policy through data on segregation in Texas convinced legislators on the committee to support the proposal, an automatic admission plan for the top 10 percent of every high school graduating class in Texas. *Hopwood* had banned affirmative action, but the data on Texas high schools showed that this policy would maintain racial diversity. Rangel and Barrientos faced opposition in the state legislature, whose Republican members were concerned that this was affirmative action by another name. When the bill was introduced in January 1997, its language of race neutrality and the governor's quiet support allowed it to be shepherded into law. Ultimately, governor George W. Bush was able to use the measure to rally his support with Hispanic voters, and Texas universities had a plan to overcome the effects of the state's affirmative action ban.

## Implementing the Top Ten Percent Law

The Top Ten Percent law had two distinct pieces. Most famously, it gave all Texas high school students in the top 10 percent of their graduating classes—as ranked by grade-point average, not standardized testing—automatic admission to state public universities. The automatic admission applied to first-year students and could be taken advantage of within two years of high school graduation. Second, the law authorized universities to use eighteen other factors in determining the admission of prospective students outside the top 10 percent. Outside the automatic admissions, admissions offices had some flexibility to innovate and prioritize. Universities could consider a prospective student's socioeconomic background, whether the student's parents had attended college, whether the student spoke multiple languages, a personal interview, and extracurricular involvement.

In implementing this legislation, University of Texas at Austin administrators reshuffled their admissions processes in a way that prioritized

Black and Hispanic applicants. Specifically, the university changed the weights given to various factors in its admissions process. Admissions Director Bruce Walker recalled:

> We lessened the weight placed on the SAT. And we upped the weight place on leadership and extra-curricular activities (e.g. work experience, community service). . . . Lessening the weight of the SAT has helped us. You have to make a choice: (1) higher and higher SAT scores in class or (2) diversity.[62]

Officers also removed any positive weighting for Advanced Placement test results because these classes and tests are not available to students at underperforming schools. The university did not want to inadvertently give more privileged students an advantage. Admissions review at Texas moved to a multivalent process, avoiding rigid formulas. Applications from students outside the top 10 percent of their high school class were read by multiple readers who were trained to compare students holistically.[63]

The Top Ten Percent plan was crafted to maintain racial diversity, but it proved to be a success story for geographic diversity. Before the law passed, the trend in UT admissions concentrated enrolled students from a handful of "feeder" schools in mostly suburban and white areas. When the top 10 percent of students in every high school were guaranteed admission, students from a wider range of high schools began arriving on UT campuses. Additionally, the admissions process was re-weighted to include a holistic review of the remaining applications that deemphasized testing and other signs of privileged educational environments, which meant students from under-resourced high schools had a better chance of being admitted. Ultimately, feeder schools declined in admissions at UT, and high school representation from small cities and rural areas increased.[64] Indeed, top UT administrators argued that increasing geographic diversity, in addition to maintaining racial diversity, was a distinct advantage of the law.[65]

Not everyone, however, welcomed the new approach of decreasing the role of feeder schools and looking holistically at applications outside the top 10 percent. Families of students at high-performing high schools felt shortchanged. In these schools, students outside the top 10 percent of the high school class could have strong standardized test scores and yet not be admitted. University officials were also frustrated. Huge numbers of students were taking advantage of the Top Ten Percent law to secure admission. From 1998 to 2002, between 41 percent and 54 percent of admitted UT students gained admission through the policy, but by 2008, 81 percent of admits secured admission this way, cutting into the spaces in the class where admissions officers could use their discretion.[66] This meant that increasingly fewer students were admitted using the eighteen holistic factors—a way for admissions officers to deprioritize educational privilege and pay greater attention to hardship. By 2007, the Texas legislature was poised to limit admissions for top 10 percent students.[67]

But legislators for white, rural Texas intervened and saved the law meant to maintain racial diversity. The new policy had increased by 26 percent the number of high schools represented at the state's premier university. This created a new constituency in the legislature for protecting the Top Ten Percent law. Representative Jim McReynolds (R-Lufkin), a self-identified "rural white guy," voted against changes to the policy. After the amendment's defeat, he colorfully announced, "I was grinning like a possum eating a sweet potato."[68] Representative Warren Chisum (R-Pampa), a rural legislator, perceived the law as necessary: "Top 10 percent is really important to the people in rural Texas. A lot of times it's the only way we can get into big universities."[69] For these rural representatives, the law succeeded in expanding access—for rural students. The Top Ten Percent law had created an unintended constituency for its policies.

## Conclusion

Race progressives in Texas resisted the affirmative action ban by continuing to prioritize the educational benefits of racial diversity in higher education student populations. However, university officials and legislative sponsors were adamant that their public policies needed to comply with the law. Meeting in fall 1996, the University of Texas academic brain trust crafted a policy response based on segregation patterns in Texas. Texas high schools were de facto segregated, so admitting the top portion from every graduating class would ensure a racially diverse student population. These academics and administrators at the University of Texas created the Top Ten Percent plan and, with advocates in the legislature, formalized it under Texas law.

The new admissions policies did not immediately replicate race-conscious affirmative action in maintaining racial diversity. According to a quantitative study by Long and Tienda in 2008, the change was not enough to replace affirmative action and restore enrollment numbers to their pre-*Hopwood* levels.[70] The University of Texas at Austin enrolls upwards of forty thousand undergraduates each year, and underrepresented minorities are a small fraction of the population. To see the drop in the numbers up close, table 1 below shows the number of students offered admission and the number who chose to enroll.

TABLE 3.1. Admissions Offers and Enrollments of Freshman Students, University of Texas at Austin.

|  | 1994 | 1995 | 1996 | 1997 | 1998 |
|---|---|---|---|---|---|
| Black | 498 offers 303 enroll | 508 offers 276 enroll | 501 offers 239 enroll | 419 offers 167 enroll | 401 offers 196 enroll |
| Hispanic | 1,724 offers 815 enroll | 1,728 offers 847 enroll | 1,761 offers 823 enroll | 1,592 offers 807 enroll | 1,620 offers 861 enroll |

Source: Texas Higher Education Coordinating Board, "Report on the Effects of the Hopwood Decision on Minority Applications, Offers, and Enrollments at Public Institutions of Higher Education in Texas." 1998.

The effect of the *Hopwood* ban can be seen in the offers of admission and in the total numbers of students enrolling. For Black students, Texas accepted almost one hundred fewer applications. In a student body in the tens of thousands, one hundred is a small number. But only a couple of hundred Black students enroll as first-year students each year, and the lack of offers cut their first-year enrollments by nearly half in 1997. At first glance, Hispanic enrollments seem static at the university: a dozen fewer enrolled after *Hopwood*, similar to the previous year's declines. But once again, looking at the constrained admissions office reveals a different story. In the year affirmative action was banned at the university, the admissions office made nearly two hundred fewer offers to Hispanic students.

The university faulted the *Hopwood* decision for these declines. Analyzing the lower enrollment of racial minorities for fall 1997, University of Texas at Austin vice provost Richard Romo noted, "We know the reason for this sharp drop—because we've been having an increase (in minority applications)—is Hopwood. Nothing else can explain it."[71] The results at the University of Texas Law School were similar. The Law School's entering fall 1997 class had the lowest number of Black students since the court had ordered that Heman Sweatt integrate the Law School in 1950.[72] Mexican American admits also declined—seventy entered in 1996, whereas only forty-five entered in 1997.[73]

But within a decade after its enactment, the Top Ten Percent law had succeeded in restoring racial diversity to the University of Texas. In January 2003, UT issued a press release declaring that minority enrollment was now above pre-*Hopwood* levels and that the policy had "effectively compensated for the loss of affirmative action."[74] Bruce Walker credits the policies put in place after *Hopwood* for this success:

> It is possible to enroll a diverse class without using race, and the numbers demonstrate that can happen. This year we broadened the (admissions) definition to include leadership, community service and work experience in addition to grades.[75]

The university trumpeted its success at maintaining diversity without race-conscious policies—until it had a chance to bring them back.

As much as they cheered their policy solution, Texas administrators reevaluated it quickly when the courts opened new opportunities for policymaking. In 2003, *Hopwood* was overruled, which meant that Texas could start practicing race-conscious admissions again. In *Grutter v. Bollinger*, the Supreme Court affirmed its 1978 decision in *University of California v. Bakke* and reinforced a constitutional path for affirmative action. It affirmed that race-conscious programs must include race as one of many variables that could advantage a student in the application process. This decision did not affect policies in states not under affirmative action bans. But *Grutter* changed the law in Texas: it abrogated *Hopwood* and replaced it with a path for race-conscious policymaking.[76]

On the day of the *Grutter* decision, University of Texas at Austin president Larry R. Faulkner announced that the post-*Hopwood* policy changes were not "a good substitute for affirmative action" and that UT would reintroduce race-based admissions policies for the next cycle.[77] No longer bound by the Fifth Circuit decision in *Hopwood*, the Texas universities could model their policies on the Michigan Law admissions review system upheld by the Supreme Court in *Grutter*. President Faulkner affirmed that he was "very pleased" that *Hopwood* was no longer controlling law for Texas and that university admissions policies would be modified accordingly.[78] UT abandoned its post-*Hopwood* race-blind criteria and instead opted for race-conscious consideration in a holistic review format. The new polices increased Black student enrollment at UT to levels above those seen before the ban.[79]

The University of Texas's enthusiasm for bringing race back into its admissions review after *Grutter* drew another legal challenge to its admissions policies. Denied white applicants sued the University in 2008, arguing in *Fisher v. Texas* that the university did not need to revert to a race-conscious process, as the policies in effect after the affirmative action ban were already maintaining a diverse student body. In 2013, the court—with new Justices Roberts and Alito—underlined this argument and put teeth into *Grutter*'s narrow tailoring requirement, remanding *Fisher* for the lower court's investigation of whether race-neutral means would have sufficed to meet the University of Texas's racial diversity goals. If the automatic admissions plan was working in Texas, then the

University of Texas did not need, and therefore the Constitution would not permit, a return to affirmative action. On remand, the appellate court upheld the new race-conscious policy, and the program was appealed again to the Supreme Court. In *Fisher II*, by one vote, the court upheld the appellate decision, although it stressed that the university must continue to assess when, or if, its admissions and demographic data "have undermined the need for a race-conscious policy."[80] This was a tenuous nod to an uncertain future. The one vote—Justice Kennedy—retired in 2018.

As of this writing, Texas is no longer bound by an affirmative action ban, as it falls under the controlling law of *Grutter* and *Fisher*. This is not the case, however, for other national universities constrained by constitutional amendments. The affirmative action ban that impacted Texas was created by the federal courts, which meant that future federal court action could change the ban (as indeed it did). Michigan and California, in contrast, were subject to state constitutional amendments, which could impose a legal mandate outside federal law. Although the source of law was different, the flagship universities in both states responded similarly to the University of Texas; all of them doubled down on their commitments to racial diversity and worked to innovate new policies in compliance with the law.

4

## Expanding Access

*Holistic Admissions at the University of California*

It was the first day of the fall semester, 1995, and Bob Laird, the University of California at Berkeley admissions director, knew he needed to telegraph one message to everyone he met: he and his colleagues would not back down. That summer, the regents of the University, who controlled policymaking systemwide, had banned affirmative action in a vote that received national attention. As Laird headed back to campus for the start of the semester, he wore a T-shirt that read "I support affirmative action," in case anyone wondered where he stood on the vote.[1] He wasn't alone. Berkeley vice chancellor for student affairs Genaro Padilla called the vote "a test of our courage" and argued that the university must "protect" its racial diversity.[2] Berkeley chancellor Chang-Lin Tien echoed the sentiment. "I'm not giving up," he reported. Instead, they would find ways to "improve."[3]

A state constitutional ban on affirmative action would challenge that commitment, and the university stood at the center of the political contest over race-conscious public policies. Despite the spotlight, Berkeley, the university's flagship campus, did not back down from its commitment. Instead, it found a way to comply with the legal mandate while changing its policies to pursue its mission. Berkeley's policy innovation was led by its interpretation of the legal mandate: the affirmative action ban prohibited a set of race-conscious policies but not the principles motivating those policies. It responded to the affirmative action ban by broadening its admissions criteria to include holistic indicators, such as whether students came from disadvantaged backgrounds or had triumphed over adversity.

This chapter begins with the historical context of affirmative action at the University of California, which by the late twentieth century was deeply committed to maintaining a racially diverse student population. It explains how the affirmative action ban came to pass in California and how University of California administrators sought to preserve the racial diversity of their student body in the face of this new legal mandate. But Berkeley was in a tough spot, caught between the law and its mission. It had one of the largest applicant pools in the country. To sort through these applications efficiently, Berkeley's admissions officers relied heavily on quick indicators of merit, like test scores and grade-point averages. Now, defining academic merit with numbers alone was no longer an option if they wanted to maintain the racial diversity of their student body. The final sections of the chapter examine how admissions procedures were reinvented so that underrepresented students could receive more attention and benefit from all of the pathways to admission at UC.

## A "Beautiful Model for Diversity"[4]: The University of California

Although our current national preoccupation with affirmative action leads some to assume that it is a modern innovation, in fact the University of California has prioritized minority admission since the late nineteenth century. Starting in the 1880s, 10 percent of spots in the incoming first-year classes were for people from unusual circumstances or disadvantaged backgrounds, a percentage that rose to 35 percent of admits after World War II during the period of the GI Bill.[5] Rising student demand in the 1950s led the state legislature to mandate in 1960 that the flagship state university system—the campuses of the University of California—must be available to the top 12.5 percent of all graduating high school seniors in the state.[6] This move winnowed the number of spaces available to students from special circumstances or backgrounds who were outside this threshold; now, only 2 percent of admits would be designated as "special action" and worthy of admission because of their circumstances.

Despite the swelling application numbers and population demands, the university remained committed to its special admissions procedure. UC sought to maintain the racial diversity of its student body by increasing its outreach, setting up special programs to recruit and guide these students through college, and increasing the special admissions set-aside. In 1967, the board of regents increased special action to 4 percent of the incoming classes and by 1979 to 6 percent in order to enroll students "whose ethnic or economic background had disadvantaged them."[7] This meant that if a student was not among the top 12.5 percent of graduating seniors statewide, there was still a chance of being admitted. Six percent of the seats in the incoming class would go to students outside this top qualifying cut through the special action admissions process. All racial minority students could receive a second look.

By the late 1970s, the pressure was mounting and scrutiny increasing. Across the University of California campuses, student protests mirrored national protests over civil rights. Nationally and at UC, university administrators and admissions officers led their universities in instituting calls for or increasing the prevalence of affirmative action policies.[8] In California, the legislature approved in 1975 a statute that maintained that University of California undergraduate enrollment should reflect the ethnic diversity and gender balance of the state. What emerged from the politics of the era was a strong internal culture at the university that favored racial diversity.[9]

The Supreme Court then prohibited separate admissions tracks for students based on race. Recall that in 1978, *Regents of the University of California v. Bakke* cut a narrow constitutional path for affirmative action—it prohibited historical discrimination by race as a justification for affirmative action, with Justice Powell's concurrence offering up the educational value of a racially diverse student population as a possible compelling interest for universities in designing race-conscious admissions policies. But even if diversity was compelling enough to allow for the use of race, Powell had still struck the set-asides of the Medical School program. He explained the sort of consideration in pursuit of racial diversity that would meet the requirement of narrow tailoring by reaching into an amicus brief filed by Harvard University in the case. Harvard had an admissions plan that was race conscious, but race was one of many variables indicative of diversity that the admissions office considered. Powell upheld this approach as a way forward in his opinion:

> When the Committee on Admissions reviews the large middle group of applicants who are "admissible" and deemed capable of doing good work in their courses, the race of an applicant may tip the balance in his favor just as geographic origin or a life spent on a farm may tip the balance in other candidates' cases. A farm boy from Idaho can bring something to Harvard College that a Bostonian cannot offer. Similarly, a black student can usually bring something that a white person cannot offer.[10]

Justice Powell upheld the constitutional use of race in university admissions as an individualized review process that considered multiple factors of a student's background in order to produce a class that was a diverse, heterogenous mix of students.

Individual UC campuses expanded their use of race in admission in accordance with the *Bakke* decision, and UC-Berkeley led them in policy development. The crush of applications to UC had already forced the university to revise its policies before *Bakke*, and in 1971, the university admissions guidelines allowed for up to 50 percent of the admitted class to include nonacademic factors, in addition to academic review.[11] These vague factors resulted in a two-tiered admission system and decentralized admissions policymaking at each of the system campuses. The board of regents supported this approach and in 1988 issued a policy statement that each campus was to "encompass" the racial and ethnic diversity of the state.[12] The UC faculty senate's admissions committee reiterated that half of the class was to be admitted based on academics alone, and half of the admissions could also include supplemental factors.[13] When the numbers of applications began to grow in the 1980s and 1990s, the faculty admissions committee gave individual campuses more control by increasing the flexibility campuses had over the tiers and by enumerating the range of supplemental criteria campuses could use, including activities and leadership, circumstances like disability or low income, and "ethnic identity, gender, and location of residence."[14]

Admissions review was now more flexible, and race played a prominent role in the supplemental factors that could help a student gain admission. Minority enrollment at the University of California doubled between 1980 and 1990.[15] The review process at Berkeley is an example of how the two-tier system worked to increase the representation of underrepresented minorities. In 1997, Black, Hispanic, and Native American students made up only 11 percent of high school seniors in the state who had taken the minimum number of academic courses required for admission. However, these underrepresented minority students were 22.5 percent of those admitted to Berkeley that year.[16] The system worked well at maintaining a racially diverse student population. In 1996, the year before the affirmative action ban went into effect, nearly half of all racial minorities who applied to the elite UC campuses, Berkeley and UCLA, received an offer of admission.[17]

Since the early twentieth century, UC had used various measures to determine the applicable academic standards for admission, including operative "special action" for students from backgrounds that the university prioritized, like racial minorities. When separate admissions tracks and quotas for racial minorities were banned by *Bakke* in 1978, the university dropped any set-aside seats and instead introduced supplemental factors that could carry weight in the admissions process, such as race. But "that all stopped in '98, the first year after the bans."[18]

## "Change the Culture of the University"[19]: Banning Affirmative Action in California

Decentralized policymaking worked against the university when the regents began to focus on affirmative action. Two administrations of Republican California governors had left the regents more conservative than the state legislature. In winter and spring 1995, the regents focused their attention on affirmative action policies, led by newly minted regent Ward Connerly, urged on by his patron and presidential-hopeful governor Pete Wilson. The UC Office of the President—the centralized UC top administration—did not have an accurate response to even the most basic questions about current affirmative action programs. In his January 1995 memo to the regents, President Peltason cited a complex array of programs across the individual campuses.[20] President Peltason and Provost Massey also gave conflicting statements about the weight given to race across UC campuses. At one point, they claimed that race was not a dispositive factor in any application, but later evidence showed that two UC campuses automatically admitted all eligible racial minorities and that both Berkeley's and UCLA's tiered systems gave race significant consideration in the process.[21] President Peltason later conceded that some admissions procedures "need to be modified."[22] Connerly used this waffling and uncertainty to add fuel to the anti–affirmative action fire, citing problems in university credibility around the use of race in admissions and fears of *Bakke* violations.[23] Governor Wilson backed him up and argued to the regents that they need to take back control from a duplicitous university administration.[24]

The contentious fight among the regents generated national interest in affirmative action at UC and laid bare both faculty dissension and the top administrators' lack of awareness of the contours of policy. On July 20, 1995, Connerly had led the board in a narrow 14–10 vote to ban affirmative action across all UC campuses, while the Reverend Jesse Jackson led protesters outside in singing "We Shall Overcome" before the national media.[25] The ban became effective in January 1997 for the entering class in fall 1997.[26]

Eager to cement this gain into a statewide victory, activists led by conservative university faculty capitalized on the regents' ban to continue fighting policies that gave preference to race. Even before the UC regents acted in 1995, academic faculty were already mobilizing to ban affirmative action policies. Thomas Wood, a philosophy scholar, was the executive director of the California Association of Scholars (CAS), the state branch of the conservative National Association of Scholars; he brought the resources and connections of that organization to California. In 1991, Wood, along with fellow CAS member and California State University professor of anthropology, Glynn Custred, led CAS in fighting (ultimately unsuccessfully) California legislation that mandated diversity in state graduate admissions.[27] The organization channeled its energy into electoral action. Their primary complaint was that multiculturalism was taking hold on college campuses, and they found their target in university affirmative action policy. As the regents were proposing a UC affirmative action ban, Wood and Custred were drafting the statewide ban later named Proposition 209, which they modeled on the language in the 1964 Civil Rights Act and called the California Civil Rights Initiative (CCRI).

Connerly's campaign against affirmative action did not start as a national effort. He initially rebuffed invitations by Wood and Custred to join the California Civil Rights Initiative, seeing his involvement as limited only to the institution for which he was a regent.[28] However, Wood and Custred ultimately brought Connerly on board by playing to his fears that state politicians would be able to erode the UC ban without a ballot initiative campaign.[29] Connerly's addition was not the only stroke of political fortune for the initiative campaign; Republicans poured resources into the campaign, eager to capitalize on affirmative action in 1996 as an issue that could peel conservative Democrats in California away from the party as it sought to reelect president Bill Clinton.[30] Ultimately, both Clinton and Connerly won California; voters opted to reelect the president and to ban affirmative action.

The California Civil Rights Initiative, with Ward Connerly at the helm, brought onto the state ballot in 1996 a ban on affirmative action policies called Proposition 209. California became the first state in the country in which a plebiscite banned affirmative action at public universities. Connerly positioned himself as the main figurehead behind the California ban on affirmative action (1996) and behind later bans, including Washington's (1998) and Michigan's (2006).[31] What started as university professors disenchanted with higher education's commitment to multiculturalism and racial diversity became a national movement that sought to ban affirmative action in multiple states over the next decade.

## Berkeley's Commitment to Racial Diversity

The California state constitution now prohibited affirmative action, and top Berkeley administrators were unwilling to relinquish their commitment to racial diversity. "There was never a discussion of abandoning those principles," notes one UC administrator.[32] Bob Laird, the admissions director who wore a T-shirt proclaiming "I support affirmative action" the day after the regents' ban passed, was outspoken in his support of the university mission surrounding racial diversity.[33] He took that support to the opinion pages of higher education publications, writing in the *Chronicle of Higher Education*, "I knew that I would lose the confidence of my staff members—and therefore my ability to lead the office—if any of them began to doubt my commitment to access for underrepresented minority students."[34] Berkeley's chancellor Chang-Lin Tien linked his job to the commitment: "I've done much soul-searching on this, and if I thought that there was not any way we could maintain the kind of diversity we want and we need here because of this new policy, I would have resigned."[35]

Berkeley administrators framed their commitments to racial diversity in the language of struggle and tenacity to overcome the affirmative action ban. "There's no question now that [diversifying the campus] will be very, very hard to continue," said Patrick Hayashi, Berkeley vice chancellor for admissions.[36] And in the words of Berkeley vice chancellor for student affairs Genaro Padilla, "This will be a tremendous test of our courage and our commitments. We've built a beautiful model for diversity. Now, we must find some way to protect it."[37] They were intent on adapting their policies to follow the law, but also on not giving up their ideals. They believed they could accomplish two seemingly irreconcilable goals: "I'm not giving up [after the ban]. Our outreach can improve. Our admissions systems can improve," stated Berkeley chancellor Chang-Lin Tien.[38]

Many progressives, however, were angry with Berkeley because of what they perceived as its submission to the law. Instead, they wanted the university to defy the law. Democrats in the state legislature threatened to get involved with university policymaking if the university did not "subvert" the law.[39] Community members expressed outrage and asked admissions leaders simply to break the law. As Bob Laird said:

> The supporters of affirmative action, on the other hand, were harshly critical of Berkeley. Many had hoped that we'd figure out a way around Proposition 209 and were severely disappointed when we didn't. It was hard for everyone in the admissions office to hear friends and colleagues say or imply, "You didn't try hard enough," or "You weren't clever enough," or "You didn't have the courage and the will to maintain your commitment to underrepresented minority students." The most exasperating comment, which I heard a lot, was "You should have broken the law." It is remarkably easy, I realized, for people to recommend that others break the law.[40]

Berkeley policymakers were maneuvering in a narrow political space; the community would accept nothing less than progressive racial policy, which was unacceptable to the conservative regents.

Indeed, administrators at Berkeley, and the wider University of California Office of the President involved in the process of admissions, continually reported a commitment to comply with the language of the law. As one administrator reflected, the tone of all policymaking was, "What can we do within the context of the law?"[41] Administrators would push questions to university counsel: "How far can we possibly stretch outreach? How far can we go out on a limb . . . without putting the university at risk? We were cognizant of risk factors, but we were always proactively looking for different ways to do things better."[42]

Understanding how they created and implemented their policies requires understanding their vision of the law. They believed it prohibited only a set of actions, not the principles that guided those actions.

Administrators immediately framed the ban on affirmative action as a ban on a method—affirmative action that selected some students for recruitment and admission programs based on their race. The California ban required that the state "not discriminate against, or grant preferential treatment to" people on the basis of race or gender.[43] Across the university, faculty and administrators reacted to this language exclusively by changing their policies. They read the law's language—"no preference" to race—and interpreted it to mean that admissions and recruitment policies could not give special consideration to students from particular racial groups.

Accordingly, the University of California broadened its language, knowing that a broader definition would still encompass racial minorities. This meant a change in the language and approach they used to discuss racial diversity—namely, eliminating racial and ethnic diversity in policies and instead talking about students who were underserved or "underrepresented" at the university. The UC president's office defined underrepresented as

> students from groups that collectively achieved eligibility for the University . . . at a rate below 12.5 percent. These include African Americans, American Indians, and Chicano/Latinos and the terms "underrepresented" and "underrepresented minority" are used throughout this report to denote students from these groups.[44]

Underrepresented minority students were racial minorities who had the lowest rates of eligibility for admission to the University of California. Essentially, as one administrator put it, "When I say underrepresented, it's African-American, Latino, American Indian."[45]

The California affirmative action bans altered the "beautiful model for diversity" at the University of California. The previous policies had explicitly considered an applicant's race in the admissions decision, so they had to change. But because administrators had not abandoned their commitments to racial diversity, the new policies would "protect" this commitment by "improv[ing]" and "expand[ing]" existing systems. At both Berkeley and UCLA, the admit rates of underrepresented minorities after the affirmative action ban plummeted. Nevertheless, the University of California doubled down on its commitment to maintaining racial diversity by interpreting the law as requiring compliance with its language: no preference to race. This meant abandoning a method at achieving racial diversity, not the commitment to doing so.

## Making Admissions Local

In the midst of the California affirmative action bans, legislators and UC faculty realized that if giving preference to specific applicants through affirmative action could not maintain representation, then community-based preferences might be the solution. In 1996, two University of California sociology professors, Richard Flacks and Rodolfo Alvarez, had seeded the idea for an admissions guarantee to all California high schools. Their goal was to make admissions local and guarantee UC admission to the top students at all California high schools, even low-performing schools that also happened to be majority-minority. The California Master Plan for Higher Education already required that a top percentile of graduating seniors be admitted to the University of California, but this policy did not consider the relative programmatic and resource strength or weakness of a high school. Instead, students from across the state were assessed against each other, using only grades and standardized testing to determine the top performers. Unless students at weaker high schools somehow achieved miraculous SAT scores well above their schools' averages, this guarantee of admission would ring hollow for many. The Flacks and Alvarez proposal noted that existing eligibility and standardized testing requirements were holding these students back, particularly the UC requirement that applicants take multiple SAT II subject-based exams, which other public universities in the state did not require.[46]

State legislators translated this local admissions idea into numbers aggressively imagined to shake up racial representation at the University of California. Democratic representative Teresa Hughes proposed to extend the UC admissions guarantee to the top 12.5 percent of graduates in each California high school, rather than just the top 12.5 percent of high school graduates statewide. The proposal was considered aggressive and extreme by UC officials, and it was too risky for the academic senate.[47] Though the policy would increase the representation of students of color and students from rural districts, the senate's admissions committee argued that such students would have a difficult time succeeding at the University.[48] In a February 1998 report, the committee argued that it would result in less-prepared students being admitted to the university, which would mean a decrease in the rate of students graduating in four years, or even at all. The plan, they concluded, was "well intentioned" but a "poorly thought out alternative."[49]

The solution would not match the sweeping legislative vision of community-based admissions, but the legislative and faculty push had put the academic senate on the ropes to come up with an alternative plan. In May 1998, the admissions committee of the academic senate recommended to President Atkinson and the board of regents a plan to guarantee admission to a smaller cohort of the top graduates of each California high school. This "eligibility in a local context" policy would offer UC admission to the top 4 percent of each California high school. Students would be evaluated for rank in their high school at the end of their junior year and offered conditional admission if they were in the top 4 percent of the class, provided that they had no grade lower than a C in college-preparation-level courses, that they ultimately filed an application with the university, and that they understood that the policy did not guarantee admission to their campus of choice. The committee's chair, Keith Widaman, left open the door to future automatic admission increases, testifying at a legislative hearing that "we may [later] wish to alter" the percentages.[50] The policy was not the far-reaching admissions guarantee legislators had hoped for, but, Widaman's testimony noted, it would have an effect on racial representation: it was projected to add between three hundred and seven hundred Black and Hispanic students to the eligibility parameters, and it could encourage their high schools to strengthen the curriculum to make more students competitive for admission at UC.[51]

The governor made a direct pitch to the board of regents, arguing that the policy did not violate the affirmative action ban. Governor Davis earned national media attention at the beginning of his tenure for his support of the policy. At his inauguration, he stressed that admitting the top 4 percent from each high school would "ensure diversity and fair play."[52] Three days later, at his State of the State address, he again pushed for the regents to support the policy:

> This is a policy that rewards excellence across the board. It is blind to ethnicity, gender and race.[53]

His spokesperson said that support for the policy was a critical point of consideration for any future Davis appointees to the board of regents.[54] Now the challenge was to convince the regents that the plan was to reward excellence, not racial diversity. Governor Davis stressed to the regents committee on educational policy that the new plan would not prevent students qualified for admission from earning it but rather would improve underperforming schools, signaling to them that their students were capable of admission at UC and should have the same rigorous curriculum as other high schools. Davis stressed that the policy was not about race but about access—"While some schools are better than others, this situation is not the fault of the students. [The top 4%] will do well at the University of California because class rank is the best determinant of success."[55]

In March 1999, the UC regents approved the local admissions policy. The committee members agreed that qualified students would not be displaced by the policy if all students set to be admitted under it still had to take the required UC prerequisite courses and meet the testing requirements. Even though he arrived at the vote undecided, Regent Connerly ultimately voted in favor, acknowledging that a policy based on neighborhoods was not a race-based policy.[56] Connerly championed the solution that "doesn't violate Proposition 209 [or] displace any students [or] diminish the quality of the University of California."[57]

In practice, this review process was race neutral. Officers reviewed the transcripts of *all* students at *all* high schools who were in the top 10 percent of their class as rising seniors. They checked to make sure these students were on track to complete all of the required academic courses for UC admissions and then recalculated their grade-point averages based on these academic courses alone. The top 4 percent were sent a letter that they would receive UC admission if they continued on their current paths.[58]

The new UC top-percent plan increased the number of underrepresented minority students receiving guaranteed admission to the University of California. In the first year of the local context policy (the fall 2001 admissions cycle), an additional 2,065 applicants were guaranteed UC admission for being in the top 4 percent of their high school classes, even though they were outside the top 12.5 percent of statewide graduating seniors. Half of these students were underrepresented minorities.[59] Additionally, the students now guaranteed UC admission because of their high school standing also had higher admission rates at Berkeley and Los Angeles.[60]

The university had attempted to capture racial diversity in a race-neutral way. Admission was already guaranteed to the top 12.5 percent of the state's graduating seniors, and now the faculty committee added the top 4 percent of an individual high school's seniors.[61] This "eligibility in a local context" policy meant that even if students graduated from a weak high school—far behind others in the state in terms of academic performance—they just had to be at the top of *their* school, not at the top among their statewide peers, to receive guaranteed admission. The

UC percent plan carried the day thanks to faculty persistence and legislative pressure to survive the regents' concerns that the plan would violate the affirmative action ban. When the dust settled and the numbers of students now enrolled at the University of California were counted, the group of new first-year students admitted through the local context focus had a higher proportion of minority students. The university had followed the language of the law. At the same time, it continued to prioritize racial diversity by designing its admissions policy to increase the enrollment of underrepresented minority students.

## Making Admissions Personal

While legislators and faculty in the academic senate pushed for a system-wide UC response to the affirmative action ban, individual campuses took action through their own policies. Berkeley responded to the regents' ban on affirmative action by considering each student's background and relative disadvantage. Before the affirmative action ban, Berkeley assigned applicants an academic index score, which combined their high school grade-point average and scores on standardized tests, and admitted 50 percent of its class based on this score. The remaining spots in the class were awarded based on both academics and background factors like race. In the 1995 ban, the regents formalized a two-tier review process, saying that 50–75 percent of the incoming class must be admitted based on "academic" criteria, and the rest could use supplemental factors, exclusive of race and gender. Berkeley began evaluating each student's academic achievement in light of the disadvantages she or he had to overcome.

To execute this two-tier review process, Berkeley revised the way it scored applications in its admissions review. Jenny Franchot, a Berkeley professor and head of the Berkeley faculty admissions committee, noted that the goal of revamping admissions procedures was to "evaluate students individually according to all they have achieved in the context in which they have done it."[62] The university added a second metric—a personal score or comprehensive score—to take the measure of a student's life outside the classroom. It included factors such as leadership, contributions to the community, and challenging life circumstances. Berkeley also adapted its academic index score into an academic score that was heavily influenced by the context of a student's academic experience: what was available—or absent—at their high school that influenced his or her success, such as the rigor of the classes and whether grades were on the rise or dropping off. In a remarkable increase of its workload, Berkeley announced that all applications would be read and would receive both scores, even though 50 percent would still be admitted based solely on the academic score.

There were two main advantages to adapting the academic score and adding the comprehensive score. First, Berkeley could use every admissions policy in its arsenal to identify high-achieving students from disadvantaged communities. Second, the UC regents had required in their 1995 affirmative action ban that at least 50 percent of students be admitted based on academic merit. Now, Berkeley's measure of academic merit also was informed by social context.

Beginning immediately after the statewide ban, readers were trained to evaluate social circumstances and adjust the academic score accordingly. Franchot and the Berkeley faculty committee recommended taking into account circumstances that framed "a high schooler's true experience or merit [such as] consideration of school and family context."[63] Mary Dubitzsky, an admissions assistant director, put it simply: "We don't penalize a person for not taking more honors courses or AP courses if those courses weren't available."[64] For example, students at well-resourced suburban feeder schools to Berkeley would now have depressed academic scores, even with all As, if they had not taken advantage of the honors and AP classes at their high school, but not so for a student, perhaps with an objectively weaker transcript, who came from a low-performing school where those courses were not offered.

Along with bringing disadvantage and context into its process through the comprehensive score, first-time indicators of student circumstances, like recommendation letters, were incorporated into the review process.[65] As Patrick Hayashi, the lead administrator on admissions policy, noted:

> Students in California come from a wide range of circumstances and backgrounds [and] it's important for us to understand these in order to make informed and fair judgments about our applicants and their achievements. . . . We are interested in students who have accomplished remarkable things. Students who have done so under unusual or challenging circumstances may be even more engaging to us.[66]

To return to the example from above, the achievement of a student from a well-resourced suburban feeder school, without challenging life circumstances, would look less remarkable next to someone with equal or lower academic "numbers" who had achieved that academic profile despite disadvantages like a weaker school environment, a difficult home life, or low educational attainment in the family.

Berkeley's new review policy required the university to dramatically ramp up its admissions staffing. Berkeley wanted more than one set of eyes on each application because the academic and comprehensive scores were now a comprehensive evaluation of student circumstances. Under the new policy, each application would receive an academic score (from 1 to 7) and a comprehensive score (from 1 to 5), from two readers working independently of each other and blind to each other's review.[67] By 1998, Berkeley had fifty-two readers—thirty-one readers in-house in the admissions office, five part-time readers for admissions review season, six volunteers from other units across the campus, and five high school counselors from the area. According to Berkeley admissions director Bob Laird, "Each application is read by two readers, which adds up to between 75,000 and 80,000 files read in an eight-week period. There are 53 total readers. . . . [The training process] begins in October [and] continuing training occurs for two hours every week."[68]

The change to a more personalized admissions process was not without critics who feared that race would seep into the review, so Berkeley put rigorous training and evaluation standards in place. The reading season began with a "norming session" meant to get all the readers on the same page; if the scale went from 1 to 5, then everyone needed to understand how a "1" differed from a "2."[69] Skeptical faculty insisted on being involved. Professor Jack Citrin attended the norming session and expressed his doubt at the outset:

> The faculty must participate in training readers, and by training I mean communicating to them our understanding of the values embedded in the new system, the kinds of criteria we believe are legitimate and those that are not.[70]

During norming sessions, readers evaluated the same group of applications and assigned scores, which trainers reported clustered together after the norming. During the reading season, top admissions officers ran weekly, and sometimes daily, evaluations of readers and reports on the application progress. According to Berkeley admissions assistant director Mary Dubitsky, who collected samples that would be fodder for the next norming conversation, statistics showed that in 93 percent of evaluations the reader scores were within one point of each other.[71]

All these changes in admissions at Berkeley were due to the change in the law. In his admissions report to Berkeley faculty and staff, Berkeley chancellor Robert Berdahl stated that the new policy would comply with the admissions bans by eliminating race in review:

> This new process is being introduced as we implement for the first time in undergraduate admissions Regents' Resolution SP-1 and the voter-approved Proposition 209, which eliminated the use of race, ethnicity and gender as considerations for admissions.[72]

The Berkeley faculty admissions committee agreed in media interviews that that bans had accelerated the switch to comprehensive review. Professor Jenny Franchot argued that the committee "was already moving in the direction of abandoning" the sole reliance on GPA and test scores as measures of academic success. Professor David Forsyth noted the switch "might have gone slower" without the bans.[73]

By spring 2001, this new admissions review policy had caught the attention of the top stakeholders at the university—the president and the board of regents. In February 2001, UC President Atkinson wrote to the academic senate in support of a review process that would broadly consider applicant background. He argued that "all campuses [should] move away from admissions processes focused on quantitative formulas and instead adopt evaluative procedures that look at applicants in a comprehensive . . . way."[74] In his letter, he also pushed for the board of regents to end the tiered admissions policy. Working closely with Atkinson was Patrick Hayashi, the former vice chancellor for admissions at Berkeley, who was heavily involved in the change in the admissions process there. Hayashi had also served on President Peltason's task force on admissions. In 1999, after the Berkeley policy change, Hayashi joined the UC Office of the President as associate president, advising the president on systemwide admissions policy and coining the term *comprehensive review* for the policy.[75]

The next step was for the UC Board of Regents to decide whether comprehensive review should be adopted across the entire UC system. While Berkeley was leading the way, the plan's system-wide success was not a guarantee, as the board of regents was initially unwilling to abandon tiered admissions. Its membership had shifted since its 1995 vote to ban affirmative action, as a Democratic governor had appointed new regents. The board had voted in May 2001 to rescind its affirmative action ban, although the move was symbolic because the university was already under the statewide ban. In this vote, the board also requested a review of undergraduate admissions procedures and a comprehensive review policy.[76] This request opened the door for the board of regents education policy committee to study the issue and approve policy recommendations.

The faculty pushed to eliminate the cap on academic-only admits and allow campuses to evaluate the full background and context of every applicant, but the regents were fearful that race would reemerge. The board was skeptical about reader opinions and subjectivity in the reading process and wondered whether applicant racial background would find its way into these reviews. In a delicate meeting in October 2001, the admissions policy arm of the faculty senate described to its counterpart at the board of regents why comprehensive review would not violate the affirmative action ban. The senate's Board of Admissions and Relations with Schools (BOARS) presented to the regents' Committee on Education Policy, whose membership included anti–affirmative action stalwarts like Ward Connerly. The regents were open to changes in admissions that would consider applicant background. This was not the first time this regents committee had considered "a more comprehensive approach" to admissions review; indeed, a form of it had been discussed after the 1995 ban, and the October meeting returned to the idea that this approach was prevalent nationally among peer institutions, as the faculty stressed.[77] The Stanford admissions director also presented at this meeting, noting that some form of comprehensive review was critical to its admissions process.[78] The legislature was in agreement. Its 2001–02 budget offered an additional $750,000 to the University of California if it made the switch to the more comprehensive—and more resource intensive—review process.[79]

The faculty presenters chose their words carefully. Comprehensive review was an adjustment, not a change, in procedure, and it was a unified, fair one for students. In addition to noting widespread use and support from stakeholders, the academic senate's admissions committee stressed to the regents that this review process was not an alteration of admissions criteria but rather a stronger method for evaluating the existing criteria. BOARS chair professor Dorothy Perry argued that "merit is best judged within the context of achievement."[80] The process was already in use at selective UC campuses. Perry stressed that this policy would unify the admissions process and treat applicants more equitably, evaluating everyone "in the context of the opportunities that were available to the applicant."[81]

The regents at the meeting returned to a familiar frame: student quality and hard work equaled high GPA and testing, and disadvantaged backgrounds were irrelevant. Most of the regents believed that merit was measured by numbers. Jack Citrin, the faculty member and frequent affirmative action critic, argued to the board that dropping the tiers and adopting a comprehensive process would not be fair to students because "the standard by which applicants are judged would be based upon their social background." This is an attempt, he argued, to "bring about a different racial and socioeconomic distribution of students."[82] Connerly was concerned about the inconsistent message the new process would send to families regarding whether UC placed a "premium on quality" over other factors and whether "it matters that students work hard and earn good grades."[83] The regents continually brought the conversation back around to the question of whether quality students would be passed over in the new policy.

The regents' educational policy committee, in short, was not convinced of the merits of looking broadly at student context. It was overwhelmingly concerned about who would no longer be admitted under the new policy, rather than about who would now receive a more careful review. At the end of its October 2001 meeting, the committee had not reached a consensus on whether to allow for an expanded comprehensive review. Too many of its members were wary of the proposed plan's lack of transparency and feared that it would lower a perceived bar for quality and bring in subjective social factors. But this reluctance did not stop the faculty.

Fourteen days after the regents' committee fell short on comprehensive review, the academic senate adopted the policy. On October 31, 2001, the UC-wide senate adopted principles to guide the implementation of the holistic admissions policy, as recommended by the senate subcommittee on admissions (BOARS). Merit needed to be about more than numbers, which was precisely the tipping point for the regents. Approving the proposal, argued BOARS chair Professor Perry, both "eliminate[d] the tiered system of review and put faculty back in control of the University's admissions policy."[84] Her statement addressed the regents' criticism directly and argued that BOARS believed student quality would be "not only maintained but enhanced" by a policy that took student background into consideration for all applicants. The motion was approved unanimously.

The academic senate's admissions committee had released criteria for the new admissions policy so that the UC campuses could continue their commitments to racial diversity in compliance with the law. The first principle was to make individualized, holistic review a common requirement. As one administrator tells it:

> They said that no student could be denied admission without an individualized review. In other words, we couldn't look at their academics and just lob them off. Even the kids that were not eligible needed to get a review.[85]

The permissible criteria included grade-point average and test scores, but they added achievement relative to what was available, such as outstanding projects, performance, or improvement; special talents, awards, or interests; academic accomplishments in light of the applicant's life experiences and special circumstances; and, additionally, whether the applicant added geographic diversity to the school.[86] Lastly, the new policy took a careful look at an applicant's high school and explicitly made consideration of a student's high school background a requirement in deciding whether she or he would be admitted.

In its 2001 guidelines, the faculty senate did away with a strict, numerical definition of merit. Comprehensive review was

> The process by which students applying to UC campuses are evaluated for admission *using multiple measures of achievement and promise while*

*considering the context* in which each student has demonstrated academic accomplishment.[87]

No stone would be left unturned in determining whether a student—from any background—might be admissible, which meant that minority students would not fail to receive the full benefit of the doubt when it came to what their academics indicated they could accomplish.

This approach might seem unremarkable—and for private colleges at that time, it would have been—but this was the largest public university system in the country, now promising to open all files and spend time carefully reading all pages. It was also a public university that, by state law, had to prioritize academics in some kind of predictable way in order to admit the top 12.5 percent of all graduating seniors. The state legislature of California had practically wedded the University of California to a rigid merit-based admissions formula decades earlier when it promised enrollment in the state's premier university to the top academic segment of graduating seniors. And yet the faculty committee on admissions was eager to tie itself in policy knots to satisfy the commitment to maintaining racial diversity while continuing to admit the top academic students, all without using race as a factor.

This was a big moment. Despite the tremendous new volume of work the change would produce for admissions staff, the faculty had redefined academic success so that students from disadvantaged backgrounds now had a better chance at being deemed academically successful. UC President Atkinson supported the change, and the full academic senate unanimously approved it. But they would need to get it through the board of regents.

Though still skeptical and worried about abuse of the new policy, the regents' educational policy arm voted in favor of comprehensive review in November 2001. Regent Connerly argued that more contextuality in reading would allow for reader preferences to seep in and give weight to applicant race. Therefore, he pushed for "a system of accountability" in response. Regent Moore shared these concerns. He had opted to observe the Berkeley process and training, concluding that with long attention to application essays, "at some point the attempt would be made to circumvent Proposition 209."[88] In her introduction of the policy, BOARS Chair Perry led by addressing concerns from the meeting two months prior. Grade point average and standardized testing—the traditional indicators of academic success—"will continue to play a central role" in the new contextualized process, she said.[89] By the meeting's end, Connerly was on board with the policy, now that it included an amended statement of accountability, policy evaluation, and faculty involvement so that comprehensive review would "not be distorted to look like racial preferences of any kind."[90] With an amendment stating that the policy would not use race and would comply with the affirmative action ban, comprehensive review passed the board of regents.

The late 2001 vote ushered in comprehensive review as the main method of admissions review at UC, replacing the overwhelming reliance on the numbers—grade-point average and standardized testing—that held back so many students from disadvantaged contexts. The 1995 affirmative action ban also included a requirement that these numerical indicators of merit be used for at least 50 percent of admitted UC students. With the 2001 vote, this would no longer be the case. All students would now receive an admissions review that evaluated the opportunities or disadvantages that surrounded their educational performance, in line with the principles developed by the academic senate's admissions policy committee and the admonitions for continual review, faculty leadership, and continued priority to the numbers.

Faculty intervened in the policymaking process in two capacities. First, they participated at the individual school level in admissions committees, such as the UC-Berkeley Committee on Admissions, Enrollment, and Preparatory Education. Second, they were involved on the UC-wide level through the academic senate admissions committee, the Board of Admissions and Relations with Schools. Throughout the postban landscape, BOARS recommendations were ultimately accepted by the wider faculty with little markup. The faculty senate and the president of the university were generally deferential to faculty committee recommendations and, although they asked for more information, did not subsequently make changes to the faculty admissions committee-recommended policy regarding a response to the affirmative action ban.[91] Even the regents, many of whom were skeptical of the commitment to racial diversity or outright hostile to it, requested only that there be continued research into the policy's effects and assurances that the law was being followed.[92]

Ultimately, the UC system relied on faculty leadership and individual campus entrepreneurship in responding to a post–affirmative action ban landscape. Berkeley acted as a UC campus leader by innovating comprehensive review, which meant revamping its entire review process to take into account the circumstances of an applicant's life that may have impeded his or her educational growth. Faculty were the main protagonists in the story of policymaking after the affirmative action ban. They led the university-wide effort in adopting Berkeley's policy innovation and shifting a massive admissions system into methods that required more time, attention, and holistic evaluation.

## Conclusion

The University of California made central policy moves in response to a total ban on affirmative action, all meant to increase the amount of attention reviewers could give to an applicant's background and context. The university already used class rank—the top percentage of students statewide—to guarantee admission. Immediately after the ban, the university retooled this top percent plan, adding a focus on individual high schools to capture the way students performed in the context of their high school quality and not against the competitive California high schools as a whole. But an elite campus at the university—Berkeley—was already testing ways to shift away from a focus on numbers to a tailored or individuated process that would highlight more details of an applicant's background. Five years after the ban, the whole university system had adopted this new reading method.

The University of California faculty led the way on policy innovation. The university complied with the language of the law by removing explicit consideration of race; however, for certain stakeholders at the university, allowing a decline in the enrollment of underrepresented minority students was not an option. University policymakers knew they needed to bring in more factors from applicant backgrounds to achieve the racial diversity they desired while still adhering to what the law required. Policymakers revised the admissions standards to redistribute the weight given to application factors in the review process. These efforts were led by the faculty, even though faculty were not the primary admissions decisionmakers. Campus committees of faculty led the innovation on policy, and when they needed the regents' permission to change, the faculty presented proposals and the regents looked to them for assurances. Faculty, the regents assumed, would not want to compromise on the quality of the students and would safeguard the process in enforcing the admissions ban.

Where there is a will, there is not always a way. This is not a story of mass resistance; the enrollment of Black and Hispanic students at elite University of California campuses took a hit after the affirmative action bans and has never recovered. The returns on UC's new policy investments were at best marginal in the short run. Overall, the affirmative action bans have depressed the enrollment of Black and Hispanic students on the elite campuses, Berkeley and UCLA. Without being able to take race explicitly into consideration, the two most selective UC campuses could not admit underrepresented minorities at their previous pre-ban admissions rates. Table 4.1 below shows the presence of underrepresented minorities at three critical points—in 1995 (the last class admitted before the affirmative action bans), in 1998 (the first class admitted after the bans went into effect), and in 2002 (the first class admitted after UC implemented both of its new admissions review policies). It displays both the total number of

underrepresented minorities in each first-year class and the proportion they made up in the class overall.

TABLE 4.1. Number and Proportion of Underrepresented First-Year Students,
Universities of California, Berkeley and Los Angeles.

|  | 1995 | | 1998 | | 2002 | |
|---|---|---|---|---|---|---|
|  | Number | % Total | Number | % Total | Number | % Total |
| Berkeley | 807 | 24.3% | 412 | 11.2% | 558 | 15.6% |
| Los Angeles | 1,108 | 30.1% | 597 | 14.3% | 806 | 19.3% |

Source: University of California Office of the President. "Undergraduate Access to the University of California
After the Elimination of Race-Conscious Policies," March 2003.

On both campuses, minority student representation plummeted after
the ban went into effect. By 2002, the new policies had made an impact,
but the numbers were nowhere near where they were before the bans.
For underrepresented minority students, the affirmative action bans severely curtailed access to the elite University of California campuses.

Table 4.2 shows increased underrepresented student enrollment at the
Universities of California Berkeley and Los Angeles. UCLA has made
significant strides in increasing the population of underrepresented minority students. This is almost entirely because of the jump in the enrollment of Hispanic students at UCLA, which has doubled in the time
between the policy responses to the bans and recently enrolled class.[93]

TABLE 4.2. Current Number and Proportion of Underrepresented First-Year
Students, Universities of California, Berkeley and Los Angeles.

|  | 2016 | | 2017 | |
|---|---|---|---|---|
|  | Number | % Total | Number | % Total |
| Berkeley | 1,020 | 16% | 1,082 | 17% |
| Los Angeles | 1,794 | 27% | 1,575 | 26% |

Source: University of California, Office of Planning and Analysis, "UC Berkeley Fall Enrollment Data"; Academic Planning and Budget, "Common Data Set," 2017.

University representatives lauded the policy changes that allowed
for some recovery of student representation at the same time that they

recognized the substantial effect of Proposition 209 on racial diversity. Berkeley chancellor Robert Berdahl acknowledged the difficulty:[94]

> I think [the new admissions review process] it's a very, very good process. It hasn't obviously turned the numbers around, and it probably won't be-cause without race as a factor it's just very difficult to get the same level of diverse people who came before.[95]

Researchers and UC faculty have noted that the outcomes for the UC policies, specifically its move to a local percent plan, were "anemic."[96] These policies made a broader pool of racially diverse students eligible for the University of California, but it did not get them into their top choice campus.

This chapter has focused on the main policy responses of the University of California in adjusting undergraduate admissions after the California affirmative action bans. However, it is worth noting that the university pivoted its educational opportunity policies in other ways as well. After the bans, the University of California tried to broaden its outreach to underserved students in public schools. For example, UC increased its minority student pipeline through outreach programs hosted at each campus site and at local community schools. These programs included funneling resources to specific K–12 schools, which in turn involved expanding college-prep and other programs through tutoring, extracurricular opportunities, and access to UC online Advanced Placement courses.[97] The campaign also included information outreach with publications on how to qualify for college admission and financial aid, with the intention of supplementing the resources available to students where high school counselors were absent or overworked.

These programs were wildly popular and, for racial progressives, gave the bans a silver lining—they had made the university put its money into the pipelines that progressives thought these institutions should be trying to expand anyway. In 1999, professor Pamela Clute, head of the University of California at Riverside partnership program, put it this way:

> Until about a year ago what outreach meant was fuzzy, feel-good stuff—come to the campus on Saturday, see the buildings, look at the daffodils. Now, it's taken on a life of its own, and it's been put at the core of the university's existence.[98]

The legislature was also on board with outreach. In 1998, the state legislature authorized $38.5 million for these efforts and required public schools to support them with an additional $31 million.[99] At Berkeley, even the students widely supported an increase in their student activity fee that would help pour resources into these outreach efforts.[100]

Resistant compliance is not limited to one policymaking arena. California, like Texas and soon Michigan, faced a ban on looking at race in the admissions process. Each state, however, approached the resulting challenge in a different way. At the University of California, with its multiple undergraduate campuses, the policy changes were led by faculty. At the University of Michigan, as the next chapter will show, it was admissions administrators and university lawyers who led the way on policy design.

5

## Preserving the Mission

*Technology as a Policy Tool at the University of Michigan*

Late at night on November 7, 2006, thousands of devastated University of Michigan students and community members gathered in the heart of their campus—the Diag—to take solace in the words of their president, Mary Sue Coleman. Earlier that day, Michigan voters had overwhelmingly approved a proposal to write into their state constitution a ban on affirmative action. The affirmative action ban was unqualified and clear.[1] In Michigan, universities could not give any benefit to race. The Diag was the main space on campus where the community congregated, celebrated, and protested. It was the natural place for people to vent their outrage.

Coleman stood above the crowd on the steps of the campus library, with top administrators surrounding her. She was unapologetic and unwavering in her support of the university's mission:

> If November 7 was the day that Proposal 2 passed, then November 8 is the day that we pledge to remain unified in our fight for diversity. . . . [Diversity] is too critical to our mission, too critical to our excellence, too critical to our future simply to abandon.[2]

She passionately defended the university's commitment to diversity twenty-one times, pausing for applause twenty-six times.[3] Her fiery call to action foreshadowed the law's effect: "We will find ways to overcome the handcuffs that Proposal 2 attempts to place on our reach for greater diversity."[4]

Coleman's passion and commitment were shared widely across the university. A theme that runs through this book is the sense of moral imperative and social justice responsibility that drives university administrators to pursue racial diversity in their student populations, even in response to bans on affirmative action. Yet Michigan did not refuse to concede its affirmative action policies. In addition to defending the university's commitment to racial diversity, Coleman made it clear that the university would "comply with the laws of the state."[5] Instead of mass resistance, the institution would find a way to prioritize diversity and enroll underrepresented students on campus without abandoning its commitment. To accomplish this goal, top admissions personnel would creatively repurpose financial aid software marketed to them as a way to boost their recruitment of student populations who could afford Michigan's hefty tuition. These administrators would run the software through previous years of applicants, looking for ways to identify underrepresented populations at Michigan in race-neutral ways. Through technology, they could comply with the ban on race-conscious admissions with new policies that still maintained the racial diversity they valued.

This chapter argues that the University of Michigan practiced resistant compliance in response to the Michigan affirmative action ban through its adoption of new computer software. It begins with the affirmative action policies in place before the ban and the context of Michigan's commitment to student body diversity. Next, it explains how Michigan's reaction to the passing of the potential constitutional amendment laid the groundwork for policymakers to look for creative ideas in unexpected places and find new purposes for technology instruments. This approach included overlaying this technology on hundreds of thousands of applications from prior admissions cycles and, once the technology was adopted, modifying the reading process to include the software variables. Michigan's commitment to student body diversity resulted in the retooling of the admissions process around underrepresented populations. Despite conservative criticism, Michigan outlined its changes in admissions practices to the public as a viable means of complying with the constitution while also resisting the intended impact of the law.

## "We're Not Making a Secret of It"[6]: Evolving Policies before the Ban

University of Michigan officials responded to the civil rights movement by acting on the responsibility their institution bore to advance equal opportunity and make their programs accessible to groups that had historically suffered discrimination. University of Michigan provost Roger Heyns, who established the Equal Opportunity Program, argued that Michigan could not sit on the sidelines as a mere witness to the struggles for racial equality. Instead, he argued, the university should "participate appropriately in the national movement to improve the status of the Negro in our society."[7] Regardless of where we place the emphasis on what motivated these policies, scholars agree that the arrival of affirmative action programs in higher education was intended to broaden access and address the past wrongs of racial discrimination.[8] The literature that positions affirmative action as a response to campus protests for greater Black representation is not off the mark. University policies simply started earlier, and in response to a wider movement, than has previously been recognized.

The University of Michigan 1964 Opportunity Awards Program (OAP) was an answer to a tense time in American political life. The civil rights movement was galvanizing the country, including administrators at Michigan and their peers at other national universities. University leaders pushed for an increase in recruitment of racial minority students.[9] Broadening admissions access, though, meant changing the procedures. Because the university's admissions system was oriented around traditional, stable categories of merit—test scores and grade-point averages—the university set up two systems with OAP.[10]

The OAP process created two tracks of admission to the University of Michigan in order to increase racial representation. In one stream, students were judged by academic numbers. Admitted students at the time had a 3.3 grade-point average and a top 25 percent SAT score. The OAP track involved a separate evaluation standard and a separate group of readers. Students referred for evaluation under this process, or recruited to apply by these administrators, were judged holistically with attention given to all the variables of their application, including a disadvantaged background and personal circumstances. Initially, race was downplayed in the establishment of the OAP program, but 85 percent of the program's first classes were Black students.[11]

The University of Michigan did not need to qualitatively assess all of its applications in order to increase the representation of racial minorities on campus. The two-track system allowed university officials to be selective, admitting only students with the highest grade point and test averages. The qualitative process was reserved for prioritizing race.

Officials at Michigan felt pressure to review their systems in light of *Bakke* to make sure that all applicants were judged with the same process and guidelines. They convened a two-day conference to carry out this review.[12] In 1980, Michigan had premiered a system of quantitative evaluation for all applicants with two separate admissions cut-offs based on race. In-state and white students needed a 1000 SAT and 3.5 GPA for admission. Underrepresented racial minorities needed an 850 SAT and 3.0 GPA for admission.[13] Into the 1990s, the grids became more complex, bringing in factors that determined admission thresholds and giving weight to indicators of diversity such as geography, race, and being from "unusual" circumstances.[14]

The university acknowledged that its standards for admission were different based on race. "It's no secret that we're taking minorities with lower GPAs than majority students," said Cliff Sjogren, Michigan admissions director, to a journalist in 1987. "We don't go out and tell the world about it, but we're not making a secret of it either."[15] However, the quantitative system maintained the goal of evaluating all applicants with the same criteria—no one was admitted without having the required admissions components or purely for having a certain racial background or possessing alumni ties.

At the University of Michigan, the choice to hew to the safest legal path meant distancing the institution from nondiscrimination justifications for affirmative action practices. University administrators alienated advocates for racial justice in their quest to invoke legal language that might carry their policies forward as constitutional. In her study of twenty-first-century language surrounding race, Ellen Berrey elucidates the politics behind the University of Michigan's choice of diversity as its affirmative action justification. In its legal mobilization during the Michigan affirmative action cases, the organization By Any Means Necessary fought for racial justice as the pillar behind race-conscious remedies. University administrators kept the organization at a distance, did not share time in oral arguments during the litigation, and did not include these racial justice advocates during its litigation PR campaign.[16] Michigan had to reject racial inequality claims for affirmative action because of its litigation strategy. Instead, the University of Michigan wholeheartedly embraced the diversity justification during the decade it was sued over its affirmative action policies, turning the potentially negative litigation spotlight into a positive campaign that featured the university as the crusader for a public good.[17]

Nationally, the *Gratz/Grutter* combination offered a way for universities to use race in admissions—they could abandon quantified policies that resembled *Gratz* and converge on holistic policies like *Grutter*. The University of Michigan undergraduate admissions office abandoned the points system at issue in the litigation and moved to an individualized assessment policy based on the Michigan Law plan that had survived judicial review. While the use of test scores and GPAs remained a part of the process, the new application was now six pages longer, with more inputs for "students' individual viewpoints, skills, and qualifications."[18] Michigan detailed the new policy in a press release and noted that increasing the size and expanding the questions would help them bring in more evidence of diversity that the applicant could contribute to the campus.[19] The old process was effected mainly by one reader, whereas the new one would require two or three reads before a final decision.

In short, Michigan's policies were developed during the civil rights movement in the 1960s and modified by the 1978 *Bakke* decision. The use of race in admissions survived the 2003 Supreme Court challenges. The Michigan undergraduate admissions office modified its policies and made admissions decisions a more holistic determination, but it was able to continue to factor in race as one of many variables. All of this changed when the state banned affirmative action.

## Michigan's Continued Commitment to Racial Diversity in Its Student Population

Racial progressives both won and lost at the end of the twentieth century. *Grutter* affirmed Powell's decision in *Bakke*—universities could use race in a holistic way. But this was a hollow victory for progressives at universities in states that banned affirmative action. On November 7, 2006, Michigan voters amended their state constitution to ban affirmative action. The vote was the end of a three-year campaign by "colorblind" conservatives; these plaintiffs and activists had failed to get the Supreme Court to end affirmative action, so they took their challenge to Michigan voters instead. The ban proponents felt morally compelled to attack and eliminate any state practices aimed at altering racial representation. In his speech founding the Michigan Civil Rights Initiative, Connerly declared, "We are not content to be governed by admissions officers instead of the Constitution."[20] Jennifer Gratz, a cofounder of the initiative and a plaintiff in the Michigan cases, pointed to the moral imperative of the civil rights movement: "There isn't middle ground when it comes to discrimination. It's wrong no matter who it's against."[21]

In response to the ratification of Proposal 2, the University of Michigan renewed its commitment to admit racially diverse classes and vowed to persevere. Michigan's commitment to increasing minority student representation on campus was more than just a value; it shaped the way administrators at Michigan understood themselves as professionals and the definition of the university itself. In her remarks the night Proposal 2 passed, Coleman used several verbs to illustrate that this mission was an inseparable part of the core identity of the university—Michigan, she said, "promotes . . . embraces . . . wants . . . believes in . . . is" its commitment to the educational value of racial diversity.[22] For top admissions administrators, the value of diversity was "hardwired in the mind." Administrators spoke of their commitment with existential conviction: "[Diversity issues are] part of my being."[23]

President's Coleman's speech did not go over well with proponents of the affirmative action ban, and they responded across the country with outrage. Conservative columnists in national newspapers claimed that Coleman's speech "exude[d] contempt" for the voters and was "breathtakingly arrogant."[24] Conservatives on campus called the speech evocative of the "diversity cult" at Michigan.[25]

Coleman's message, however, had already filtered to all levels of the university: racial diversity was a priority everyone was expected to embrace. According to one admissions officer, "You're [at Michigan] not just to do a job, you're there because you believe in the institution's mission [surrounding prioritizing racial diversity]."[26] Michigan administrators entrenched this view further: "It's way beyond the law. It's way beyond everything that anyone can put on us. It's part of us. It's what this place was built on. If you don't believe in that you shouldn't be here."[27] Michigan philosophy professor Carl Cohen, a prominent affirmative action opponent, described the university's commitment to racial diversity as "unqualified enthusiasm," noting that Michigan "left no doubt that faculty members who opposed it here would put themselves outside of the mainstream."[28]

Any institution that maintained its selectivity and academic prestige while becoming increasingly white would be a failed institution, according to top Michigan administrators. President Coleman defined Michigan as diversity—"we are Michigan and we are diversity."[29]

The defeat of diversity would lead Michigan "down the path to me-diocrity."[30] The less senior university administrators made sure policy meetings and changes were in line with the administrative stance. The admissions office needed the belief in the "core mission" from the re-gents, president, and provost to implement its response to Proposal 2. The directors of admissions, though highly motivated, were careful to make sure these high-level actors and legal counsel were "online" with the same "vision and mission."[31] All agreed that the top administration set the tone for "how much they want to press. Are they comfortable in the spotlight?"[32]

However, university administrators did not see resistance, or refusing to follow the law, as an option. Everyone at Michigan articulated a firm desire to be in compliance with the law. Although President Coleman stressed that all legal opinion would be guided by the importance of diversity ("I have asked our attorneys for their full and undivided sup-port in defending diversity"), the legal counsel was tasked with answer-ing the questions of "how do we stay true to the mission given these constraints?" and "how do we solve this problem in a legal way?"[33] The commitment to racial diversity did not lead the university away from the law, but it defined the organization's response.

Ultimately, the university policymakers concluded, the law targeted only the university's current race-conscious method of increasing the representation of minority students on campus. The law stated they could give "no preference" to race, so that is what they would do. The message from university legal counsel was that responding to Proposal 2 was "ultimately" and "first and foremost a legal question of 'what does the law require?'"[34] The attorneys determined, in agreement with the leaders of Michigan's administrative hierarchy, that the affirmative ac-tion ban limited the methods by which the university could pursue its goals, but not the goals themselves.

University administrators focused on what the law did not say—it was silent about the priorities surrounding racial diversity. They framed the law as prohibiting one set of policies, which would allow the university to draft a new set of policies that complied with the language of the law. In the reasoning of one administration official,

> Prop 2 tells you, you might need to rethink the way you're going to achieve goals that have some kind of consideration of racial diversity or gender diversity. . . . It doesn't say that racial diversity is no longer important or that there is no longer a compelling governmental interest in achieving the educational benefits that flow from a diverse student body.[35]

It was what the law "said" that mattered.

## Michigan's Initial Response

At first, the university proceeded along two tracks—policy change and litigation. While the specifics of the litigation are not relevant to this book, the university did not give up on affirmative action with the passage of the ban. One month after the ban, the university won an injunction to delay implementation of the new law until July 2007, arguing that it needed time to change its policies and should not admit the fall 2007 entering class under two separate admissions policies (one with the consideration of race, prior to the November vote, and one without the consideration of race, after the ban went into effect).[36] Soon, however, the anti–affirmative action group Towards a Fair Michigan (led by *Grutter* plaintiff Barbara Grutter) and the Michigan attorney general filed an emergency appeal to the Sixth Circuit. On December 29, 2006, a three-judge panel lifted the injunction and ordered the immediate implementation of Proposal 2.[37] Affirmative action activists carried the fight forward. In 2007, the group By Any Means Necessary sued to overturn the ban in Michigan, and in 2014, the Supreme Court ended its challenge, upholding the state's new constitutional amendment.[38] In December 2006, an affirmative action ban became the law in Michigan.

The university immediately changed its policies for application review, although not without controversy. The admissions cycle was fully underway, with half of the incoming class already admitted under a process that considered race, and another half yet to be admitted by admissions staff who were scrambling to eliminate race from consideration.[39] Proposal 2 went into effect on December 23, 2006, typically the halfway point in the admissions review season. Controversially, admissions administrators decided to keep race visible to readers on the applications, whereas Michigan State University and other Michigan public universities chose to make applicants' race invisible in the reading process.[40] The University of Michigan argued that it was required by federal law to collect information on the race of applicants, so why not let the readers see the applications as they arrived? Admissions director Erica Sanders reasoned that their instructions to the readers sufficed: "We simply have stated [to application readers] that race and gender cannot be considered in the process."[41]

Michigan also quickly authorized a new essay prompt for the upcoming cycle. The old essay question, in place since the Supreme Court decision in 2003, asked merely that applicants explain how they would contribute "diverse talents, experiences, opinions, and cultural backgrounds" to Michigan. Now, starting in fall 2007, the application essay began with a quote from president Mary Sue Coleman on the benefits of diversity and asked students to respond, with specific reference to experiences from their own lives.[42]

Simultaneously, Michigan initiated a task force to crowdsource ideas from the university community and find creative ways to respond to the new mandate, while still maintaining their commitment to a broad diversity that included race. On November 21, 2006—just weeks after the ban's passage—Michigan formed a fifty-five-member Diversity Blueprints Task Force composed of students, faculty, staff, and alumni, with the aim of collecting feedback. The task force released a report in February 2007 with 155 recommendations for how to proceed. For the most part, the recommendations were broad: applications should be read holistically as a way to give attention to the diverse characteristics of students; partnerships with underserved schools should be strengthened as a way to generate enthusiasm for Michigan among diverse populations.[43] However, one immediate result of the task force's recommendations was the creation of the Center for Educational Outreach and Academic Success, in charge of forming these K–12 partnerships throughout the state.[44]

The Diversity Blueprints Task Force final report revealed another way Michigan's racial diversity priorities could survive—the university would get by with a little help from its friends. Recall that Michigan was not the first elite university to face an affirmative action ban. The flagship campuses of the University of Texas (Austin), the University of California (Berkeley and Los Angeles), and the University of Washington (Seattle) had all survived similar tests, Texas and California in 1996 and Washington in 1998. As top Michigan administrators wrote in 2007:

> Ongoing conversations with these and other universities will help us avoid blind alleys, prepare for on-going challenges, capitalize on best practices, and prevent unintended consequences. Because of this, we anticipate that many of our setbacks and discouraging moments will be short-lived. Indeed, we see ourselves as uniquely situated to be at the leading edge of the questions and challenges posed to our nation through ballot initiatives like Proposal 2.[45]

Michigan's administrators acknowledged their predecessors and at the same time were aware of their presence in the spotlight, and they were determined that the university would continue its role as a trailblazer in the fight to maintain racial diversity among its priorities.[46]

Professional ties with similarly situated institutions provided motivation and encouragement, if not comprehensive solutions. Between 2006 and 2009, Michigan sent its administrators on site visits at the Universities of Washington-Seattle, California-Berkeley and Los Angeles, and Texas-Austin. In early 2008, Michigan hosted a symposium in Ann Arbor with representatives from these institutions.[47] Interviewees who attended that meeting could not think of specific policy changes that resulted, though they were interviewed almost ten years after the fact. Instead, they pointed to a sense of camaraderie and understanding that resulted, which made them feel supported and empowered.[48] However, nearly all top administrators at Michigan interviewed felt that because of the spotlight on Michigan from the recent lawsuit, and Michigan's greater selectivity in comparison to other national institutions, the university would have to craft a unique response and could not rely entirely on the means used by other universities in response to similar bans.

What other institutions did give Michigan, however, was top personnel. The university looked to other universities in similar circumstances when filling administrator positions that included admissions policy-making. Right before the Proposal 2 vote, Michigan was hiring a provost and a top academic officer, and it turned to the University of Texas at Austin in search of expertise. In 2006, Michigan hired the executive vice chancellor of the University of Texas system, Teresa Sullivan, as provost and executive vice president for academic affairs.[49] Sullivan had close knowledge of how the University of Texas at Austin had navigated its affirmative action ban; she was the co-principal investigator of the Texas Higher Education Opportunity Project, a multiyear study of the effects of the Texas Top Ten Percent law. In 2014, Michigan again looked to Texas for admissions expertise, hiring Kedra Ishop, the vice provost and admissions director at the University of Texas at Austin, as the new vice president of enrollment management at the University of Michigan. In her departing interview, Ishop acknowledged that Michigan had sought her out for the position because of her experience at Texas.[50] It appears that Michigan's instincts were not misplaced; in her first year managing the application process, Ishop oversaw the highest enrollment of under-represented minorities in a Michigan first year class since 2005, the year before the affirmative action ban.[51]

Michigan, a Big Ten powerhouse, at first responded offensively to the affirmative action ban. As it had in response to the *Grutter* and *Gratz* challenges, Michigan sought a way forward, refusing to backtrack on its commitments. The University of Michigan never entertained the idea of outright resistance to the new affirmative action ban. During the weeks after the law's passage and while considering its options, university administrators maintained that they would both comply with the law *and* continue the university's commitment to racial diversity. The debate was about how, not whether, the university would comply with a ban on the explicit use of race in admissions.

Though broadening access to recruitment and programs that reached younger students was important, it was not enough. Michigan wanted a way—beyond a retooled diversity essay—to guarantee that an applicant's diverse background would be considered in the admissions process. It knew that its admitted students came predominantly from white, affluent backgrounds; indeed, these students were overrepresented at Michigan in proportion to their representation in the entire Michigan college-age population. Paying explicit attention to race in the process was one way to correct for this. Was there another way? Well, if certain populations were overrepresented, others had to be underrepresented. Accordingly, the university removed attention to race and replaced it with attention to underrepresentation. If the readers were to know whether a given applicant was underrepresented, they needed a computer program that would crunch a lot of data and give each applicant a tag. Enter "Descriptor Plus."

## Seeking New Technology and Descriptor Plus

Descriptor Plus was a software idea taken from savvy commercial marketing campaigns. In the mid-2000s, the College Board—the educational company that runs the SAT—took a page from commercial industries. Corporations had long relied on the practice of profiling consumers' behavior to tailor their marketing to specific kinds of customers. Why not apply the same principle to higher education? According to the College Board's marketing pitch for Descriptor Plus, the current means that universities used to market were inadequate because universities did not have "analytical capabilities . . . or communication budget/flexibility to achieve commercial levels of hyper-targeting" the way the commercial industries could.[52] The College Board knew that typically, universities and colleges market to students they find through data purchased from test score companies like the College Board. Yet all they had were test scores and brief demographic data (perhaps sex, race, and high school), which was not a lot to go on when the goal was to figure out if a student was likely to apply or enroll.

The College Board developed a solution: software that exploited the fact that in the twenty-first century, computers could process hundreds of thousands of data points quickly and with concise results. The program divided the United State into 180,000 geographic neighborhoods and then grouped them into similar clusters. It used four sources to determine which cluster a student would fit into: individual test results and individual patterns in where they sent their scores; student answers to questions on College Board "assessment questionnaires"; College Board "high school and college files" data; and data collected from the census and the American Community Survey. In the end, the program produced thirty-three educational neighborhood clusters and twenty-nine high school clusters.[53]

The result was a country divided into a few dozen similar neighborhoods and high schools based on profiles of the students who lived there. The College Board called this software Descriptor Plus, a "geodemographic segmentation service" that clustered students together based on demographic factors and behaviors, or "the art and science of profiling people based on where they live."[54] The software, argued the College Board, "profiles students' *college choice behavior* based on where they live and where they go to school."[55] Clusters allowed colleges to make assumptions about what high schoolers in similar neighborhoods might expect from the college process.

The software clusters gave universities the ability to make more sophisticated guesses about who might be interested in attending or who might be able to pay full tuition. "Birds of a Feather" was the title of the College Board presentation to universities with the potential to purchase the product. Neighborhoods contain people of common "cultural backgrounds, financial means, outlook and perspectives," it went on. People "emulate" their neighbors and will have "similar patterns of consumer behavior" and "similar values and expectations":

> College expectations are formed in-part by where the neighbors are sending their kids. College-going patterns in different communities can be analyzed and categorized using Geodemography.[56]

Corporate America was already taking this approach to marketing, argued the College Board; this is why we see different stores in different neighborhoods. The same logic could be applied to admissions.

Top Michigan administrators began post Proposal 2 planning in earnest in late 2004, meeting informally as the Plan B Committee.[57] By chance, the College Board regional representative was passing through at this time. He presented to two of the admissions executives on the state of the admissions field, trends in statistics, and the new software available. What would typically have been a commonplace meeting ended with a lightning bolt when the representative presented the new program, Descriptor Plus, as a way to highlight the demographic background of students in the admissions process. After the meeting, two administrators in conversation with one another understood for the first time that Descriptor Plus was the way forward.[58]

Descriptor Plus was exciting to Michigan admissions officers because it was an efficient way to bring into the process the socioeconomic and background factors that frequently correlate with race, without using race as a variable. Each applicant could be identified with a high school and a neighborhood cluster tag, which were assigned to them without respect to race. For example, High School Cluster 26 meant a high school where most students had a lower socioeconomic status and few educational opportunities. In the state of Michigan, many of the nearly all-Black, urban Detroit high schools had a tag of 26, or a similar number, but so did many of the small, rural, nearly all-white high schools in Michigan's Upper Peninsula.

The University of Michigan's inventive policy solution to the affirmative action ban was the use of sophisticated computer software in its admissions process. Descriptor Plus let the university continue to prioritize what it could no longer make legible—race—by including racial minorities along with other students who were underrepresented at Michigan. The technology did not single out race, let it stand alone in student applications, or even make it visible to readers. But it did include race as a demographic factor in ways that segmented students together. If Michigan was giving priority to disadvantaged groups, then among the populations that stood to gain from that priority were racial minorities.

## Backtagging Data and Adopting Descriptor Plus

Admissions officers were excited about technology that could precisely and effectively focus their attention on students who were underrepresented at Michigan. But before shelling out thousands of dollars on an annual subscription, retraining staff around the tool, and figuring out where to integrate the clusters into the admissions process, they needed to check whether it would work. The ballot initiative to ban affirmative action in Michigan had survived the initial legal challenges and collected enough signatures, and it was headed toward the 2006 ballot. If it passed, Michigan needed to have a system in place.

Throughout the 2005–6 academic year, the Office of Undergraduate Admissions data crunchers back-tagged the 2004 and 2005 enrolled classes of students to see how Descriptor Plus clusters were represented in the current Michigan student population, including racial diversity. This meant they pulled the information on students already admitted and enrolled at Michigan and tagged them with the neighborhood and high school cluster numbers that the College Board would have assigned to them at the time of application. The admissions staff wanted to answer the question, Who is at Michigan now? They knew Michigan was predominantly affluent and white, and that the proportion of this population dramatically exceeded the proportion of white, affluent college-aged individuals in the state. Would looking at the Michigan student population, as represented by Descriptor Plus cluster tags, bear out this observation? They found that it did.

Descriptor Plus cluster tags, as applied to the University of Michigan student population, showed admissions officers in greater detail what they already knew. Affluent neighborhoods and high schools were over-represented at the University of Michigan. For the class of 2008 and 2009, a mere five of the thirty neighborhood clusters made up three-quarters of the class, and in these affluent clusters, 90 percent of the students were white.[59] Approximately 28 percent of the enrolled 2004 and 2005 classes at Michigan were tagged as neighborhood cluster 1—which was dominated by "well-educated, fairly affluent families."[60] Correspondingly, clusters with lower-than-average parent income were not well represented at the university. Fewer than 2 percent of students each year came from high school clusters 8 and 15, and only 7 percent of students were from cluster 23. Racial background varied; some of these underrepresented clusters were predominantly Black and some predominantly white.[61]

Descriptor Plus put the Michigan undergraduate population in stark relief. Now instead of talking about Michigan undergraduates as predominantly white and skewing affluent, officers could say that cluster 1 was overrepresented and clusters 8, 15, and 23 were underrepresented.

The stumbling block, however, was how to translate clusters into admissions priorities. All applicants had a cluster tag that corresponded with a prose description of the cluster's demographics, but which ones should be prioritized in the admissions process? Which clusters were represented in such a low percentage of the existing student population that it would be deemed underrepresented or highly underrepresented? "That was always the sticking point with everyone, where do you decide to draw the line?"[62] The Plan B Committee used the "university's goals" surrounding diversity in tandem with the "descriptions of the clusters" to determine at what proportion a cluster was underrepresented at Michigan. To admissions, clusters represented "segments of society"—a "purely" race-neutral concept—and their task was to figure out which segments were "not well represented."[63] Where underrepresented clusters actually had "high [socioeconomic status]," admissions staff perceived "access and opportunity [as] not a problem," and these clusters were not designated as high priority.[64] Ultimately, the office decided that any cluster below 5 percent of the enrolled Michigan class was underrepresented at the university, and less than 2.5 percent of the enrolled class was highly underrepresented.[65]

Underrepresented clusters were where Michigan could find diversity for its student population. Specific Descriptor Plus cluster and high school numbers lined up with high schools and neighborhoods that were under resourced and low income. Therefore, targeting admissions efforts in these areas could bring the racial diversity that Michigan sought, an approach that also gave more attention to under resourced areas that were also nearly all-white, like Michigan's Upper Peninsula. Michigan's plan was to identify applicants with their respective neighborhood and high school cluster tags and then give weight in the admissions process to those clusters that were underrepresented at the university.

The University of Michigan announced that it had adopted Descriptor Plus in March 2007, six months after the affirmative action ban passed, and paid $15,000 annually for the software subscription.[66] Michigan administrators briefed journalists on the technology and released a press release. Top university administrators were enthusiastic about the new software tool. Senior vice provost Lester Monts proclaimed that they saw "great promise" in how the "tool . . . identifies underrepresented high schools and neighborhoods."[67]

Michigan's narrow interpretation of the new legal mandate supported its adoption of the new technology. University administrators remained committed to the same diversity goals; the ban required them only to change the policy tools that accomplished the goal. In its press release after the affirmative action ban passed, the university discussed its new policy tool, the specialized computer software. It argued:

> U-M remains committed to diversity, and diversity remains a lawful goal. Proposal 2 removed affirmative action as a means to achieve diversity in undergraduate admissions, but other methods to achieve a diverse undergraduate student body remain permissible under current law. The University is making full use of these methods.[68]

With a clear prohibition only on its former methods, Michigan concluded that all it needed was a new, legally compliant way to continue to achieve its goal.

Top admissions officials were careful to note that Descriptor Plus helped them gain a better sense of all students who faced disadvantage and adversity, and they chose to highlight how the software would benefit white students as well. At a meeting with top administrators, undergraduate admissions executive director Ted Spencer took them through a case study of an admitted white male student with a low GPA (3.1) who worked on a farm to help with the family income. He relayed how the admissions evaluation summary notes the student's leadership and strong extracurriculars but also that his high school and neighborhood were "high-interest" and underrepresented at Michigan. The student was admitted with the help of Descriptor Plus, said Spencer: "We want more kids from those types of schools that have done these types of things."[69] In an interview with the campus newspaper, Chris Lucier, director of admissions recruitment and operations, also spoke about the technology in a way that emphasized how Descriptor Plus was compliant with Proposal 2:

> It's not a device that's oriented solely at social or ethnic diversity. It's another tool for us to identify populations that might not have the same access to higher education as other populations.[70]

The technology was appealing as a way to capture diversity in a way that was consistent with an affirmative action ban, precisely because diversity was not the focus of the computer product.

For a slim number of applicants, their Descriptor Plus designation was the decisive factor in being accepted to the University of Michigan. This is because Michigan admitted students in batches, not as individuals. Each student received multiple reads that took account of all the components of his or her application and was assigned an academic rating from 1 (highest) through 15. The assignment followed a strictly academic path in most cases. A seasoned admissions reader—the "validator"—then assessed all the applicant's reads and assigned a final academic rating. A numerical ranking of 1 through 15 was where individual consideration ended, but a rating was not the same as an admissions decision of admit, waitlist, or deny. A select group of university administrators called the Enrollment Working Group (EWG) met every month or so during application season to decide which numbered ratings to admit. Most EWG meetings ended with large batches admitted and a reserved number of seats, typically in the hundreds, for admissions directors to admit at their discretion, typically with only a rating recommendation to limit them, if at all. Recalls a top admissions official, "We would walk out and say, 'now we'll need to go pick these 500 [rating level] 3s.'"[71]

High-level admissions directors could use these reserved seats and Descriptor Plus tags to give attention to university priorities, such as admitting underrepresented students to the university. The top admissions directors, frequently on their own, pulled all applicants at a particular rating level and sorted them by various characteristics to figure out which priority combinations could fill the reserved seats. They called this process "cherry picking," and it involved sorting through a Microsoft Excel document, called a "pivot table," filled with applicant data:

It was sorting that massive Excel document by different things to grab groups of people, because you knew you could only admit 1,000 out of

8,000 kids that were all in the 4 category or something like that . . . and do that well and protect the university as you're doing it.[72]

Tags on applicants sorted out categories like legacy students, students of interest to top administrators, in-state and out-of-state students, and students with underrepresented cluster tags.

Running the pivot tables was a closely guarded activity that took place behind the scenes in the admissions office. While EWG authorized the reserved admits, no one outside the admissions directors saw the final lists, made recommendations, or approved the selection criteria. The sentiment was if the top admissions guard "wanted more students from a certain high priority cluster to be admitted, they would make the decision" through the pivot tables.[73]

Administrators were careful not to insert race into the reading process, the Descriptor Plus categories, or the final choices for applicants selected for admission. However, the adoption of new software was intended to help the university succeed in its mission. Descriptor Plus and the massive pivot tables spreadsheet were the technologies that enabled the University of Michigan to adopt new policies in compliance with Proposal 2. These new policies allowed it to pursue the same mission—enhancing racial diversity and multiculturalism at the university.

## Defending Descriptor Plus

The University of Michigan defended Descriptor Plus by claiming that it was in line with the policies peer institutions had developed in response to affirmative action bans. The technology distilled the background and context of applicants into geographical stickers pinned on applications, allowing administrators to sort huge volumes of applicants and pull ones from particular backgrounds at the touch of a button. Descriptor Plus let officers use geography as a way to categorize people—in this respect, the university argued, it was similar to the solutions of other universities that had gone unchallenged and were sometimes even celebrated by conservative critics.

Top policymakers at the University saw Descriptor Plus as being compliant with the language of Proposal 2—giving no preference to race. Admissions presented Descriptor Plus to legal counsel as "a means that we feel we can create a diverse community in a way that's essentially using a race-neutral means."[74] The lawyers were positive; they had a "this could work" reaction.[75] One administrator recalls that the reaction of counsel to Michigan's use of Descriptor Plus was that the software complied with the law "as long as you're consistent within that cluster, as long as you treat everybody within the school the same way."[76] Interviewees reported that somewhere in the excitement, the provost and the president were likely briefed on the software. Admissions directors could not remember exactly how but reiterated that major policy changes often went through the top, including likely the board of regents. Legal counsel also confirmed that their opinion would have only been advice; the final sign off came from the top.

Michigan's provost, Teresa Sullivan, compared Michigan's computer technology with Texas's top students plan. It was all about geography, she claimed, whether a university was prioritizing the top-performing students at a high school or prioritizing students from particular kinds of high schools. She argued that courts had supported looking at geography as one of many indicators of diversity, including courts deciding affirmative action and desegregation measures.[77] She recommended geography-based policies, like the Texas Top Ten Percent plan and Descriptor Plus, as a way to pursue diversity: "Just as geography once broadened an education through travel, today geographical diversity can broaden the experience of everyone on the college campus."[78] Sullivan was quite familiar with both policies. As discussed in previous chapters, she had been a top administrator at Texas and had run a study on the effects of the Top Ten Percent law before coming to Michigan in 2006 and navigating the institution through Descriptor Plus.

Like generations of racial progressives before them, Michigan administrators sought a legally compliant way to continue to prioritize diversity of all kinds, including racial diversity, in their student populations. They could not act based on race, so they pivoted to geography as way to capture underrepresented student populations. In an edited volume released four years after the affirmative action ban, *The Future of Diversity*, aimed at sympathetic audiences within higher education, Sullivan argued that the way forward was through geography:

> The consideration of micro-geographic origins, such as the composition of neighborhoods and high schools, offers one proxy means for increasing the diversity of public universities. Even increasing the number of high schools represented within a freshman class represents an important means of strengthening a university's links to its publics, and may contribute at least some of the diversity that is currently sought through affirmative action.[79]

Racial affirmative action was banned, but geography could still be considered, and in Michigan (as the United States as a whole), race has a lot to do with geography.

The race-neutral, geographic message about Descriptor Plus was one the university hammered away at in press releases, presentations, and interviews. As noted above, Ted Spencer focused on a white applicant's success under Descriptor Plus when previewing the tool in 2007. Chris Lucier, director of admissions at Michigan, also argued that the technology complied with the mandate because it was based on geographic and educational information.[80] And the boilerplate press release language Michigan used for Descriptor Plus always emphasized its basis in the geography of neighborhoods and high schools.[81]

The conservative reaction was mixed. Roger Clegg, president and general counsel of the Center for Equal Opportunity, was skeptical. First, he said, look at the makers of the technology, the College Board.

The organization historically had a strong commitment to affirmative action and had spoken out against the bans as they began to appear. They were "less interested in education than in guaranteeing a predetermined and politically correct racial and ethnic mix," and that would extend to its computer software. Clegg was concerned that *demographic* just meant *race*. "It sounds like it may be not just a proxy for race or ethnicity in an application, but be race or ethnicity itself."[82] One group of the proponents of Proposal 2, in their later book on the campaign, would take this position and call the software a "proxy for race" when Michigan announced its adoption.[83]

Others were more strident in their criticism. Richard Sander and Stuart Taylor, the authors of *Mismatch* and some of the most outspoken critics of affirmative action and the diversity imperative in higher education, argued that Descriptor Plus was a matter of straightforward resistance, not compliance. In their book arguing that affirmative action actually hurts minority students, they assert that the software "was a screen for business as usual."[84] In a later interview, Sander was considerably more blunt, stating that the idea that the technology was race-neutral was "total bulls***"[85]

In practical terms, conservative lawyers noted the challenges involved in litigating a tool like Descriptor Plus. "It certainty raises some questions," remarked Terry Pell, lead counsel at the Center for Individual Rights, which had litigated the Michigan cases. But he went on to note that if the review tool used socio-economic factors in its analysis, it would comply with the law.[86] Alan Foutz, of the conservative Pacific Legal Foundation, also believed it would be hard to mount a legal challenge to the software:

[Litigants against Descriptor Plus] would have to establish that the criteria they are using are subterfuge for actual racial profiling, which would be a difficult case to establish. If they are in fact taking into consideration the whole panoply of demographics that are attached to a particular geographic area, that is most likely not a violation of Michigan's Proposal 2.[87]

Conservatives may not have liked the adoption of Descriptor Plus, but they treated it as categorically different from giving preference to race in admissions review.

The staff of the conservative newspaper on campus saw the new software as an attempt at compliance and resistance. There was something else about the law, they argued, that Michigan was resisting, and that was the goal of getting the university out of the business of prioritizing diversity:

> The University should not only comply with the letter of the law, but the spirit of it, as well. The University should not use tactics that have the secondary effect of affirmative action policies under a facially-neutral primary tactic.[88]

Was this a legally cognizable claim? Lawyers from the Center for Individual Rights and the Pacific Legal Foundation did not seem to think so. But whether the university was "against" something that seemed fundamental about the law was a different question. Michigan was resisting something; it just might not be something that courts or litigation could reach.

Was Descriptor Plus affirmative action by another name? The technology was decidedly different from the old forms of race consciousness. In affirmative action policies, readers could take explicit account of an applicant's race in their assessment, an accounting that had been narrowed over the decades. At one time, readers could evaluate racial minorities for separately reserved spots in the class (ended by *Bakke*), give them extra "points" to boost them toward admission (ended by *Gratz*), or prioritize the admission of applicants who were racial minorities (ended by Proposal 2 and other states' affirmative action bans). Using Descriptor Plus meant doing none of these things. Underrepresented neighborhoods and high schools may be populated predominantly by racial minorities, like many areas of Detroit, Michigan, or they may be almost entirely white, like the communities in Michigan's rural Upper

Peninsula. Each of these two geographies received a boost through Descriptor Plus. As Chris Lucier said at the time of its adoption, Descriptor Plus—unlike traditional affirmative action—was not "solely" about race or ethnicity but about expanding access.

As Richard Sander's salty comment suggests, Descriptor Plus resembles certain longstanding methods of affirmative action. And yet, as the comments from Terry Pell and Alan Foutz indicate, the software also seems to achieve what conservatives spent years asking and advocating for: affirmative action based on socio-economic status rather than race. Prior policies that were adopted and then abandoned were motivated by the desire to give greater access in higher education to underrepresented racial minorities. The reasons for this quest have changed; consider, for example, the shift from justifying affirmative action based on historical discrimination to arguing that these policies stem from the belief that diversity is an educational benefit. Descriptor Plus was adopted to boost the numbers of admitted students from underrepresented neighborhoods and high schools because these were the places where white, affluent students were not present. The effort was a far cry from the 1960s attempts to remedy prior discrimination based on race. But Descriptor Plus was still about changing access and disrupting the patterns that give more representation to privileged students.

## Conclusion

As the Universities of Texas and California had done before it, the University of Michigan led with its educational commitments when finding a way to comply with the new law. The University of Michigan did not declare defiance when it implemented these new policies, nor did it reject its previous mission of maintaining and enhancing racial diversity. Instead, the university exercised its will to pursue racial policymaking by finding a way around the language of the law. While creativity and flexibility may not be common hallmarks of administration in higher education, Michigan's responses to Proposal 2 demonstrate that these qualities remain vital to the university's image and mission. Administrators had to pivot, finding a new means to pursue these ends within the now altered legal landscape.

At Michigan, this pivot centered on repurposing marketing technology. A software tool that could capture new communities within which to advertise about the university could also be used to target admissions at communities underrepresented in the student population. Michigan's narrow interpretation of the affirmative action ban helped it incorporate this new technology into its admissions practices. Counsel for the university clarified that Proposal 2 banned a method of affirmative action, not a commitment to racial diversity. The Descriptor Plus technology did not take race into account when assigning student categories.

Unlike other universities responding to affirmative action bans, Michigan administrators had autonomy over policy changes independent from state legislative mandates. The idea to use Descriptor Plus as an admissions tool came from top admissions directors, unlike the University of Texas, where the automatic admissions plan was spearheaded by legislators. Unlike the University of California at Berkeley, where guidance often came from the governance of the University of California system, Michigan could craft a solution tailored to its student population and based on data regarding the students its campus was able to attract from year to year.

The affirmative action ban had the effect of reducing the representation of racial minorities on campus. As they had after the affirmative action ban at the flagship University of California campuses, underrepresented minority students lost out when it came to the affirmative action ban at the University of Michigan. The Table below summarizes their decline in representation. The year before the ban at the University of Michigan, underrepresented minority students (defined at Michigan as all Black, Hispanic, and Native students) made up 13.6 percent of all undergraduate students at the university. The year after the ban, that number dropped to 12.4 percent of students. Five years after the ban Michigan had recovered slightly, up to 12.7 percent of undergraduates were underrepresented minority students. Table 1 below breaks this percentage down by group, with the exact numbers of Black, Hispanic, and Native American students painting an even bleaker picture.[89]

TABLE 5.1. Number and Proportion of Undergraduate Enrollment, University of Michigan.

|  | 2005 | | 2007 | | 2011 | |
|---|---|---|---|---|---|---|
|  | Number | % Total | Number | % Total | Number | % Total |
| Black | 1,840 | 7.6% | 1,633 | 6.6% | 1,212 | 4.7% |
| Hispanic | 1,215 | 5.0% | 1,212 | 4.9% | 1,123 | 4.4% |
| Native American | 235 | 0.97% | 242 | 0.98% | 42 | 0.16% |
| 2+ groups | N/A | N/A | N/A | N/A | 912 | 3.54% |

Source: University of Michigan Office of the Registrar, "Ethnicity Reports/Undergraduate Enrollment by Ethnicity," 2015.

Fast-forward a decade, and the University of Michigan still struggles to enroll these student populations. Table 2 below reflects a more recent enrollment of underrepresented students. Representation for these groups of students has remained fairly consistent. Though Hispanic students are now more numerous at the university than in the mid-2000s, an increase in the overall student population means these students are even less proportionally represented on campus.

TABLE 5.2. Number and Proportion of Undergraduate Enrollment, University of Michigan.

|  | 2014 | | 2015 | |
|---|---|---|---|---|
|  | Number | % Total | Number | % Total |
| Black | 1,166 | 3.4% | 1,216 | 4.6% |
| Hispanic | 1,209 | 4.6% | 1,300 | 4.9% |
| Native American | 44 | 0.16% | 53 | 0.20% |
| 2+ groups | 897 | 3.4% | 969 | 3.7% |

Source: University of Michigan Office of the Registrar, "Ethnicity Reports/Undergraduate Enrollment by Ethnicity," 2015.

The numbers highlight the reason for progressives' frustration. Whether the University of Michigan succeeded in maintaining its commitment to racial diversity depends on one's point of view. Administrators report doing all that they could, given the narrowed legal path. Even a decade after the ban, the university claimed defeat and bemoaned the ban's effect on racial diversity.[90] But progressive backlash at the University has been swift. In the decade between 2005 and 2015, the population of Black undergraduate students at Michigan dropped by more than six hundred students. Student organizations and activists in the state have accused the university of not doing enough surrounding racial diversity, and they launched the Being Black at Michigan movement—#BBUM—to highlight these concerns. The commitment of universities, including the University of Michigan, to improving the representation of underrepresented minority students on campus remains contested. Both scholars and campus protesters, for instance, are critical of universities' intentions.[91]

# 6

## Equality by Other Means

*Rethinking Policy on the Basis of Race*

On January 15, 1991, two days before the anniversary of Martin Luther King Jr.'s birth, the Supreme Court effectively ended the *Oklahoma City Board of Education v. Dowell* desegregation litigation. The Oklahoma City schools had re-segregated, and control over school policy was handed back to the local school board. The original plaintiff, Dr. Alfonso Dowell, had persevered through the resistant compliance of the board of education and decades of litigation. He greeted the court's decision with anger and frustration: "We are no better off now than when we got off slavery. The only thing is, we can eat in a few more places."[1] Yet he remained resolute in his fight for desegregation. "It isn't going to kill me. But I'm not going to throw in the towel. I'd like to see someday, before my eyes are closed, equal justice for all."[2]

Dr. Dowell died in 2001 at the age of eighty-four. The Oklahoma City schools are still segregated, and they have lost half their population to white flight since the litigation began.[3] Dowell had spent almost half his lifetime fighting for desegregated schools in his hometown, having brought the case three decades earlier. The optometrist sued the board of education after his son was denied a transfer to a white school, although transfers were commonly granted to white students. He was raised in West Virginia by parents who were also dedicated to the civil rights movement. When he was a child, there were no schools for Black children in their small coal-mining town until his parents protested. "My daddy took a whipping for that," he recalled nearly forty years later while waiting for the Supreme Court judgment in his desegregation challenge on behalf of his own son: "I've always told [my children] you've got to fight for what you believe."[4]

Dr. Dowell initiated the litigation when his son, Robert L. Dowell, was thirteen years old and trying to take a few advanced courses that were only offered at the white high school. He planned to become a doctor like his father and wanted to take Latin.[5] The case would consume his high school career. By the time Robert Dowell was twenty-five, he was the main named plaintiff in the litigation; the 1972 decision that required the Oklahoma City Board of Education to implement an expert's desegregation plan was issued only in Robert's name. When the case reached the Supreme Court in 1991, Robert Dowell was a business executive and was dedicated to the cause, like his father. Robert died in 2020 at the age of seventy-three, having spent over forty years of his life fighting for desegregated schools in Oklahoma City.

## Resistant Compliance in Racial Politics

This book is an effort to understand how governmental, institutional, and organizational actors have resisted legal mandates based on race, in ways that look quite different from the familiar images of mass defiance to civil rights. Resistance, as this book demonstrates, sometimes takes the unexpected form of compliance. Institutions craft racial policies with an eye toward meeting the terms of a legal mandate while also working persistently and creatively to maintain their own understanding of and commitment to advancing or resisting racial equality. If we see resistance to law only as openly defiant refusal, then we miss the many ways the recipients of law diminish or expand its impact.

Creative responses to law exist in areas where the law seems to invite none. Currently, to the extent that scholars see organizations as shaping compliance, their analyses usually focus on laws drafted in abstract or ambiguous language, open to varying interpretations. Ambiguous laws invite a range of responses, all with plausible arguments that favor compliance. Organizations comply by choosing a plausible interpretation of the law's facial language. Resistant compliance is a response to forms of law that are different from those that typically occupy the scholarly imagination. When the language of the law unambiguously bans the organizations' desired goal, the organizations must search for a new method. Choosing resistant compliance as a policymaking strategy, they comply with the language of the law while resisting its manifest intent.

The Oklahoma City Board of Education doggedly delayed its compliance with desegregation orders, seeking all options for legal protection and writing policies on paper that the district minimized in implementation. Faculty at the University of Texas had an entirely different policy agenda. They joined with state legislators to improvise an innovative university admissions plan based on the recognized reality of racial segregation in the state's public high schools. The predictable demographics of the state meant that the new plan was race neutral in its criteria but in effect maintained a racially diverse student population. In this resistant compliance response, policymakers relied on social structures— like segregation—to produce a predictable effect. At the University of California, administrators and faculty also relied on a local admissions program and then creatively reimagined the concept of "merit" in their review process to include student background factors such as adversity. Here, resistant compliance consisted of expanding preexisting thresholds, categories, and requirements so that they could passively catch what the organization could not seek out directly. Lastly, admissions directors at the University of Michigan repurposed computer software that categorized students in a race-neutral way and still took into account communities that were underrepresented at the university. Universities under affirmative action bans did not give up their racial diversity projects, only their affirmative action practices.

White supremacist local government officials and racially progressive admissions officers have radically different ideas about civil rights and equality. Segregationist school boards and progressive university admissions officers are about as far apart as possible where egalitarian visions of the Constitution are concerned. Their similarities lie only in their persistence when various constitutional developments have struck at the root of their projects. Both groups used an understudied policymaking tool in response to racial legal mandates that limited the actions they could take. This dynamic of similar responses to legal regulation across ideologically diverse groups heightens the value of studying resistant compliance. Regardless of the legal mandate and goals of the targeted organization, resistant compliance is a feature of US racial policy and a key shaper of its legal impact. In other words, complying in ways that resist is a recurring pattern in American political life. The story of the Fourteenth Amendment's jurisprudence on race is one of legal innovation in response to resistant compliance from both racially conservative *and* progressive social movements.

## The Future of Affirmative Action in Higher Education

Affirmative action bans negatively impact the enrollments of racial minorities. Huge literatures in the fields of education, public administration, and sociology have focused on studying the numerical effects of admissions changes on racial minority populations. The numbers of students of color declined at universities under the jurisdiction of affirmative action bans.[6] For example, at the University of Michigan in 2006, before Proposal 2 was the law, Black students made up 6.4 percent of the Michigan undergraduate first-year class. By 2012, they made up only 4.6 percent, and by 2013 only 4.1 percent. Similarly, in 2006, Latino students made up 5.3 percent of the first-year class, which was down to 3.9 percent in 2012.[7] When universities cannot use affirmative action, they have no equivalent way to maintain the same levels of racial representation in their student populations. Race-neutral strategies do not replicate the racial representation results of race-conscious affirmative action; they are less effective than affirmative action at producing racial diversity.[8] Strategies focused on socioeconomic status that aim to recruit and admit a diverse group of students are less effective than race-conscious affirmative action, unless they are used at universities that are less selective and therefore place little weight on race in the first place.[9]

Should the Supreme Court ban affirmative action the list of universities affected might be shorter than the sweeping constitutional change would suggest. Scholars have shown that nationally, public statements on race by universities have declined in number. In 1994, 60 percent of institutions of higher education said they used race in their admissions process, and by 2014, that number was down to 35 percent.[10] This decline in policy statements that emphasize race cannot be explained by the presence of affirmative action bans.[11] Many state flagship public universities have already pivoted away from race-conscious policies. In three states that now ban affirmative action—Nebraska, New Hampshire, and Oklahoma—the new law did not have an effect on state flagship institutions. This is because the Universities of Nebraska, New Hampshire, and Oklahoma already did not consider race or ethnicity in their undergraduate admissions review processes.[12]

Instead of viewing courts as weak and therefore a "hollow hope" in partnership for social change, we should recognize that courts are armed with the power to exclude certain means, but not the ends.[13] Even if race-conscious affirmative action is struck down by the Supreme Court, race consciousness among higher education administrators cannot be eliminated in the same way. As this book has explained, in some states that formalized legal bans on affirmative action, the change in the law spurred people to devise alternative means to maintain their institutions' policy priorities. University administrators consistently viewed affirmative action bans as a prohibition on a method used to achieve a goal, but not on the goal itself.

In response to affirmative action bans, universities developed admissions policies based on non-racial demographic factors, like socioeconomic status. Nationally, colleges and universities see socioeconomic consideration as a substitute if they cannot use race in policies aimed at promoting student body diversity. If the Supreme Court ends the use of race in admissions, directors at universities across the country report that they will incorporate more review based on student disadvantage, give more weight to factors that bring out disadvantage, and give less weight in the process to student characteristics that are heavily influenced by wealth and access. For example, 10 percent of public and 13 percent of private schools would drop standardized testing as a requirement in their applications; 16 percent of public and 8 percent of private universities would admit some kind of top percent from each in-state high school; 20 percent of public and 22 percent of private schools would give more weight to socioeconomic factors; and 30 percent of public and private schools would give more weight to first generation in college status.[14]

Indeed, even without a national ban, socioeconomic-based polices have caught on nationally as a middle ground between a tradition- ally numbers-based system (with heavy influence from grade-point average and standardized testing) and one that gives consideration to race. Daniel Hirschman and Ellen Berrey argue, this approach shows "spillover effects" from elite institutions and theorize that less selective universities "quietly backed away from considering race, even as elite schools increased their vocal commitments to diversity in general and to race-conscious admissions in particular."[15]

The most elite universities still emphasize race as part of their ad- missions and recruitment process, except at those required to drop race-conscious action through affirmative action bans; however, this emphasis drops off considerably as the institution becomes less selec- tive.[16] On the whole, United States universities are moving away from their emphasis on race.

The College Board—the creator of the SAT and Descriptor Plus—is already trying to get ahead of this trend. In 2019, it announced a plan to pilot an "adversity score" attached to each student taking the SAT and visible only to admissions officers. Researchers in consultation with the College Board on this project have found that admissions readers who use context data are more likely to admit socioeconomically disadvan- taged students.[17] The College Board ultimately pulled back from this new measure due to criticisms of its methodology, but it now releases all of its scores accompanied by information regarding a student's school and neighborhood.[18]

Even universities committed to maintaining racial diversity have backed away from using the word *race* in public statements. One study suggests that language prioritizing racial representation in campus diversity is already on the way out at the University of Michigan. A study of Michigan administrators and staff found that they perceived that the Michigan ban had

> silenced conversations related to race and racism[; made] less visible efforts in support of racial diversity[; created] feelings of personal disempowerment in advocating for racial diversity[; and created] concerns that the law undermined a proud institutional history and commitment to racial diversity.[19]

The findings included interviewees' perceptions that the university had scaled back on its actions and commitment—that without a formal structure, commitments seemed to have eroded.[20] Ellen Berrey finds that University of Michigan administrators substituted direct talk of race with broad language about perspectives, geography, and background.[21]

The switch to affirmative action based on socioeconomic disadvantage is attracting wide support. Prominent conservatives have backed away from a strict meritocracy view of admissions and instead support some preferences for students from disadvantaged backgrounds.[22] Richard Kahlenberg argues that public policy should be in line with public values; by 2016, over 60 percent of Americans supported class-based and not race-based affirmative action.[23] Democratic politicians have also lent their support. While on the presidential campaign trail in 2008, Barack Obama said that his daughters—with the advantages of educated, financially successful parents—should not receive affirmative action. Indeed, he said, race-conscious affirmative action should change "in such a way where some of our children who are advantaged aren't getting more favorable treatment than a poor white kid who has struggled more."[24]

If a future Supreme Court upholds affirmative action, efforts to expand the practice will face headwinds. In 2020, voters in California had the opportunity to repeal the state's constitutional amendment banning affirmative action. Proposition 16 would have allowed universities to consider race in admissions.[25] Yet the vote was not even close. Voters rejected the amendment; 57 percent chose to maintain the affirmative action ban, and 42 percent voted to repeal it.[26] Those in favor of affirmative action were not at a financial disadvantage; almost $20 million was contributed in support of restoring affirmative action to California, and only slightly over $1 million was contributed in favor of maintaining the ban.[27]

## Constitutionalism and Universities

Ultimately, higher education as a whole may trend away from race-conscious affirmative action on its own. However, as the research above demonstrates, prestigious, selective universities have maintained the practice where they can. "Colorblind" cause lawyering has recognized this trend. Recent litigation challenges to university admissions practices have focused on institutions that are selective; the Universities of Texas and North Carolina have a 31 percent and 23 percent admissions rate, respectively. Yale and Harvard are much more difficult to attend, with admissions rates of 6 percent and 4 percent. Yet resistant compliance suggests that winning lawsuits, ballot initiatives, and the sought-after legal mandate may not bring about the desired social change. Dr. Dowell fought for thirty years to end segregation in the Oklahoma City schools. "Colorblind" activists sought bans on affirmative action by bringing lawsuits against universities and organizing ballot initiative campaigns for voters to amend state constitutions. Both legal efforts worked in the short term: the courts ordered Oklahoma City to desegregate its schools and affirmative action bans were written into law. The long-term effects of those efforts were somewhat different.

Law is not just one thing. Even if we can point to a constitution or a statute book to answer the question of what the law is, the language we read is only part of the answer. Studying formal law provides an incomplete education if it is our exclusive focus.[28] Law as it is received in the world is distinct from laws as they are produced by courts, by legislatures, and at the ballot box. Desegregation policy and post–affirmative action policies were implemented by people within the institution targeted by the law. The Oklahoma City Board of Education was influenced by community protests but ultimately made its own decisions about student assignment policies and legal strategy. Similarly, admissions officers and university administration officials wrote and researched post-ban legislation in Texas, created new admissions review systems in California, and repurposed computer software in Michigan.

The existence of resistant compliance is a cautionary tale for those who seek to change society through law. Understanding how these targets resisted law not only increases our understanding of legal effectiveness but also allows for broader consideration of law's political context and salience. A new political regime determined to create social change can target universities and civil society organizations for legal change. The targeted organizations, however, have in their toolboxes the capacity to resist while complying, combining a legal and political response through organizational action. This suggests that the ultimate success of a new political regime in upending social policies might depend less on the laws it can pass or the judges it can put on courts than on the particular capacities of the organizations these laws target.

To achieve social transformations through law, it may be necessary to go beyond law and to shift the commitments of insiders or replace them with new ones. The conservative legal movement of the late twentieth century arguably achieved this feat with respect to federal courts and legal academia.[29] Protests from within the Catholic Church and the military, two traditionally patriarchal institutions, produced policy movement on equality for women.[30] In these instances, new ideas arrived through infiltration. To overcome resistant compliance, it may be necessary to follow this strategy.

Studies of American constitutional and political development must attend more to the ideas that shape legal implementation. If organizations can resist while still following law, they can blunt the impact of the laws intended to govern them. Each of these organizations made policy choices with an eye toward complying with the law and maintaining its organizational commitments at the same time. The board of education in Oklahoma City was able to create compliance policies that failed at actually desegregating schools for eighteen years after *Brown v. Board of Education*. The Universities of Texas, California, and Michigan all experienced decreases in their populations of underrepresented racial minority students on campus but were able to build back these populations to some extent after implementing their adaptive policies. In each case, the commitments and ideas of the targeted organization shaped the policies that followed.

Universities play a role in constitutional politics. Who is in charge of admissions policy is as worthy a subject of inquiry as which judge will hear the constitutional challenge. We know that social movements are influential in creating constitutional change.[31] We can advance this understanding by studying universities as sites of political contestation over racial politics and constitutional protections. Throughout this book, we have seen university actors embracing progressive policy ideas and implementing admissions programs in pursuit of them. Affirmative action is one important area in which universities are simultaneously state actors and civic reformers, but there are certainly many others. Universities regulate controversial ideas on campus.[32] Their role in implementing policies that expanded citizenship makes higher education policies a crucial and overlooked area of the American welfare state.[33] Higher education politics are also critiqued for exacerbating inequality.[34] Universities have appeared before the Supreme Court defending policies that broaden and limit education and access for students.[35] Questions about race, identity, belonging, and who gets to decide are constantly emerging, and universities will continue to play a central (but not yet centered) role in the constitutional politics and development of the United States.

## ACKNOWLEDGMENTS

My work in universities and American political development found its first champions in Adam Sheingate and Steve Teles, who were always available to meet, share ideas, and provide encouragement. Emily Zackin taught me how to write "bird by bird" and shepherded this project as my dissertation chair. Annie Gillman and I turned to Bootcamp, then and now, as a way to write paragraphs and navigate life. My fellow dissertating friends Yoni Abramson, David Dagan, Devin Fernandes, Denva Gallant, Ayako Hiramatsu, and Tristan Klingelhöfer provided camaraderie, humor, and a kindhearted interest in talking about law.

This book exists because of the generosity of scholars and editors in lending their time, ideas, and intellect to the project. I was fortunate to finish my dissertation as a Jefferson Scholars National Fellow at the University of Virginia. My thanks go to Brian Balogh for the opportunity and his enthusiasm. Rogers Smith served as my "Dream Mentor" through this fellowship and provided the sparks that transitioned this project from dissertation to book. Mark Graber is a tremendous champion of all young scholars in public law, and our conversations have shaped my core arguments. Stephan Stohler and Charlton Copeland pushed my thinking forward, encouraged this project, and helped me see how to present it. I am grateful to Austin Sarat and the reviewers at *Studies in Law, Politics, and Society* for the opportunity to present some of the early work. Sonia Tsuruoka saw merit early in this project and enthusiastically championed it at NYU Press. Four anonymous reviewers added helpful suggestions and sharpened the arguments. Allison Van Deventer strengthened every chapter, and it is a more compelling story because of her guidance. My colleagues in the Department of Political Science at Western Michigan University provided enthusiasm, protection, and support, particularly Priscilla Lambert in her commitment to our weekly writing time. I'm excited to begin my career in their good company.

That I can pursue my dreams in academia is a testament to the abiding, unconditional well of support from my family. I am profoundly grateful that it is impossible to disappoint them. Mike Kaplan has always been present in my life with a gentle, open mind. My parents, Sallie and Steve, and my siblings, Jessica and Rob, have never doubted I would take each step that I attempted. Sallie, with persistence and flowers, held the hope for me when my ambition started to wobble. My dear wife, Melinda, has confidently predicted my future since our first meeting and held steadfast in her patience and love. To our children, Reed and Ava: we will believe in you and your dreams as she has believed in mine.

I do not think it is possible to survive as a woman in academia without mentorship. I have been blessed to have brilliant minds believe in my career before I could believe in it myself. Kristine Bowman gave me my first glimpse of research and writing in law school. Doug Edlin led the way with steadiness and faith in me that has shone now for twenty years. Emily Zackin finds ways to bring other women along with her as she rises, and she asks the best questions. All I can do is thank you and hope to pay forward your collective generosity to my own students.

I received a book contract and three weeks later lost all my childcare in the pandemic shutdown. This book is a testament to the sheer force of will it took to keep going in the bits of time I could chisel away from the rest of my life. I dedicate it to all the working mothers in the pandemic.

# NOTES

## 1. BEYOND THE LETTER OF THE LAW

1   Connerly, "Taking It to Michigan." This is, of course, a reference to James Meredith's enrollment in and integration of the University of Mississippi.

2   The ban's language was modeled after the 1964 Civil Rights Act and read in part, "The University of Michigan [and other public universities in the state] shall not discriminate against, or grant preferential treatment to, any individual or group on the basis of race" (Michigan Constitution Article I, Section 26). Among its public university peers across the country, the University of Michigan has the distinction of being explicitly named in its state ban.

3   California (1996), Washington (1998), Michigan (2006), Nebraska (2008), Arizona (2010), and Oklahoma (2012) instituted these bans by ballot initiative, Florida (1999) by executive order, and New Hampshire (2011) through legislation.

4   Hopwood v. Texas, 78 F.3d 932 (5th Cir. 1996); Grutter v. Bollinger, 539 U.S. 206 (2003).

5   This is not meant, of course, to capture the full range of the forms of white resistance. Some of that resistance has involved (and continues to involve) physical violence through such tactics as beatings, bombings, and shootings.

6   Fisher v. University of Texas at Austin, 579 U.S. 365 (2016) (Fisher II); Liptak, "Supreme Court Upholds Affirmative Action Program at University of Texas."

7   *Fisher II*, 579 US.

8   Chotiner, "How Trump Transformed the Supreme Court"; Bains, "Amy Coney Barrett Could Bring Down Decades of Anti-Discrimination Law"; Riley, "With Justice Barrett, Is the End Near for Racial Preferences?"; Sunstein, "Gorsuch Paves Way for Attack on Affirmative Action"; Harpalani, "Chicago-Kent College of Law ISCOTUS Now"; Bravin, "Brett Kavanaugh's Complicated History with Racial Preferences"; Jaschik, "Kavanaugh Evades Questions on Affirmative Action"; Marimow, "Brett Kavanaugh Once Predicted 'One Race' in the Eyes of Government"; Savage, "Leaked Kavanaugh Documents Discuss Abortion and Affirmative Action"; Hasen, "Neil Gorsuch Got Where He Is Because of a Form of Affirmative Action."

9   Smith, *Civic Ideals*.

10   Karabel, *The Chosen*.

11   Karabel; Chen and Stulberg, "Before Bakke"; Skrentny, *The Minority Rights Revolution*; Bowen and Bok, *The Shape of the River*; Schuck, *Diversity in America*.

12 Okechukwu, *To Fulfill These Rights*; Williamson, *Black Power on Campus*; Biondi, *The Black Revolution on Campus*; Deslippe, *Protesting Affirmative Action*; Karabel, *The Chosen*; Skrentny, *The Minority Rights Revolution*; Bowen and Bok, *The Shape of the River*.

13 "Affirmative action was not a 'steam valve' implemented by institutions of higher education to shore up their legitimacy—and the legitimacy of the larger social order—in the face of student protests and urban riots." Stulberg and Chen, "The Origins of Race-Conscious Affirmative Action," 47.

14 Stulberg and Chen, 41, 43.

15 Messer-Davidow, *The Making of Reverse Discrimination*, 185.

16 Regents of the University of California v. Bakke, 438 U.S. at 265.

17 Regents of the University of California v. Bakke, 438 U.S. at 265.

18 This was early in Justice Stevens's tenure on the Supreme Court. Over the next few decades, he would move left on issues of affirmative action. See Stohler, *Reconstructing Rights*, 31–66; Eisgruber, "How the Maverick Became a Lion"; Amann, "John Paul Stevens and Equally Impartial Government." "The meaning of the Title VI ban on exclusion is crystal clear: race cannot be the basis of excluding anyone from participation in a federally funded program." Regents of the University of California v. Bakke, 438 U.S. at 418.

19 "Government may take race into account when it acts not to demean or insult any racial group, but to remedy disadvantages cast on minorities by past racial prejudice." Regents of the University of California v. Bakke, 438 U.S. at 325.

20 Regents of the University of California v. Bakke, 438 U.S. at 314.

21 A tremendous amount of scholarly ink has been spilled in the intervening decades concerning whether Justice Powell's opinion should be viewed as controlling precedent. According to the court's ruling in *Marks v. United States*, 430 U.S. 188 (1977), "the holding of the court may be viewed as that position taken by those Members who concurred in the judgments on the narrowest grounds"; *Id.* at 193 (citation omitted). Applying *Marks* to *Bakke*, Justice Powell's opinion is commonly understood as the controlling precedent (until *Grutter*) for determining the constitutionality of affirmative action programs in higher education. The Powell opinion in *Bakke* provided this path and was viewed as established precedent. See, for example, Friedl, "Making a Compelling Case for Diversity in College Admissions"; Killenbeck, "Pushing Things up to Their First Principles"; Scalia, "The Disease as Cure." Antonin Scalia, writing before his appointment to the Supreme Court, characterized the Powell opinion in *Bakke* as "[what] we must work with as the law of the land." Scalia, 148.

22 Hirschman, Berrey, and Rose-Greenland, "Dequantifying Diversity"; Warikoo, *The Diversity Bargain*; Berrey, *The Enigma of Diversity*; Berrey, "Why Diversity Became Orthodox in Higher Education"; Stulberg and Chen, "A Long View on 'Diversity'"; Stevens and Roksa, "The Diversity Imperative in Elite Admissions"; Lipson, "Embracing Diversity"; Green, "Fighting the Battle for Racial Diversity";

Skrentny, *The Minority Rights Revolution*; Bell, "Diversity's Distractions";
Goodwin, "Affirmative Action in Higher Education"; Lynch, *The Diversity Machine*.

23 Berrey, "Making a Civil Rights Claim for Affirmative Action"; Lipson, "Where's the Justice?"

24 James, "White like Me"; Leong, "Racial Capitalism"; Stevens and Roksa, "The Diversity Imperative in Elite Admissions"; Bell, "Diversity's Distractions"; Lipson, "Where's the Justice?"

25 Adarand Constructors Inc. v. Pena, 515 U.S. 200 (1995); City of Richmond v. J.A. Croson Co., 488 U.S. 469 (1989).

26 Scholars have documented how across education, employment, and contracting organizations deemphasized justifications for affirmative action as compensation and instead shifted to justify these policies as in keeping with commitments to increase diversity. The orientation around diversity is a "bargain" (Warikoo, *The Diversity Bargain*), a "machine" (Lynch, *The Diversity Machine*), and the "remedy" (Kahlenberg, *The Remedy*). The push for diversity is an "enigma" (Berrey, *The Enigma of Diversity*) that professionals have made "manag[erial]" (Kelly and Dobbin, "How Affirmative Action Became Diversity Management") and "embrac[ed]" (Lipson, "Embracing Diversity").

27 Stephan Stohler expands on the court's shifting political alignments and legal development of the diversity rationale in the period between *Bakke* and *Grutter*. Stohler, *Reconstructing Rights*, 31–66.

28 *See* Gratz v. Bollinger, 539 U.S. 244 (2003); Grutter v. Bollinger, 539 U.S. 306 (2003).

29 *Grutter*, 539 U.S. at 309.

30 *Grutter*, 539 U.S. at 334.

31 Hirschman, Berrey, and Rose-Greenland, "Dequantifying Diversity," 285–89. During oral argument in the Michigan cases, the university's attorney denied that the amount of points was set to guarantee admission for racial minorities. "The design is not 'Gee, admit all qualified minorities,'" he argued to the court. But archival research in 2016 by Hirschman, Berrey, and Rose-Greenland indicated that "at least through the mid-1990s, the University's undergraduate admissions policy seems explicitly intended to admit all qualified minority students." Hirschman, Berrey, and Rose-Greenland, 289n43.

32 *Gratz*, 539 U.S. at 276 (O'Connor, J. concurring).

33 "Diminishing the force of [racial] stereotypes is both a crucial part of the Law School's mission, and one that it cannot accomplish with only token numbers of minority students. Just as growing up in a particular region or having particular professional experiences is likely to affect an individual's views, so too is one's own, unique experience of being a racial minority in a society, like our own, in which race unfortunately still matters." *Grutter*, 539 U.S. at 333.

34 "The Law School does not, however, limit in any way the broad range of qualities and experiences that may be considered valuable contributions to student body

diversity. . . . [The Admissions policy] makes clear '[t]here are many possible bases for diversity admissions,' and provides examples of admittees who have lived or traveled widely abroad, are fluent in several languages, have overcome personal adversity and family hardship, have exceptional records of extensive community service, and have had successful careers in other fields." *Grutter*, 539 U.S. at 338.

35 Justice Ginsburg in her *Gratz* dissent made note of this point: "If honesty is the best policy, surely Michigan's accurately described, fully disclosed College affirmative action program is preferable to achieving similar numbers through winks, nods, and disguises." *Gratz*, 539 U.S. at 304.

36 Kluger, *Simple Justice*; Klarman, *Unfinished Business*; Klinkner and Smith, *The Unsteady March*; Badger, "'The Forerunner of Our Opposition'"; Aucoin, "The Southern Manifesto"; Rosenberg, *The Hollow Hope*; Bartley, *The Rise of Massive Resistance*.

37 Sweet, *Merely Judgment*; Gould, *Speak No Evil*; Dolbeare and Hammond, *The School Prayer Decisions*.

38 Kagan, *Adversarial Legalism*, 11.

39 Kagan, 16.

40 Silverstein, *Law's Allure*, 15.

41 We want the "purity, clarity, and efficiency of judicial rulings" over the "gray ambiguity and frustrating inefficiency of the political process." Silverstein, 27.

42 Epp, *The Rights Revolution*.

43 Francis, *Civil Rights*; Feeley and Rubin, *Judicial Policy Making*.

44 Gash, *Below the Radar*.

45 Rosenberg, *The Hollow Hope*.

46 Epp, *Making Rights Real*, 9.

47 Friedman, *Impact*, 88.

48 Friedman, 61.

49 "Much of the complexity [of the tax code] is due to the arms race between the government, on the one side, trying desperately to feed Leviathan's appetite for revenue, and on the other side, nimble lawyers and accountants looking for weak spots in the sea monster's hide." Friedman, 176.

50 Ayres and Braithwaite, *Responsive Regulation*, 26.

51 Bulman-Pozen and Pozen, "Uncivil Obedience"; Johnson, "Do Strikes and Work-to-Rule Campaigns Change Elementary School Assessment Results?"

52 Melnick, *The Crucible of Desegregation*; King and Smith, "Racial Orders in American Political Development"; Katznelson, *When Affirmative Action Was White*; Klinkner and Smith, *The Unsteady March*.

53 King and Smith, "Racial Orders in American Political Development," 75.

54 Frymer, *Black and Blue*.

55 Brown v. Board of Education of Topeka, 347 U.S. at 483.

56 Hopwood v. Texas, 78 F.3d at 944.

57 California Constitution, Article I, Section 31.

58 Michigan Constitution Article I, Section 26.

59 I take the term *affirmative action* from a civil rights based remedial understanding as "a policy that provides special consideration to women or racial minority applicants in an effort to further equality by including members of groups that have historically been subordinated." Lipson, "Where's the Justice?," 693. These programs have changed throughout the last fifty years of American constitutional politics. Before *Bakke*, affirmative action programs were justified as corrective justice for underrepresented minorities and after *Bakke* universities shifted to emphasize the pedagogical benefits of educational diversity. Keck, *Judicial Politics in Polarized Times*, 237.

60 King and Smith, "'Without Regard to Race'"; Novkov, "The Conservative Attack on Affirmative Action."

61 Bonilla-Silva, *Racism without Racists*; Brown et al., *White-Washing Race*; Gallagher, "Color-Blind Privilege."

62 Katznelson, *When Affirmative Action Was White*; King and Smith, "Racial Orders in American Political Development"; Klinkner and Smith, *The Unsteady March*.

63 Dobbin, *Inventing Equal Opportunity*.

64 Epp, *Making Rights Real*.

65 Skrentny, *The Ironies of Affirmative Action*.

66 Edelman, *Working Law*, 34–35.

67 Barnes and Burke, "The Diffusion of Rights"; Edelman, *Working Law*; Dobbin and Sutton, "The Strength of a Weak State"; Dobbin and Kelly, "How to Stop Harassment"; Kalev, Dobbin, and Kelly, "Best Practices or Best Guesses?"; Epp, *Making Rights Real*.

68 Edelman, *Working Law*; Dobbin, *Inventing Equal Opportunity*; Barnes and Burke, "The Diffusion of Rights."

69 Skrentny, *After Civil Rights*, 4.

70 Skrentny, 4.

71 Skrentny, 30–31.

72 In recent years, both organizations have also supported the organization Students for Fair Admission in its litigation against Harvard and the University of North Carolina. "Brief Amicus Curiae of Pacific Legal Foundation, Reason Foundation, Center for Equal Opportunity, Individual Rights Foundation, Chinese American Citizens Alliance-Greater New York, Coalition for TJ, and Yi Fang Chen in Support of Petitioner," US Supreme Court, March 30, 2021; "Brief Amici Curiae of the Center for Equal Opportunity, the Independent Women's Forum, and the American Civil Rights Institute in Support of Petitioner," US Supreme Court, January 16, 2003.

73 Melnick, The Crucible of Desegregation; Klarman, *Unfinished Business*; Frymer, *Black and Blue*; Valelly, *The Two Reconstructions*; Klinkner and Smith, *The Unsteady March*.

74 Valelly, *The Two Reconstructions*, 162.

75 Edelman, *Working Law*, 11.
76 Klarman, *From Jim Crow to Civil Rights*; Rosenberg, *The Hollow Hope*.
77 Brandwein, *Rethinking the Judicial Settlement of Reconstruction*.
78 Klarman, *Unfinished Business*.

## 2. DELAYING PROGRESS

1 Reid, "Friction Seen."
2 William, "Ignoring the Soul of Brown"; Hannel, "Future of Desegregation after Dowell."
3 *Compare* Dowell v. Board of Education, 795 F.2d 1516 (10th Cir. 1986), *cert denied*, 479 U.S. 938 (1986), *with* Riddick v. School Board, 784 F.2d 521 (4th Cir. 1986), *cert denied*, 479 U.S. 938 (1986). The 1980s and 1970s were marked by district courts unsure of how to carry out the mandate to desegregate once systems were declared unitary. Days, "School Desegregation Law in the 1980's."
4 William, "Ignoring the Soul of Brown," 615n2.
5 Killackey and McCarthy, "School Desegregation."
6 Oklahoma Constitution, Article XIII, Section 3 § (1907).
7 Title 70, Section 5 Oklahoma Code §.
8 Dowell v. School Board of Oklahoma City Public Schools, 219 F. Supp. 427 (W.D. Okla. 1963).
9 Throughout this book, I use the term *Black* when referring to African American students and African American communities. I do not capitalize *white* when referring to white schoolchildren or communities. I made this choice in recognition of a cultural identity among African American communities and in line with usage in current social science scholarship.
10 Brown v. Board of Education of Topeka, 347 U.S. 483 (1954).
11 Green v. County School Board, 391 U.S. 430 (1968).
12 In 1991, the Supreme Court in *Dowell* declined a precise definition, saying it would not be "useful" to do so. The court proceeded in its opinion after only a cursory mention that "dual" systems have historically "engaged in intentional segregation" whereas "unitary" systems are "in compliance with the command of the Constitution." Board of Education v. Dowell, 498 U.S. 237 (1991). Leaving the definition broad led the *Dowell* court to favor short-term desegregation decrees and more local control.
13 Thurgood Marshall and other dissenting justices in *Dowell* followed this line of reasoning. Their dissent argued that the command of the Constitution is a public education without racial stigma, compliance with which would require further judicial supervision, in Oklahoma City and other districts currently under court orders.
14 Kluger, *Simple Justice*, 765.
15 Milliken v. Bradley, 418 U.S. 717, 741 (1974).
16 Refusing to reopen court-ordered desegregation after the schools resegregated, the *Dowell* court instead focused on the importance of allowing local school

boards to control education policies "so that school programs can fit local needs." Federal court "supervision of local school systems was intended as a temporary measure." *Dowell*, 498 U.S. at 248 (citing to *Milliken v. Bradley*, 418 U.S. 717 [1974]); San Antonio Independent School District v. Rodriguez, 411 U.S. 1 (1973).

17  Smith, *Civic Ideals.*

18  In 1984, after the district court ended its supervision, the board was able to return to its policies of anti-busing and neighborhood schools unimpeded. Indeed, because the court had ended its jurisdiction, Black families were not able to reopen the case even when board policies reverted the school system to a segregated one.

19  Kluger, *Simple Justice*; McAdam, *Political Process*; Klarman, *Unfinished Business*; Klinkner and Smith, *The Unsteady March*; Rosenberg, *The Hollow Hope.*

20  Aucoin, "The Southern Manifesto."

21  Kluger, *Simple Justice*, 752.

22  Woodward, *The Strange Career of Jim Crow*, 156–67.

23  "Murray Declines Bid to Southern Parley on Segregation Issue," *Daily Oklahoman*, May 21, 1954.

24  Oklahoma City School Board, "Statement Concerning Integration of Oklahoma Public Schools, 1955–1956," August 1, 1955.

25  Oklahoma City School Board.

26  *Dowell*, 219 F. Supp. at 443.

27  *Dowell*, 219 F. Supp. at 430.

28  *Dowell*, 219 F. Supp. at 446.

29  *Dowell*, 219 F. Supp. at 444.

30  *Dowell*, 219 F. Supp. at 431.

31  Board of Education of the Oklahoma City Public Schools v. Dowell, 375 F.2d 158 (10th Cir. 1967).

32  *Dowell*, 219 F. Supp. at 434.

33  *Dowell*, 219 F. Supp. at 439.

34  *Dowell*, 219 F. Supp. at 441.

35  *Dowell*, 219 F. Supp. at 445.

36  *Dowell*, 219 F. Supp. at 441.

37  "Father Glad at Decision," *Daily Oklahoman*, July 12, 1963, sec. 1.

38  Reid, "Friction Seen; Schools Plan Racial Appeal."

39  One local psychiatrist testified that desegregation was not advisable for Black students because then schools would have to "bring the subject matter down to the level of the Negro student [and] hold the white students back." The newspaper account noted that while the mayor's committee was receptive to this pro-segregation argument, the reporter could not get board members to comment on it due to its "controversial nature." The committee did note that the apparent gap in academic ability was evident only after third grade, when, they reasoned, "socio economic and environmental factors" start to impede students' development.

"School Board between Rock and Hard Place on Integration," *Daily Oklahoman*, July 24, 1963.

40 "Teachers Accept Integration," *Daily Oklahoman*, July 12, 1963.

41 "School Board between Rock and Hard Place on Integration."

42 "School Board Hit by Urban League," *Daily Oklahoman*, July 14, 1963.

43 "Teacher Plan Under Attack By Negroes," *Daily Oklahoman*, August 7, 1963.

44 "Board for School Integration Urged," *Daily Oklahoman*, August 20, 1963.

45 "School Board Imposes Strict Transfer Rule," *Daily Oklahoman*, August 6, 1963, sec. 1.

46 Editorial Board, "No Easy Solutions," *Daily Oklahoman*, August 7, 1963.

47 "Teacher Plan under Attack By Negroes," *Daily Oklahoman*, August 7, 1963, quoting E. Melvin Porter, president of the Oklahoma City chapter.

48 *Dowell*, 375 F.2d at 163–64.

49 *Dowell*, 244 F. Supp. at 973–74.

50 "U.S. Judge Instructs City Schools to Seek Expert on Integration," *Daily Oklahoman*, February 29, 1965.

51 "U.S. Judge Instructs City Schools to Seek Expert on Integration."

52 "City School Plan Unwise Parents Say," *Daily Oklahoman*, February 15, 1965.

53 "Segregated Schools Deprive City Children Full Benefit?," *Daily Oklahoman*, August 10, 1965.

54 "Segregated Schools Deprive City Children Full Benefit?"

55 *Dowell*, 244 F. Supp. at 978.

56 *Dowell*, 375 F.2d at 166.

57 *Dowell*, 244 F. Supp. at 976.

58 *Dowell*, 375 F.2d at 164.

59 *Dowell*, 244 F. Supp. at 974.

60 *Dowell*, 244 F. Supp. at 975.

61 *Dowell*, 244 F. Supp. at 975.

62 *Dowell*, 244 F. Supp. at 975–76.

63 *Dowell*, 244 F. Supp. at 977.

64 *Dowell*, 375 F.2d at 166.

65 *Dowell*, 244 F. Supp. at 977.

66 *Dowell*, 244 F. Supp. at 978.

67 *Dowell*, 244 F. Supp. at 977–78.

68 Reid, "Judge's School Order Called Unwarranted."

69 Reid, "School to Appeal Integration Order."

70 *Dowell*, 375 F.2d.

71 Reid, "Integration Appeal Machinery Starts."

72 Hatch, "New Desegregation Plan."

73 Reid, "Integration Appeal Machinery Starts."

74 Reid, "City Schools Tackle Job of Carrying Out Court's Racial Plan."

75 "Only 33 Pupils Seek Racial Minority School Transfers," *Daily Oklahoman*, August 19, 1967.

76  Reid, "City Schools Tackle Job of Carrying Out Court's Racial Plan."
77  "School Advisory Panel to Meet," *Daily Oklahoman*, December 6, 1967.
78  "Petition Urges School Action," *Daily Oklahoman*, July 18, 1967.
79  Reid, "School Board Urges Judge to Reconsider Integration 'Pairing.'"
80  Reid, "School Board Urges Judge to Reconsider Integration 'Pairing.'"
81  Reid, "School Pairings Protested Anew."
82  Reid, "School Board Urges Judge to Reconsider Integration 'Pairing.'"
83  Reid, "School Board Urges Judge to Reconsider Integration 'Pairing.'"
84  Reid, "School Pairings Protested Anew."
85  Mays, "School Board Chief Backs Drive."
86  Mays.
87  Reid, "Plan Adopted on Integration."
88  Reid.
89  Hatch, "City Integration Plan Criticized."
90  Hatch, "City Integration Plan Criticized."
91  Hatch, "School Board Chief Doubts Voluntary Integration Possible."
92  Hatch, "School Board Chief Doubts Voluntary Integration Possible."
93  Hatch, "School Board Chief Doubts Voluntary Integration Possible."
94  Hatch, "School Board Chief Doubts Voluntary Integration Possible."
95  Hatch, "School Board Chief Doubts Voluntary Integration Possible."
96  Reid, "School Board Votes to Follow Bohanon's Edict on Integration."
97  "School Factions View Integration," *Daily Oklahoman*, July 30, 1969.
98  "Meeting Held in Belle Isle," *Daily Oklahoman*, August 7, 1969; "Irate Patrons Call on Harris with Protests," *Daily Oklahoman*, August 16, 1969.
99  Reid, "School Board, OU Experts Seek Integration Answers."
100 Hatch, "City School Order Vacated."
101 Fulkerson, "It's Probably Last Year's Boundaries."
102 Hatch, "City School Order Vacated."
103 "High Court Gets City School Plea," *Daily Oklahoman*, October 18, 1969.
104 Fulkerson, "It's Probably Last Year's Boundaries."
105 Reid, "'Home Base' School Plan Wins Approval of Board."
106 Hatch, "'Cluster' Plan Given Tentative Approval."
107 Hatch, "'Cluster' Plan Given Tentative Approval."
108 Reid, "School Board Splits 3 to 2."
109 "Board Acts to Block 'White Flight' Transfers," *Daily Oklahoman*, June 3, 1970.
110 Reid, "School Board Splits 3 to 2."
111 Hatch, "Books Closed by Bohanon on City Integration Case."
112 Reid, "Pupils Have Option Not to Shift Schools."
113 Boone, "Neighborhood School Plan Voted by Board."
114 Boone, "Schools to Seek Integration Consultant."
115 Boone, "Strengthened Cluster Plan for City Schools Drafted in Report by Consultants."

116  Boone, "Strengthened Cluster Plan for City Schools Drafted in Report by Consultants."

117  Dowell v. Board of Education of the Oklahoma City Public Schools, 338 F. Supp. 1256 (W.D. Okla. 1972).

118  *Dowell*, 338 F. Supp. at 1273.

119  Boone, "School Ruling Due in Week."

120  Boone, "School Ruling Due in Week."

121  *Dowell*, 338 F. Supp. at 1270, notes 11, 14.

122  *Dowell*, 338 F. Supp. at 1270.

123  *Dowell*, 338 F. Supp. at 1263.

124  *Dowell*, 338 F. Supp. at 1258.

125  *Dowell*, 338 F. Supp. at 1265.

126  *Dowell*, 338 F. Supp. at 1271.

127  *Dowell*, 338 F. Supp. at 1271.

128  Killackey, "Board Told to Pay Lawyers."

129  Killackey, "Board Told to Pay Lawyers."

130  Boone, "Bohanon Requested to Stay School Order."

131  Boone, "Bohanon Requested to Stay School Order."

132  Boone, "School Board Rejects Defiance Pleas."

133  Boone, "School Board Rejects Defiance Pleas."

134  Boone, "School Board Rejects Defiance Pleas."

135  Patterson, "Judge Rejects Schools Plans."

136  Killackey, "Arguments Heard on Principal Shift."

137  Killackey, "NAACP Letter Asks Judge to Retain City School Case."

138  Killackey, "NAACP Letter Asks Judge to Retain City School Case."

139  W.D. Okla., "Order Terminating Case, No. CIV-9452," January 18, 1977.

140  W. .D. Okla., "Order Terminating Case, No. CIV-9452," January 18, 1977.

141  Killackey, "Integration Goals Met, Judge Feels."

142  McCarthy, "Bohanon Gives Up City School Reins."

143  McCarthy, "Bohanon Gives Up City School Reins."

144  Singleterry, "City School Proposal Draws Large Protest."

145  Singleterry, "City Board Approves School Plan."

146  Singleterry, "City Board Approves School Plan."

147  Singleterry, "Angry Moms Balk at Long Bus Rides."

148  Fossett and Singleterry, "City School Plans Challenged in Court."

149  Dowell v. Board of Education of the Oklahoma City Public Schools, 606 F. Supp. 1548 (W.D. Okla. 1985).

150  *Dowell*, 606 F. Supp. at 1554.

151  Dowell v. Board of Education, 795 F.2d.

152  Dowell v. Board of Education of the Oklahoma City Public Schools, 677 F. Supp. 1503 (W.D. Okla. 1987).

153  *Dowell*, 677 F. Supp. at 1506.

154 Dowell v. Board of Education of the Oklahoma City Public Schools, 890 F.2d 1483 (10th Cir. 1989).

155 *Dowell*, 498 U.S.

156 *Dowell*, 498 U.S. at 249–50.

157 *Dowell*, 498 U.S. at 250.

158 *Dowell*, 498 U.S. at 249.

159 *Dowell*, 498 U.S. at 262 (emphasis in original) (Marshall, J., dissenting).

160 *Dowell*, 498 U.S. at 262 (Marshall, J., dissenting).

161 *Dowell*, 498 U.S. at 259; citing to *Milliken v. Bradley* (1977)(emphasis in original) (Marshall, J., dissenting).

162 *Dowell*, 498 U.S. at 259 (Marshall, J., dissenting).

163 *Dowell*, 498 U.S. at 265 (Marshall, J., dissenting).

## 3. PRIORITIZING DIVERSITY

1 Hopwood v. Texas, 78 F.3d. 932 (5th Cir. 1996).

2 Gonzalo Barrientos, University of Texas at Austin Voces Oral History Center, available at https://voces.lib.utexas.edu/collections/stories/gonzalo-barrientos.

3 Gonzalo Barrientos.

4 Gonzalo Barrientos.

5 The Law School issued color-coded applications by race, had lower test score and GPA requirements for minority applicants, and had separate admissions review committees and waiting lists for minority applicants. Hopwood v. Texas, 861 F. Supp. 551, 560–62 (W.D. Texas 1994).

6 Burka, "Law-Cheryl Hopwood."

7 In 2003, *Grutter v. Bollinger* resulted in a constitutionally permissible path for affirmative action and replaced *Hopwood* as controlling law in Texas.

8 Hired by CIR and representing Cheryl Hopwood was prestigious appellate litigator Theodore Olson. Olson's clients would later include governor George W. Bush in his ultimately successful quest to stop recounting ballots in the 2000 presidential election in *Bush v. Gore*. Fifteen years later, Olson and his *Bush v. Gore* litigator-opponent David Boies would represent Californian LGBT couples in their successful bid to reinstate same-sex marriage in California in *Perry v. Schwarzenegger*.

9 *Hopwood*, 78 F.3d at 945.

10 *Hopwood*, 78 F.3d at 945.

11 *Bakke* authorizes race-conscious affirmative action to implement desegregation orders. Public universities in Louisiana and Mississippi were already under these orders and so were unaffected by *Hopwood*. The decision noted that the University of Texas was not under such orders and therefore could not justify any affirmative action programs as necessary to remedy past acts of discrimination. *Hopwood*, 78 F.3d at 962.

12 The university appealed the case, but state policymakers were divided. The regents were worried about the competitive disadvantage against peer institutions if Texas

could not practice affirmative action. They were also under pressure from groups like MALDEF and the NAACP that claimed they had not fought hard enough for affirmative action. Republican governor George W. Bush and attorney general Dan Morales did not support an appeal. Roser, "Groups Call UT's Efforts Lacking."

13 Morales, "Letter Opinion No. 97–001."

14 Morales, "Hopwood Opens New Era in Pursuit of Diversity."

15 Lipson, "Affirmative Action As We Don't Know It," 303.

16 Montejano, "On Hopwood," 139.

17 Montejano, 134, 139.

18 Merle, "Court Rules against Affirmative Action at UT Law School."

19 Montejano, "On Hopwood," 134.

20 Robert Berdahl, editorial in *Daily Texan* as quoted in Munoz, "The Politics of Supporting Diversity in Higher Education," 6.

21 Walt and Hughes, "Minorities Say They Might Ax Funding for UT."

22 Stutz, "Senators OK Bill Tracking Colleges' Minority Enrollees."

23 Brooks, "Rival States Lure Minority Students."

24 Brooks, "Morales Reiterates Affirmative Action Rules."

25 Montejano, "Maintaining Diversity at the University of Texas," 358n9.

26 Montejano, "On Hopwood: The Continuing Challenge," 140.

27 "Although somewhat crude . . . these estimates nonetheless suggested that a 10 percent plan, even under the 50 percent scenario described above, yielded a pool of African Americans and Mexican Americans greater than their current percentages at the University of Texas of 3.9 percent African American and 12 percent Hispanic." Montejano, 140.

28 Montejano, "Maintaining Diversity at the University of Texas," 363.

29 Montejano, "On Hopwood: The Continuing Challenge," 143.

30 Munoz, "The Politics of Supporting Diversity in Higher Education: Texas Legislature's Enactment of House Bill 588," 99.

31 Texas House of Representatives, House debate on HB 588, Tape 58, Side B, 10:31.

32 Thompson and Tobias, "The Texas Ten Percent Plan," 1126.

33 Montejano, "On Hopwood: The Continuing Challenge," 141.

34 Munoz, "The Politics of Supporting Diversity in Higher Education: Texas Legislature's Enactment of House Bill 588," 99.

35 Montejano, "On Hopwood: The Continuing Challenge," 142.

36 Montejano, 142.

37 Montejano, 144.

38 Montejano, 144.

39 This plan would have had three tiered levels for admission. Up to 50 percent would be admitted based on grades and scores with automatic admission for top 10 percent standing in high school class. Then up to 40 percent would be admitted based on grades, scores, and certain demographic factors, such as "whether students are bilingual, have parents with college degrees, held jobs

during high school or live in economically disadvantaged areas." Lastly, up to 10 percent would be admitted at the college's discretion based on "student's potential to succeed." Brooks, "Bill Seeks to Balance Court Ruling."

40  Fikac, "University Admission Policy Bill Filed."

41  Brooks, "Bill Seeks to Balance Court Ruling."

42  Montejano, "On Hopwood," 147.

43  Montejano, 145.

44  Texas Legislature Online, "SB 1419/HB 588 Legislative History, Session 75(R)."

45  Munoz, "The Politics of Supporting Diversity in Higher Education," 103.

46  Texas House of Representatives, House debate on HB 588, Tape 58, Side A, 15:29.

47  Texas House of Representatives, Tape 58, Side A, 15:40.

48  Texas House of Representatives, Tape 59, Side A, 8:44.

49  Texas House of Representatives, Tape 58, Side B, 45:39.

50  Texas House of Representatives, Tape 59, Side A, 8:44.

51  "I don't believe in quotas. . . . I believe in an equal, level field where we can all obtain and receive an accessibility to higher education . . . [this bill] will reach the areas of Texas that have been under-served [by higher education]." Texas House of Representatives, Tape 58, Side B, 13:27.

52  Munoz, "The Politics of Supporting Diversity in Higher Education," 108.

53  Montejano, "On Hopwood: The Continuing Challenge," 148.

54  Munoz, "The Politics of Supporting Diversity in Higher Education," 79.

55  Texas Legislature Online, "SB 1419/HB 588 Legislative History, Session 75(R)."

56  Munoz, "The Politics of Supporting Diversity in Higher Education," 93.

57  Texas House of Representatives, House debate on HB 588, Tape 58, Side A, 24:01.

58  Texas House of Representatives, Tape 58, Side A, 28:00.

59  Munoz, "The Politics of Supporting Diversity in Higher Education," 101.

60  Villafranca, "Bush Extols Hispanic Businesses, Reiterates Opposition to Quotas."

61  Texas Legislature Online, "SB 1419/HB 588 Legislative History, Session 75(R)."

62  Walker argued that this resulted in indistinguishable academic difference within the incoming class: "Faculty believe that students are better. I would challenge any faculty member to say that you can tell a difference between a 1220 and 1235" SAT scores in terms of students who had earned them. Lipson, 368–69.

63  Bruce Walker recalled the training process:
    Our essays we score holistically, 1 being low and 6 being high. We take a random sample of 200. We have a professional reader—a faculty member in English who is a trainer for Advanced Placement. He takes 200 resumes and 200 essays. He takes examples of what he picks as a 6, 5, 4, 3, 2, 1. We all go through the training every year . . . The 1s and 6s are easy to distinguish. The middle scores are harder to distinguish. He distributed a packet seeing if we can all agree on what an essay score is. After a while, everyone can recognize a 6, what you're looking for is a clear example of each score to go into a 'range finder' notebook . . . We don't have formulas. Lipson, 369.

64  Between 1992 and 2002, the number of high schools sending students to UT rose from 678 to 798, including schools with large numbers of underrepresented minority students and schools in rural west Texas that were economically underprivileged. Long, Saenz, and Tienda, "Policy Transparency and College Enrollment," 84, 96.

65  Sullivan, "College Access, Geography, and Diversity," 154–55.

66  Long, Saenz, and Tienda, "Policy Transparency and College Enrollment," 91.

67  Root, "UT-Austin Pushes Lawmakers to Modify 'top 10 Percent' Rule"; Jaschik, "The 10 Percent Fight Is Back."

68  Hughes and Tresaugue, "Small-Town GOP behind Survival of the Top 10 Percent Rule."

69  Hughes and Tresaugue. This was not actually the case. When researchers analyzed quantitatively the admissions stats from pre- and post-*Hopwood* and the Top Ten Percent law, they found that admitting the top 10 percent was the de facto rule in UT admissions and all the law did was make it de jure. Perhaps the publicity made people in rural areas feel that they could get in and therefore motivated them to apply. Long, Saenz, and Tienda, "Policy Transparency and College Enrollment." Their data does show that once one student in a "new to UT" high school was admitted and attended, others in future classes continued to apply, suggesting that broadened access is resilient once achieved.

70  Long and Tienda, "Winners and Losers," 257.

71  Brooks, "Texas College Applications."

72  Sweatt v. Painter, 339 U.S. 629 (1950).

73  Montejano, "On Hopwood," 137.

74  University of Texas press release, "Enrollment of First-Time Freshman Minority Students No Higher than before Hopwood Court Decision," January 29, 2003, https://news.utexas.edu.

75  Brooks, "Fewer Hispanics, Blacks Start at UT."

76  Grutter v. Bollinger, 539 U.S.

77  University of Texas press release, "Enrollment of First-Time Freshman Minority Students No Higher than before Hopwood Court Decision"; Nissimov, "UT Austin to Reintroduce Race-Based Criteria."

78  University of Texas press release, "The University of Texas at Austin Reacts to the Supreme Court's Affirmative Action Decisions," June 23, 2003, https://news.utexas.edu.

79  Okechukwu, *To Fulfill These Rights*, 191.

80  *Fisher*, 579 US at 19.

## 4. EXPANDING ACCESS

1  Laird, "Bending Admissions to Political Ends."

2  Sanchez, "Struggling to Maintain Diversity."

3  Sanchez.

4 The characterization as "a beautiful model of diversity" is from Genaro Padilla, University of California, Berkeley vice chancellor for student affairs, quoted in Sanchez, "Struggling to Maintain Diversity."

5 These two tracks were the regular admits with about a B grade average, or about the top 15 percent of graduating California seniors, and then special admits from special and/or disadvantaged backgrounds. Douglass, "The Evolution of a Social Contract," 397.

6 This plan was meant to "specify a floor of preparation needed to pursue study at UC and also function as an entitlement: anyone who meets these requirements is guaranteed a place at UC—although not necessarily at the campus nor in the major of his or her choice." University of California Office of the President, "Undergraduate Access to the University of California after the Elimination of Race-Conscious Policies," 5, www.ucop.edu.

7 Douglass, "Anatomy of a Conflict," 126.

8 Stulberg and Chen, "A Long View on 'Diversity.'"

9 Douglass, "Anatomy of a Conflict," 126.

10 *Bakke*, 438 U.S. at 316.

11 University of California Office of the President, "Undergraduate Access to the University of California After the Elimination of Race-Conscious Policies," 5, www.ucop.edu.

12 University of California Board of Regents, "Regents Policy 2102: Policy on Undergraduate Admissions," https://regents.universityofcalifornia.edu.

13 Most campuses used formulas—an academic one for Tier 1 admits with a grade-point average and testing combination. Officers then gave points to various supplemental factors, like race. This formula later developed into a matrix in which students were given an academic score and a supplemental score and then admitted with some combination of academic and supplemental scores. University of California Office of the President, "Undergraduate Access to the University of California After the Elimination of Race-Conscious Policies," 7–8.

14 University of California Office of the President, 5.

15 University of California Office of the President, 8.

16 At Berkeley, only Black, Hispanic, and Native American students received a race-based admissions bump under supplemental review because Asian-American students were considered overrepresented on campus. Lipson, "Affirmative Action As We Don't Know It," 178–79.

17 During the 1996 admissions season, nearly 50 percent of underrepresented minority applicants were admitted at the two University of California flagship campuses, Los Angeles (44 percent) and Berkeley (49 percent). This is compared to a 39 percent overall admissions rate for applicants that year to UCLA and a 36 percent overall admissions rate for applicants at Berkeley. University of California Office of the President, "Undergraduate Access to the University of California After the Elimination of Race-Conscious Policies," 35–42.

18 Anonymous University of California administration official, personal interview, November 2017.

19 The phrase "change the culture of the university " is from Connerly, *Creating Equal*, 139.

20 Peltason, "Letter to the University of California Board of Regents," January 19, 1995.

21 Douglass, "A Brief on the Events Leading to SP1," 11.

22 Peltason, "Statement to the Regents, University of California Board of Regents Meeting."

23 Burdman, "Regent's Idea to Drop UC Race Preferences."

24 "It has become clear despite official claims to the contrary . . . race has played a central role in admissions practices at many UC campuses." Wilson, "Statement to the Regents, University of California Board of Regents Meeting."

25 Connerly was particularly agitated and aggrieved by these demonstrations, comparing himself to King and Jackson and his demonstrators to white supremacist segregationists. "They are the heirs of George Wallace and all the others who stood in those doorways of the past, protecting a corrupt and outmoded way of life. 'Preferences today!' these bitter-enders are saying by their actions. 'Preferences tomorrow! Preferences forever!'" Connerly, *Creating Equal*, 241.

26 University of California Board of Regents, "Policy Ensuring Equal Treatment Admissions (SP-1)."

27 Chavez, *The Color Bind*, 11; Johnson, "Scholars Touch off an 'avalanche' on Affirmative Action."

28 Connerly, *Creating Equal*, 165.

29 Wood wrote to Connerly in November, 1995: "You and the others who voted for your resolutions have, I am afraid, much to fear if the vote on July 20 is not ratified by the voters in November 1996. A clear victory for CCRI [California Civil Rights Initiative] at the polls is the only thing that will silence the opposition." Chavez, *The Color Bind*, 74.

30 Ayres, "Conservatives Forge New Strategy to Challenge Affirmative Action"; Brown, "Clinton's Dilemma"; Chavez, *The Color Bind*, 24–43.

31 Allen, *Ending Racial Preferences*; Connerly, *Creating Equal*; Chavez, *The Color Bind*.

32 Anonymous University of California administration official, personal interview, November 2017.

33 Citrin, "Desperately Seeking Diversity."

34 Laird, "Bending Admissions to Political Ends."

35 Sanchez, "Struggling to Maintain Diversity."

36 Sanchez.

37 Sanchez.

38 Sanchez.

39  Democrats in the state assembly and senate were "explicit to the Chancellor that they will punish the University of California, Berkeley if [the university administrators] do not subvert [Proposition 209]." Lipson, "Affirmative Action As We Don't Know It," 365–66.

40  Laird, "Bending Admissions to Political Ends."

41  Anonymous University of California administration official, personal interview, November 2017.

42  Anonymous University of California administration official, personal interview November 2017.

43  Relevant language from the regents' ban, affecting only the University of California: "Section 2. Effective January 1, 1997, the University of California shall not use race, religion, sex, color, ethnicity or national origin as a criterion for admission to the university or to any program of study." University of California Board of Regents, "Policy Ensuring Equal Treatment Admissions (SP-1)." Relevant language from Proposition 209, affecting all state actors: "(a) The state shall not discriminate against, or grant preferential treatment to, any individual or group on the basis of race, sex, color, ethnicity, or national origin in the operation of public employment, public education, or public contracting." California Constitution, Article I, Section 31.

44  University of California Office of the President, "Undergraduate Access to the University of California After the Elimination of Race-Conscious Policies," 3n2.

45  Anonymous University of California administration official, personal interview, November 2017.

46  Flacks and Alvarez, "Towards Fairness in UC Admissions." Professors Flacks and Alvarez submitted the proposal to the admissions committee of the UC faculty academic senate, called the Board of Admissions and Relations with Schools (BOARS).

47  Burdman, "Two Challenges Set for UC's Race-Blind Admissions."

48  "A high percentage of students who are not now UC eligible, and hence do not meet minimum academic requirements, would now become eligible. In turn, it appeared a strong likelihood that the number of students matriculating and graduating would also decline." Academic Senate, University of California, "Report of the Board of Admissions and Relations with Schools."

49  Academic Senate, University of California.

50  Widaman testimony before the hearing of the California State Senate Select Subcommittee on Higher Education Admissions and Outreach, Sacramento, CA, May 5, 1998.

51  Widaman testimony before the hearing of the California State Senate Select Subcommittee on Higher Education Admissions and Outreach, Sacramento, CA, May 5, 1998.

52  Davis, "First Inaugural Address."

53  Davis, "State of the State Address."

54  Burdman, "Two Challenges Set for UC's Race-Blind Admissions."

55  Committee on Educational Policy, "March 18, 1999, Minutes."

56  Committee on Educational Policy.

57  Burdman, "UC Regents to Approve 4 percent Admissions Policy."

58  University of California Office of the President, "Undergraduate Access to the University of California After the Elimination of Race-Conscious Policies," 13.

59  University of California Office of the President, 27.

60  At Berkeley in the first year of the policy change, 61 percent of these local context students were admitted, as compared to a 23.9 percent overall admit rate of all applicants. At UCLA, 53.6 percent of the students newly eligible because of high school standing were admitted, compared to 24.2 percent as an overall admit rate. University of California Office of the President, 27.

61  Academic Senate, University of California, "Guidelines," 3–5.

62  Price.

63  Cockrell and Mena, "1998 Admissions Report."

64  Cockrell and Mena.

65  Sanchez, "Struggling to Maintain Diversity."

66  Patrick Hayashi, vice chancellor for admissions, UC Berkeley. Kell and Mena, "Selecting the Freshman Class."

67  Sanchez, "Struggling to Maintain Diversity."

68  Lipson, "Affirmative Action as We Don't Know It," 163.

69  According to one reader: "Becoming reacquainted with the norming and other readers' perspectives brings me back to center. When scores are tallied and they appear on the board, closely clustered, it reassures me that I'm on the right track. And that this daunting task is doable." Cockrell and Mena, "1998 Admissions Report."

70  Cockrell and Mena.

71  Cockrell and Mena.

72  Berdahl, "1998 Admissions Report."

73  Price, "New Admission Policy."

74  Richard C. Atkinson, "Letter to Academic Senate," February 17, 2001.

75  Douglass, The Conditions for Admission, 207

76  Board of Regents, University of California, "May 16, 2001, Minutes."

77  Committee on Educational Policy, "October 17, 2001, Minutes," attachment 1. In reviewing proposals, BOARS staff talked to Stanford, Harvard, Yale, MIT, and the Universities of Illinois, Maryland, Michigan, North Carolina, and Wisconsin.

78  Committee on Educational Policy, "October 17, 2001, Minutes," 15.

79  Committee on Educational Policy, "October 17, 2001, Minutes," attachment 2.

80  Committee on Educational Policy, 6.

81  Committee on Educational Policy, 6.

82  Committee on Educational Policy, 9–10.

83  Committee on Educational Policy, 8.

84  Academic Senate, University of California, "October 31, 2001, Minutes," 7.

85  Anonymous University of California administration official, personal interview, November 2017.

86  Special talents, awards, or interests could include interest in "exploration of other cultures" or "experiences that demonstrate unusual promise for leadership." Life experiences and special circumstances included "disabilities, low family income, first generation to attend college, need to work, disadvantaged social or educational environment, difficult personal and family situations or circumstances, refugee status, or veteran status." Academic Senate, University of California, "Guidelines for Implementation of University Policy on Undergraduate Admissions Guiding Principles for Comprehensive Review by the Board of Admissions and Relations with Schools."

87  Academic Senate, University of California, "Guidelines," 1 (emphasis added).

88  Committee on Educational Policy, "November 14, 2001, Minutes," 6.

89  Committee on Educational Policy, 4.

90  Committee on Educational Policy, 10–11. Amendment approved by committee: "There shall be an annual review and reporting to The Regents of the effect of this action and that, in approving the action, the board of Regents states that these comprehensive review policies shall be used fairly, shall not use racial preferences of any kind, and shall comply with Proposition 209."

91  Hurtado, "BOARS Recommendations"; Brown, "Academic Assembly"; Atkinson, "Letter to Academic Senate," February 17, 2001; Academic Senate, University of California, "Guidelines for Implementation of University Policy on Undergraduate Admissions Guiding Principles for Comprehensive Review by the Board of Admissions and Relations with Schools"; Academic Senate, University of California, "Guidelines for Implementation of University Policy on Undergraduate Admissions by the Board of Admissions and Relations with Schools"; University of California Office of the President, "Memo to Members of the Committee on Educational Policy: Proposal for Comprehensive Review in Undergraduate Admissions"; Burdman, "UC Regents to Approve 4 percent Admissions Policy"; University of California Office of the President, "Memo to Members of the Committee on Educational Policy: Proposal for Comprehensive Review in Undergraduate Admissions."

92  See, for example, Committee on Educational Policy, Regents of the University of California, "November 14, 2001, Minutes."

93  In 2002, the first-year class at UCLA had 622 Hispanic students, and by 2017, there were 1,361 Hispanic students in the first-year class. In comparison, the population of Black students at UCLA has barely shifted. The fall 2017 class had an increase of only thirty Black students over the fall 2002 class. Academic Planning and Budget, University of California, Los Angeles. "Common Data Set," 2017.

94 Berdahl started as chancellor of Berkeley in July 1997, the year after the affirmative action ban passed. He brought with him experience specific to the challenge of operating in a post–affirmative action world. Since January 1993, he had been the president of the University of Texas at Austin, including seeing the university through the *Hopwood* case and its immediate aftermath.

95 Lipson, "Affirmative Action as We Don't Know It," 169.

96 Kidder and Gandara, "Two Decades after the Affirmative Action Ban," 23.

97 Douglass, *The Conditions for Admission*, 184–214; University of California Outreach Task Force, "Report to University of California Board of Regents"; Weiss, "UC Proposes Push."

98 Pamela Clute, University of California, Riverside, faculty member and partnership program. Traub, "The Class of Prop. 209."

99 Traub.

100 Traub.

## 5. PRESERVING THE MISSION

1 The constitution was amended to "ban public institutions from discriminating against or giving preferential treatment to groups or individuals based on their race, gender, color, ethnicity, or national origin." Michigan Constitution, Article I, Section 26.

2 Mary Sue Coleman, "Remarks on Passing of Proposal 2" (Ann Arbor, MI, November 7, 2006).

3 "Prop 2 Snippets," *Michigan Daily*, November 9, 2006.

4 Coleman, "Remarks on Passing of Proposal 2."

5 Coleman.

6 "We're not making a secret of it" is from Cliff Sjogren, quoted in Hirschman, Berrey, and Rose-Greenland, "Dequantifying Diversity," 283.

7 He continued, "As social, legal, moral, and political forces continually succeed in reducing discriminatory practices, a major educational task is the preparation of the Negro and other deprived students for a greater role in all aspects of American life." Memo from Roger Heyns to the Ad-Hoc Advisory Committee on the Negro in Higher Education, May 31, 1963, box 1, UM Provost Records.

8 Skrentny, *The Minority Rights Revolution*; Bowen and Bok, *The Shape of the River*; Graham, "Unintended Consequences."

9 Hirschman, Berrey, and Rose-Greenland, "Dequantifying Diversity"; Stulberg and Chen, "The Origins of Race-Conscious Affirmative Action in Undergraduate Admissions."

10 Hirschman, Berrey, and Rose-Greenland, "Dequantifying Diversity," 276.

11 Hirschman, Berrey, and Rose-Greenland, 277.

12 Hirschman, Berrey, and Rose-Greenland, 279.

13 The measures of admission—SAT and GPA—were the same for all applicants; the guidelines were transparent and ensured consistency across admissions readers,

and "race was a literal plus factor" in obtaining an admit decision. Hirschman, Berrey, and Rose-Greenland, 278–80.

14 See, for example, the SCUGA (school, curriculum, unusual, geography and alumni) grid developed by admissions director Cliff Sjogren, who presented the approach as a model for national admissions at a College Board meeting in June 1986. Hirschman, Berrey, and Rose-Greenland, 283.

15 Hirschman, Berrey, and Rose-Greenland, 283.

16 Berrey, *The Enigma of Diversity*, 105.

17 Berrey, 90–91.

18 Hirschman, Berrey, and Rose-Greenland, "Dequantifying Diversity," 293.

19 "The new application . . . includes several new questions designed to elicit more information about a student's background, personal achievement, and ways in which that student may contribute to the intellectual vibrancy and diversity of the student body." University of Michigan, "Press Release: New U-M Undergraduate Admissions Process to Involve More Information, Individual Review," August 27, 2003.

20 Connerly, "Taking It to Michigan."

21 Jennifer Gratz, "Speech to the Young Americans for Freedom," Michigan State University, East Lansing, MI, November 13, 2008.

22 Coleman, "Remarks on Passing of Proposal 2."

23 Anonymous University of Michigan administration official, personal interview, 2015.

24 Writers called it filled with "contempt" (Steve Chapman, *Chicago Tribune*) and "arrogant" (Thomas Bray, *New York Sun*). Werder, "Affirmative Action and Reaction in Michigan," *Nation*, January 25, 2007.

25 Quoting the conservative *Michigan Review*'s editor-in-chief. Werder.

26 Anonymous University of Michigan administration official, personal interview, 2015.

27 Anonymous University of Michigan Administration Official.

28 Cohen, *A Conflict of Principles*.

29 Coleman, "Remarks on Passing of Proposal 2."

30 Coleman.

31 Anonymous University of Michigan administration official, personal interview, 2015.

32 Anonymous University of Michigan administration official.

33 Coleman, "Remarks on Passing of Proposal 2." Anonymous University of Michigan administration official.

34 Anonymous University of Michigan administration official.

35 Anonymous University of Michigan administration official.

36 Amended Order Granting Temporary Injunction, No. 06–15024 (Eastern District of Michigan December 19, 2006).

37 Coalition to Defend Affirmative Action v. Granholm, 501 F.3d 775 (6th Cir. 2007).

38 The group By Any Means Necessary argued that a popular vote banning affirmative action was a violation of Equal Protection. Its case made its way up to the Supreme Court in *Schuette v. Coalition to Defend Affirmative Action*, with a majority upholding the ban in 2014 and a plurality opinion that refused to go against the will of the voters' policy decision. Schuette v. Coalition to Defend Affirmative Action, 572 U.S. 291 (2014).

39 The review season restarted January 10, 2007, and Michigan distributed a press release that this process would not give weight to "race, gender, national origin, and ethnicity." University of Michigan, "Press Release: UM Enrollment up in 2007–08," November 1, 2007.

40 Allen, *Ending Racial Preferences*, 291.

41 McNamara, "Race to Stay on This Year's App."

42 The essay quotes President Coleman: "We know that diversity makes us a better university—better for learning, for reaching, and conducting research." Students were then asked to respond and "share an experience through which you have gained respect for intellectual, social or cultural differences." McNamara, 7A.

43 Rose, "Proposal 2 and the Ban on Affirmative Action."

44 Wade-Golden and Matlock, "Working through the Challenge," 4.

45 Monts and Sullivan, "University of Michigan Diversity Blueprints Final Report," 6.

46 Acknowledgment of predecessors came in the form of consulting with other universities because they have, according to the recommendations from the task force, "cleared a path through the territory we now walk." Monts and Sullivan, 6. Lester Monts chaired the task force, and when its recommendations were announced, he argued boldly that "the world is watching to see how we will respond to the challenges posed by Proposal 2." Greene, "Diversity Blueprints Task Force Issues Report."

47 Wade-Golden and Matlock, "Working through the Challenge," 16.

48 Anonymous University of Michigan admissions official, personal interview, 2015.

49 Sullivan left Michigan in 2010 to become the president of the University of Virginia.

50 O'Connell, "Kedra Ishop Resigns."

51 Comments Ishop: "The campus . . . worked together in response to the charge to achieve our target class size and find ways, consistent with state law, to bring further diversity to our student body. We are pleased with the progress and want to continue our forward momentum." In a press release, she attributed the increase to "being more strategic with our early-action process, bringing additional clarity and targeted messaging to our financial aid awards and with aggressive recruitment, we were able to enroll a class that is excellent in all the ways that are consistent with our mission and enables us to provide a Michigan education to a broader range of students." Fitzgerald, "Student Enrollment Stable."

52 Geslani.

53  Key data for educational neighborhood clusters included mean SAT subsection scores, percent of students who are first generation or likely to apply out of state, percent of the population that is college aged, percent of the population that is non-white, percent of the population speaking English only, percent of students interested in financial aid, percent of community adults in professional jobs, and median family income. Key data for high school clusters included mean SAT subsection scores, average number of advanced courses and AP exams taken by students, average admission rate to colleges, percent of students of color or first generation, and percent of families below the poverty level or are interested in financial aid. Geslani.

54  Geslani.

55  Geslani (emphasis in original).

56  Geslani.

57  This committee was a reunion of sorts. The same group of admissions directors had come together before the Supreme Court's decision to work out options should their admissions review be struck down.

58  Anonymous University of Michigan administration official, personal interview, 2015.

59  Nelson, "'U' Gauges Geographic Diversity."

60  Neighborhood cluster 1: "College-bound students come from well-educated, fairly affluent families. They gravitate toward more expensive, selective private college farther from home, and away from public institutions closer to home. Academically, they are high-achievers with very strong test scores and strong writing skills. They will be active in college and seek-out leadership roles. The neighborhood is young and predominantly professional, although parents are interested in financial aid (probably merit-based)." The College Board, "Descriptor Plus: Educational Neighborhood Clusters and High School Clusters," 2001, http://secure-media.collegeboard.org/digitalServices/pdf/miscellaneous /ClusterDescriptionGuide.pdf.

61  "'U' Gauges Geographic Diversity."

62  Anonymous University of Michigan administration official, personal interview, 2015.

63  Anonymous University of Michigan administration official.

64  Lucier, "Using Geodemographics to Achieve Diversity."

65  Lucier.

66  Associated Press, "Univ. of Michigan Uses Computer Program to Achieve Diversity."

67  University of Michigan, "Press Release: Preliminary U-M Admissions Figures."

68  University of Michigan.

69  Associated Press, "Univ. of Michigan Uses Computer Program to Achieve Diversity."

70  University of Michigan, "Press Release: Preliminary U-M Admissions Figures."

71 Anonymous University of Michigan administration official, personal interview, 2015.

72 Anonymous University of Michigan administration official.

73 Anonymous University of Michigan administration official.

74 Anonymous University of Michigan administration official.

75 Anonymous University of Michigan administration official.

76 Anonymous University of Michigan administration official.

77 In a 2010 academic piece arguing for a greater role for geography, Sullivan found court support in *Hopwood*, noting that "an admissions process may also consider an applicant's home state" and also the school busing decision in *Milliken v. Bradley* that protected the geographic rights to local control over integrating a central metropolitan area. Sullivan, "College Access, Geography, and Diversity," 153.

78 Sullivan, 153–54.

79 Sullivan, 157.

80 Nelson, "'U' Gauges Geographic Diversity."

81 "As part of its prospective student outreach and its individualized and holistic review of applicants, the Office of Undergraduate Admissions also uses the College Board's geodemographic tool, called Descriptor PLUS, to identify high school and neighborhood clusters that are not well represented among the U-M student community." Greene, "Press Release: Applications to U-M for 2012–13"; University of Michigan, "Press Release: U-M Applications, Projected Freshman Enrollment at All-Time High."

82 Stieber, "University Uses Descriptor Plus Program to Pursue Diversity."

83 Allen, *Ending Racial Preferences*, 292.

84 Sander and Taylor, *Mismatch*, 170.

85 Dalmia, "The Supreme Court Can't Fix University Admissions Policies."

86 Associated Press, "Univ. of Michigan Uses Computer Program to Achieve Diversity."

87 Nelson, "'U' Gauges Geographic Diversity."

88 Stieber, "University Uses Descriptor Plus Program to Pursue Diversity."

89 Though, an important caveat, Michigan started collecting data differently in 2010, offering students the possibility of self-identifying as multiracial. There is certainly the possibility that the numbers for some individual groups, particularly the stark decline in Native students, results from students selecting this new option.

90 "With the inability to use race or ethnicity at all," acknowledged then president Mark Schlissel, "our campus has become less diverse." Barnes, "University of Michigan Offers to Be Test Case for Race Admissions."

91 Berrey, "Why Diversity Became Orthodox in Higher Education." The Being Black at Michigan (#BBUM) campus protests of the last five years reenergized lingering

student critique since the 1980s regarding the depth of Michigan's commitment both to recruiting students of color and toward addressing a hostile campus atmosphere. James, "Michigan in Color"; Brandon, "Reflections on #BBUM"; Gringlas and Adamczyk, "#BBUM Goes Viral on Twitter." In a 2017 op-ed, a Michigan Department of Afroamerican and African Studies professor continued this critique, pointing to the university's commitment to racial diversity as taking a backseat to its financial interest in recruiting students who can afford full tuition. Kurashige, "Commentary."

## 6. EQUALITY BY OTHER MEANS

1 Hamilton, "Oklahoma City Blacks Criticize School Ruling."
2 Perry, "Reactions to Desegregation Ruling Varied."
3 Felder, "A Generation of School Desegregation"; Rolland, "Integration Drastically Reduced Oklahoma City Schools' Population."
4 Perry, "Desegregation Suit's Originator Waits."
5 Perry.
6 Blume and Long, "Changes in Levels of Affirmative Action in College Admissions"; Backes, "Do Affirmative Action Bans Lower Minority College Enrollment and Attainment?"; Garces, "Racial Diversity, Legitimacy, and the Citizenry"; Hinrichs, "The Effects of Affirmative Action Bans"; Howell, "Assessing the Impact of Eliminating Affirmative Action in Higher Education"; Long and Tienda, "Winners and Losers"; Long, "Race and College Admission"; Tienda et al., "Closing the Gap?"
7 Garces and Cogburn, "Beyond Declines in Student Body Diversity," 836.
8 Kidder, "How Workable Are Class-Based and Race-Neutral Alternatives," 100; Reardon et al., "Can Socioeconomic Status Substitute for Race in Affirmative Action College Admission Policies? Evidence from a Simulation Model"; Andrews and Swinton, "The Persistent Myths of 'Acting White.'"
9 Gaertner and Hart, "Considering Class."
10 Hirschman and Berrey, "The Partial Deinstitutionalization of Affirmative Action in U.S. Higher Education," 450. The decline begins in 1996 with the first affirmative action bans in California and the Fifth Circuit states, like Texas. Grodsky and Kalogrides, "The Declining Significance of Race in College Admissions Decisions."
11 Hirschman and Berrey, "The Partial Deinstitutionalization of Affirmative Action in U.S. Higher Education."
12 Potter, "What Can We Learn from States That Ban Affirmative Action," 79.
13 Rosenberg, *The Hollow Hope*.
14 Kattner, "How to Prepare for Fisher."
15 Hirschman and Berrey, "The Partial Deinstitutionalization of Affirmative Action in U.S. Higher Education," 463.

16  Among the next tier of schools—the highly competitive—there was more movement dropping race conscious policies. Ninety-one percent of these schools had policies that emphasized race in 1995, and by 2014, only 76 percent did, and of the 17 percent that dropped off only four schools were in ban states (the University of California at San Diego, Florida State University, the University of Florida, and the University of Michigan). Very competitive schools declined in maintaining affirmative action policies during the same years from 75 percent to 47 percent, and merely competitive schools declined from 46 percent to 18 percent. Hirschman and Berrey, 458.

17  Michael Bastedo et al., "What Are We Talking about When We Talk about Holistic Review?" Context data potentially increases the admissions rates of these students by 25 percent. Bastedo and Bowman, "Improving Admission of Low-SES Students at Selective Colleges."

18  Hartocollis, "SAT 'Adversity Score' Is Abandoned in Wake of Criticism."

19  Garces and Cogburn, "Beyond Declines in Student Body Diversity," 841.

20  Garces and Cogburn, 846.

21  Berrey, *The Enigma of Diversity*, 113.

22  For example, "colorblind" conservatives Ward Connerly, Dinesh D'Souza, Richard Kahlenberg, Antonin Scalia, and Clarence Thomas all supported disadvantage preferences as an alternative to race preferences. Connerly, *Creating Equal*; Kahlenberg, *The Remedy*; D'Souza, *Illiberal Education*; Thomas, "Affirmative Action Goals and Timetables"; Scalia, "The Disease as Cure."

23  Kahlenberg, "Affirmative Action Should Be Based on Class, Not Race."

24  Kuhn, "Obama Shifts Affirmative Action Rhetoric."

25  Willon, "Voters Reject Prop. 16."

26  Padilla, "Statement of the Vote."

27  Secretary of State, "2020 Ballot Measure Contribution Totals: Proposition-16-ACA 5," October 14, 2020.

28  Ellickson, *Order without Law*; Sarat and Kearns, "Editorial Introduction"; Silbey and Sarat, "Critical Traditions in Law and Society Research," 173.

29  Hollis-Brusky, *Ideas with Consequences*; Teles, *The Rise of the Conservative Legal Movement*.

30  Which is not, of course, to say that either institution achieved equality for women. Katzenstein, *Faithful and Fearless*.

31  Beaumont, *The Civic Constitution*; Francis, *Civil Rights and the Making of the Modern American State*; Zackin, *Looking for Rights in All the Wrong Places*; Siegel, "Constitutional Culture, Social Movement Conflict and the Constitutional Change," 1323.

32  Gould, *Speak No Evil*.

33  Rose, *Citizens by Degree*; Loss, *Between Citizens and the State*.

34  Mettler, *Degrees of Inequality*.

35 Grutter v. Bollinger, 539 U.S. 306 (2003); Gratz v. Bollinger, 539 U.S. 244 (2003); Regents of the University of California v. Bakke, 438 U.S. 265 (1978) universities argued for broadening education and access. United States v. Virginia, 518 U.S. 515 (1996); Mississippi University for Women v. Hogan, 458 U.S. 718 (1982); Sweatt v. Painter, 339 U.S. 629 (1950); and Sipuel v. Board of Regents, 332 U.S. 631 (1948) universities argued for limiting them.

# BIBLIOGRAPHY

Academic Senate, University of California. "Guidelines for Implementation of University Policy on Undergraduate Admissions by the Board of Admissions and Relations with Schools," 2001.

———. "Guidelines for Implementation of University Policy on Undergraduate Admissions Guiding Principles for Comprehensive Review by the Board of Admissions and Relations with Schools," 2001.

———. "October 31, 2001, Minutes," 2001. https://senate.universityofcalifornia.edu.

———. "Report of the Board of Admissions and Relations with Schools." University of California, February 24, 1998.

Allen, Carol. *Ending Racial Preferences: The Michigan Story.* Lanham, MD: Lexington, 2008.

Amann, Diane Marie. "John Paul Stevens and Equally Impartial Government." *University of California Davis Law Review* 43, no. 3 (2010): 885–925.

Andrews, Rodney J., and Omari H. Swinton. "The Persistent Myths of 'Acting White' and Race Neutral Alternatives to Affirmative Action in Admissions." *Review of Black Political Economy* 41, no. 3 (2014): 357–71.

Associated Press. "Univ. of Michigan Uses Computer Program to Achieve Diversity." *Diverse Magazine*, March 29, 2007.

Aucoin, Brent. "The Southern Manifesto and Southern Opposition to Desegregation." *Arkansas Historical Quarterly* 55, no. 2 (1996): 173–93.

Ayres, B. Drummond. "Conservatives Forge New Strategy to Challenge Affirmative Action." *New York Times*, February 16, 1995.

Ayres, Ian, and John Braithwaite. *Responsive Regulation: Transcending the Deregulation Debate.* New York: Oxford University Press, 1992.

Backes, Ben. "Do Affirmative Action Bans Lower Minority College Enrollment and Attainment? Evidence from Statewide Bans." *Journal of Human Resources* 47, no. 2 (2012): 435–55.

Badger, Tony. "'The Forerunner of Our Opposition': Arkansas and the Southern Manifesto of 1956." *Arkansas Historical Quarterly* 56 (1997): 353–60.

Bains, Chiraag. "Amy Coney Barrett Could Bring Down Decades of Anti-Discrimination Law." *Slate*, October 26, 2020.

Barnes, Jeb, and Thomas F. Burke. "The Diffusion of Rights: From Law on the Books to Organizational Rights Practices." *Law and Society Review* 40, no. 3 (2006): 493–524.

Barnes, Robert. "University of Michigan Offers to Be Test Case for Race Admissions." *Washington Post*, December 8, 2015.

Bartley, Numan V. *The Rise of Massive Resistance: Race and Politics in the South during the 1950s.* Baton Rouge: Louisiana State University Press, 1969.

Bastedo, Michael, and Nicholas Bowman. "Improving Admission of Low-SES Students at Selective Colleges: Results from an Experimental Simulation." *Educational Researcher* 46, no. 2 (2017): 67–77.

Bastedo, Michael, Nicholas Bowman, Kristen Glasener, and Jandi Kelly. "What Are We Talking about When We Talk about Holistic Review? Selective College Admissions and Its Effects on Low-SES Students." *Journal of Higher Education* 89, no. 5 (2018): 782–805.

Beaumont, Elizabeth. *The Civic Constitution: Civic Visions and Struggles in the Path toward Constitutional Democracy.* Oxford: Oxford University Press, 2014.

Bell, Derrick. "Diversity's Distractions." *Columbia Law Review* 103, no. 6 (2003): 1622–33.

Berdahl, Robert. "1998 Admissions Report." *Berkeleyan*, March 4, 1998. www.publicaffairs.berkeley.edu/berkeleyan.

Berrey, Ellen C. "Making a Civil Rights Claim for Affirmative Action: BAMN's Legal Mobilization and the Legacy of Race-Conscious Policies." *Du Bois Review* 12, no. 2 (2015): 375–405.

———. *The Enigma of Diversity: The Language of Race and the Limits of Racial Justice.* Chicago: University of Chicago Press, 2015.

———. "Why Diversity Became Orthodox in Higher Education, and How It Changed the Meaning of Race on Campus." *Critical Sociology* 37, no. 5 (2011): 573–96.

Biondi, Martha. *The Black Revolution on Campus.* Berkeley: University of California Press, 2012.

Blume, Grant H., and Mark C. Long. "Changes in Levels of Affirmative Action in College Admissions in Response to Statewide Bans and Judicial Rulings." *Educational Evaluation and Policy Analysis* 36 (2014): 228–52.

Board of Regents, University of California. "May 16, 2001, Minutes," 2001. https://regents.universityofcalifornia.edu.

Bonilla-Silva, Eduardo. *Racism without Racists: Color-Blind Racism and the Persistence of Racial Inequality in America.* Lanham, MD: Rowman & Littlefield, 2009.

Boone, Tom. "Bohanon Requested to Stay School Order." *Daily Oklahoman*, February 8, 1972.

———. "Neighborhood School Plan Voted by Board." *Daily Oklahoman*, October 30, 1970.

———. "School Board Rejects Defiance Pleas." *Daily Oklahoman*, August 18, 1972.

———. "School Ruling Due in Week." *Daily Oklahoman*, December 10, 1971.

———. "Schools to Seek Integration Consultant." *Daily Oklahoman*, June 8, 1971.

———. "Strengthened Cluster Plan for City Schools Drafted in Report by Consultants." *Daily Oklahoman*, November 2, 1971.

Bowen, William, and Derek Bok. *The Shape of the River: Long-Term Consequences of Considering Race in College and University Admissions.* Princeton, NJ: Princeton University Press, 1998.

Brandon, Alyssa. "Reflections on #BBUM Two Years after Launch." *Michigan Daily*, November 18, 2015.

Brandwein, Pamela. *Rethinking the Judicial Settlement of Reconstruction*. Cambridge, UK: Cambridge University Press, 2011.

Bravin, Jess. "Brett Kavanaugh's Complicated History with Racial Preferences." *Wall Street Journal*, September 4, 2018.

Brooks, A. Phillips. "Bill Seeks to Balance Court Ruling, Diversity-Proposed Legislation Intended to Help Texas Universities Attract Minorities." *Austin American-Statesman*, March 14, 1997.

———. "Fewer Hispanics, Blacks Start at UT." *Austin American-Statesman*, September 16, 1997.

———. "Morales Reiterates Affirmative Action Rules." *Austin American-Statesman*, February 6, 1997.

———. "Rival States Lure Minority Students." *Austin American-Statesman*, March 16, 1997.

———. "Texas College Applications by Minorities Drop—52 Percent Decline an Early Indication of Race Ruling's Impact." *Austin American-Statesman*, February 16, 1997.

Brown, Michael. "Academic Assembly Passes the Academic Council's Modification of BOARS' Proposal to Reform UC's Freshman Eligibility Policy." University of California, Academic Senate, June 18, 2008. https://senate.universityofcalifornia.edu.

Brown, Michael K., Martin Carnoy, Elliott Currie, Troy Duster, David B. Oppenheimer, Marjorie Shultz, and David Wellman. *White-Washing Race: The Myth of a Color-Blind Society*. Berkeley: University of California Press, 2003.

Brown, Peter. "Clinton's Dilemma Opposing Anti-Affirmative Action Proposal Could Cost Him California in '96." *San Francisco Examiner*, February 5, 1995.

Bulman-Pozen, Jessica, and David Pozen. "Uncivil Obedience." *Columbia Law Review* 115, no. 4 (2015): 809–72.

Burdman, Pamela. "Regent's Idea to Drop UC Race Preferences." *San Francisco Chronicle*, July 6, 1995, sec. A1.

———. "Two Challenges Set for UC's Race-Blind Admissions." *San Francisco Chronicle*, February 8, 1999.

———. "UC Regents to Approve 4 percent Admissions Policy." *San Francisco Chronicle*, March 19, 1999.

Burka, Paul. "Law-Cheryl Hopwood." *Texas Monthly*, September 1996.

Californian Secretary of State. "2020 Ballot Measure Contribution Totals: Proposition-16-ACA 5," October 14, 2020. www.sos.ca.gov.

Chavez, Lydia. *The Color Bind: California's Battle to End Affirmative Action*. Berkeley: University of California Press, 1998.

Chen, Anthony S., and Lisa M. Stulberg. "Before Bakke: The Hidden History of the Diversity Rationale." *University of Chicago Law Review Online* (blog), October 30, 2020. https://lawreviewblog.uchicago.edu.

Chotiner, Isaac. "How Trump Transformed the Supreme Court." *New Yorker*, November 11, 2021.

Citrin, Jack. "Desperately Seeking Diversity." *Sacramento Bee*, March 28, 1999.

Cockrell, Cathy, and Jesus Mena. "1998 Admissions Report: The Crucial Task of Training the Readers." *Berkeleyan Public Affairs*, March 4, 1998. www.publicaffairs.berkeley.edu/berkeleyan.

Cohen, Carl. *A Conflict of Principles: The Battle over Affirmative Action at the University of Michigan*. Lawrence: University Press of Kansas, 2014.

Coleman, Mary Sue. "Remarks on Passing of Proposal 2." Ann Arbor, MI, November 7, 2006. https://news.umich.edu.

Committee on Educational Policy, Regents of the University of California. "March 18, 1999, Minutes," 1999. https://regents.universityofcalifornia.edu.

———. "October 17, 2001, Minutes," 2001. https://regents.universityofcalifornia.edu.

Connerly, Ward. *Creating Equal: My Fight Against Race Preferences*. San Francisco: Encounter Books, 2000.

———. "Taking It to Michigan." University of Michigan, Ann Arbor, MI, July 8, 2003. https://www.nationalreview.com.

Dalmia, Shikha. "The Supreme Court Can't Fix University Admissions Policies." *Reason* (blog), March 13, 2012.

Davidson, Amelia. "Students for Fair Admissions Sues Yale Petitions to Escalate Harvard Case to Supreme Court." *Yale Daily News*, February 25, 2021.

Davis, Gray. "First Inaugural Address." January 4, 1999. https://governors.library.ca.gov.

———. "State of the State Address." Sacramento, CA, January 7, 1999. https://governors.library.ca.gov.

Days, Drew S., III. "School Desegregation Law in the 1980's: Why Isn't Anybody Laughing." *Yale Law Journal* 95 (1986): 1737–68.

Deslippe, Dennis. *Protesting Affirmative Action: The Struggle over Equality after the Civil Rights Revolution*. Baltimore, MD: Johns Hopkins University Press, 2012.

Dobbin, Frank. *Inventing Equal Opportunity*. Princeton, NJ: Princeton University Press, 2009.

Dobbin, Frank, and Erin L. Kelly. "How to Stop Harassment: Professional Construction of Legal Compliance in Organizations." *American Journal of Sociology* 112, no. 4 (2007): 1203–43.

Dobbin, Frank, and John R. Sutton. "The Strength of a Weak State: The Rights Revolution and the Rise of Human Resources Management Divisions." *American Journal of Sociology* 104, no. 2 (1998): 441–76.

Dolbeare, Kenneth M., and Phillip E. Hammond. *The School Prayer Decisions from Court Policy to Local Practice*. Chicago: University of Chicago Press, 1971.

Douglass, John. "A Brief on the Events Leading to SP1." Task Force on Governance, University of California, February 28, 1997. http://senate.universityofcalifornia.edu.

———. "Anatomy of a Conflict: The Making and Unmaking of Affirmative Action at the University of California." In *Colorlines*, edited by John D. Skrentny, 118–44. Chicago: University of Chicago Press, 2001.

———. *The Conditions for Admission: Access, Equity, and the Social Contract of Public Universities*. Stanford, CA: Stanford University Press, 2007.

———. "The Evolution of a Social Contract: The University of California before and in the Aftermath of Affirmative Action." *European Journal of Education* 34, no. 4 (1999): 393–412.

D'Souza, Dinesh. *Illiberal Education: The Politics of Race and Sex on Campus*. New York: Free Press, 1991.

Edelman, Lauren B. *Working Law: Courts, Corporations, and Symbolic Civil Rights*. Chicago: University of Chicago Press, 2016.

Eisgruber, Christopher L. "How the Maverick Became a Lion: Affirmative Action in the Jurisprudence of John Paul Stevens." *Georgetown Law Journal* 99, no. 5 (2011): 1279–88.

Ellickson, Robert C. *Order without Law: How Neighbors Settle Disputes*. Cambridge, MA: Harvard University Press, 1994.

Epp, Charles R. *Making Rights Real: Activists, Bureaucrats, and the Creation of the Legalistic State*. Chicago: University of Chicago Press, 2010.

———. *The Rights Revolution: Lawyers, Activists, and Supreme Courts in Comparative Perspective*. Chicago: University of Chicago Press, 1998.

Feeley, Malcolm M., and Edward L. Rubin. *Judicial Policy Making and the Modern State: How the Courts Reformed America's Prisons*. Cambridge, UK: Cambridge University Press, 1999.

Felder, Ben. "A Generation of School Desegregation." *Oklahoman*, October 29, 2017.

Fikac, Peggy. "University Admission Policy Bill Filed." *Houston Chronicle*, March 14, 1997.

Fitzgerald, Rick. "Student Enrollment Stable, More Diverse for Fall 2015." *University Record*, October 12, 2015.

Flacks, Richard, and Rodolfo Alvarez. "Towards Fairness in UC Admissions." Center for Research on Chicano Studies, University of California, Los Angeles, November 1996.

Fossett, Judy, and Wayne Singleterry. "City School Plans Challenged in Court." *Daily Oklahoman*, February 20, 1985.

Francis, Megan Ming. *Civil Rights and the Making of the Modern American State*. New York: Cambridge University Press, 2014.

Friedl, John. "Making a Compelling Case for Diversity in College Admissions." *University of Pittsburgh Law Review* 61, no. 1 (1999): 1–44.

Friedman, Lawrence. *Impact: How Law Affects Behavior*. Cambridge, MA: Harvard University Press, 2016.

Frymer, Paul. *Black and Blue: African Americans, the Labor Movement, and the Decline of the Democratic Party*. Princeton, NJ: Princeton University Press, 2007.

Fulkerson, Ron. "It's Probably Last Year's Boundaries." *Daily Oklahoman*, August 28, 1969.

Gaertner, Matthew N., and Melissa Hart. "Considering Class: College Access and Diversity." *Harvard Law and Policy Review* 7 (2013): 367–403.

Gallagher, Charles. "Color-Blind Privilege: The Social and Political Functions of Erasing the Color Line in Post Race America." *Race, Gender & Class* 10, no. 4 (2003): 22–37.

Garces, Liliana. "Racial Diversity, Legitimacy, and the Citizenry: The Impact of Affirmative Action Bans on Graduate School Enrollment." *Review of Higher Education* 36, no. 2 (2012): 93–132.

Garces, Liliana, and Courtney Cogburn. "Beyond Declines in Student Body Diversity: How Campus-Level Administrators Understand a Prohibition on Race-Conscious Postsecondary Admissions Policies." *American Educational Research Journal* 52, no. 5 (2015): 828–60.

Gash, Alison. *Below the Radar: How Silence Can Save Civil Rights.* Oxford: Oxford University Press, 2015.

Geslani, Marc. "Birds of a Feather: Using Geodemography in Student Search." Presented at the Illinois Association for College Admission Counseling Meeting, Itasca, IL, May 3, 2012.

Gonzalo Barrientos. University of Texas at Austin Voces Oral History Center, October 9, 2013. https://voces.lib.utexas.edu.

Goodwin, Liu. "Affirmative Action in Higher Education: The Diversity Rationale and the Compelling Interest Test." *Harvard Civil Rights-Civil Liberties Review* 33, no. 2 (1998): 381–442.

Gould, Jon B. *Speak No Evil: The Triumph of Hate Speech Regulation.* Chicago: University of Chicago Press, 2005.

Graham, Hugh Davis. "Unintended Consequences: The Convergence of Affirmative Action and Immigration Policy." *American Behavioral Scientist* 41, no. 7 (1998): 938–59.

Gratz, Jennifer. "Speech to the Young Americans for Freedom." Michigan State University, East Lansing, MI, November 13, 2008.

Green, Denise O'Neil. "Fighting the Battle for Racial Diversity: A Case Study of Michigan's Institutional Responses to Gratz and Grutter." *Educational Policy* 18, no. 5 (2004): 733–51.

Greene, Deborah. "Diversity Blueprints Task Force Issues Report." *University Record,* March 19, 2007.

———. "Applications to U-M for 2012–13 Are Highest in School's History." *UMich News,* July 16, 2012.

Gringlas, Sam, and Alicia Adamczyk. "#BBUM Goes Viral on Twitter." *Michigan Daily,* November 19, 2013.

Grodsky, Eric, and Demetra Kalogrides. "The Declining Significance of Race in College Admissions Decisions." *American Journal of Education* 115, no. 1 (2008): 1–33.

Hamilton, Arnold. "Oklahoma City Blacks Criticize School Ruling." *Dallas Morning News,* January 16, 1991.

Hannel, Joy. "Future of Desegregation after Dowell: Returning to Pre-Brown Days." *Missouri Law Review* 56, no. 4 (1991): 1141–56.

Harpalani, Vinay. "Chicago-Kent College of Law ISCOTUS Now." *The Supreme Court and the Future of Affirmative Action* (blog), October 24, 2019. http://blogs.kentlaw.iit.edu.

Hartocollis, Anemona. "SAT 'Adversity Score' Is Abandoned in Wake of Criticism." *New York Times*, August 27, 2019.

Hasen, Richard. "Neil Gorsuch Got Where He is because of a Form of Affirmative Action." *Washington Post*, April 3, 2017.

Hatch, Katherine. "Books Closed by Bohanon on City Integration Case." *Daily Oklahoman*, August 22, 1970.

———. "City Integration Plan Criticized, Applauded." *Daily Oklahoman*, May 31, 1969.

———. "City School Order Vacated." *Daily Oklahoman*, August 28, 1969.

———. "'Cluster' Plan Given Tentative Approval." *Daily Oklahoman*, December 17, 1969.

———. "New Desegregation Plan Being Prepared for City Schools, Lillard Discloses." *Daily Oklahoman*, June 15, 1967.

———. "School Board Chief Doubts Voluntary Integration Possible." *Daily Oklahoman*, July 24, 1969.

Hinrichs, Peter. "The Effects of Affirmative Action Bans on College Enrollment, Educational Attainment, and the Demographic Composition of Universities." *Review of Economics and Statistics* 94, no. 3 (2012): 712–22.

Hirschman, Daniel, and Ellen Berrey. "The Partial Deinstitutionalization of Affirmative Action in U.S. Higher Education." *Sociological Science* 4 (2017): 449–68.

Hirschman, Daniel, Ellen C. Berrey, and Fiona Rose-Greenland. "Dequantifying Diversity: Affirmative Action and Admissions at the University of Michigan." *Theory and Society* 45, no. 3 (2016).

Hollis-Brusky, Amanda. *Ideas with Consequences: The Federalist Society and the Conservative Counterrevolution*. New York: Oxford University Press, 2015.

Howe, Amy. "Justices Request Government's Views on Harvard Affirmative-Action Dispute." *SCOTUSblog* (blog), June 14, 2021. www.scotusblog.com.

Howell, Jessica. "Assessing the Impact of Eliminating Affirmative Action in Higher Education." *Journal of Labor Economics* 28, no. 1 (2010): 113–66.

Hughes, Polly, and Matthew Tresaugue. "Small-Town GOP behind Survival of the Top 10 Percent Rule; Republicans from Rural Cities Say Law Essential for Their Students." *Houston Chronicle*, May 30, 2007.

Hurtado, Sylvia. "BOARS Recommendations for President Yudof on Comprehensive Review and Holistic Admissions." University of California, Assembly of Academic Senate, June 29, 2010. https://senate.universityofcalifornia.edu.

James, Elizabeth. "Michigan in Color: #BBUM and Sankofa-Looking Back to Move Forward." *Michigan Daily*, November 18, 2015.

James, Osamudia. "White like Me: The Negative Impact of the Diversity Rationale on White Identity Formation." *New York University Law Review* 89, no. 2 (May 2014): 425–512.

Jaschik, Scott. "Kavanaugh Evades Questions on Affirmative Action." *Inside Higher Ed*, September 14, 2018.

———. "The 10 Percent Fight Is Back." *Inside Higher Ed*, January 12, 2009.

———. "UNC Wins Affirmative Action Case, for Now." *Inside Higher Ed*, October 25, 2021.

Johnson, David R. "Do Strikes and Work-to-Rule Campaigns Change Elementary School Assessment Results?" *Canadian Public Policy* 37, no. 4 (2011): 479–94.

Johnson, Kevin. "Scholars Touch off an 'Avalanche' on Affirmative Action." *USA Today*, April 4, 1995.

Kagan, Robert A. *Adversarial Legalism: The American Way of Law*. Cambridge, MA: Harvard University Press, 2001.

Kahlenberg, Richard D. "Affirmative Action Should Be Based on Class, Not Race." *Economist*, September 4, 2018.

———. *The Remedy: Class, Race, and Affirmative Action*. New York: Basic Books, 1996.

Kalev, Alexandra, Frank Dobbin, and Erin Kelly. "Best Practices or Best Guesses? Assessing the Efficacy of Corporate Affirmative Action and Diversity Policies." *American Sociological Review* 71 (2006): 589–617.

Karabel, Jerome. *The Chosen: The Hidden History of Admission and Exclusion at Harvard, Yale, and Princeton*. Boston: Houghton Mifflin Harcourt, 2005.

Kattner, Therese. "How to Prepare for Fisher." *Recruitment & Retention in Higher Education* 27, no. 2 (February 2013).

Katzenstein, Mary Fainsod. *Faithful and Fearless: Moving Feminist Protest inside the Church and Military*. Princeton, NJ: Princeton University Press, 1999.

Katznelson, Ira. *When Affirmative Action Was White: An Untold History of Racial Inequality in Twentieth-Century America*. W. W. Norton, 2005.

Keck, Thomas M. *Judicial Politics in Polarized Times*. University of Chicago Press, 2014.

Kell, Gretchen, and Jesus Mena. "Selecting the Freshman Class." *Berkeleyan*, March 4, 1998. https://publicaffairs.berkeley.edu/berkeleyan.

Kelly, Erin L., and Frank Dobbin. "How Affirmative Action Became Diversity Management: Employer Response to Antidiscrimination Law, 1961 to 1996." *American Behavioral Scientist* 41, no. 7 (1998): 960–84.

Kidder, William. "How Workable Are Class-Based and Race-Neutral Alternatives at Leading American Universities?" *UCLA Law Review Discourse* 64 (2016): 100.

Kidder, William, and Patricia Gandara. "Two Decades after the Affirmative Action Ban: Evaluating the University of California's Race-Neutral Efforts." Educational Testing Service, 2015.

Killackey, Jim. "Arguments Heard on Principal Shift." *Daily Oklahoman*, November 12, 1974.

———. "Board Told to Pay Lawyers." *Daily Oklahoman*, March 27, 1976.

———. "Integration Goals Met, Judge Feels." *Daily Oklahoman*, January 19, 1977.

———. "NAACP Letter Asks Judge to Retain City School Case." *Daily Oklahoman*, June 27, 1975.

Killackey, Jim, and Tom McCarthy. "School Desegregation Most Emotional of Civil Rights Issues." *Daily Oklahoman*, February 14, 1974.

Killenbeck, Mark. "Pushing Things up to Their First Principles: Reflections on the Values of Affirmative Action." *California Law Review* 87, no. 6 (1999): 1299–1407.

King, Desmond S., and Rogers M. Smith. "Racial Orders in American Political Development." *American Political Science Review* 99, no. 1 (2005): 75–92.

———. "'Without Regard to Race': Critical Ideational Development in Modern American Politics." *Journal of Politics* 76, no. 4 (2014): 958–71.

Klarman, Michael J. *From Jim Crow to Civil Rights: The Supreme Court and the Struggle for Racial Equality*. New York: Oxford University Press, 2006.

———. *Unfinished Business: Racial Equality in American History*. Oxford: Oxford University Press, 2007.

Klinkner, Philip, and Rogers M. Smith. *The Unsteady March: The Rise and Decline of Racial Equality in America*. Chicago: University of Chicago Press, 2002.

Kluger, Richard. *Simple Justice: The History of Brown v. Board of Education and Black America's Struggle for Equality*. New York: Vintage, 2011.

Kuhn, David. "Obama Shifts Affirmative Action Rhetoric." *Politico*, August 10, 2008.

Kurashige, Scott. "Commentary: In Diversity Gap at Michigan Flagship, Signs of a Lost Public Mission." *Chronicle of Higher Education*, March 3, 2014.

Laird, Bob. "Bending Admissions to Political Ends." *Chronicle of Higher Education*, May 17, 2002.

Leong, Nancy. "Racial Capitalism." *Harvard Law Review* 126, no. 8 (2013): 2151–2226.

Lipson, Daniel. "Affirmative Action as We Don't Know It: The Evolution of Undergraduate Admissions Policy at UC-Berkeley, UT-Austin, and UW-Madison. PhD diss., University of Wisconsin-Madison, 2002.

———. "Affirmative Action as We Don't Know It: The Rise of Individual Assessment in Undergraduate Admissions at UC-Berkeley and UT-Austin." *Studies in Law, Politics, and Society* 23 (2001): 137–84.

———. "Embracing Diversity: The Institutionalization of Affirmative Action as Diversity Management at UC-Berkeley, UT-Austin, and UW-Madison." *Law & Social Inquiry* 32, no. 4 (Fall 2007): 985–1026.

———. "Where's the Justice? Affirmative Action's Severed Civil Rights Roots in the Age of Diversity." *Perspectives on Politics* 6, no. 04 (2008): 691–706.

Liptak, Adam. "Supreme Court Upholds Affirmative Action Program at University of Texas." *New York Times*, June 23, 2016.

Long, Mark. "Race and College Admission: An Alternative to Affirmative Action?" *Review of Economics and Statistics* 86, no. 4 (2004): 1020–33.

Long, Mark C., and Marta Tienda. "Winners and Losers: Changes in Texas University Admissions Post-Hopwood." *Educational Evaluation and Policy Analysis* 30, no. 3 (2008): 255–80.

Long, Mark C., Victor Saenz, and Marta Tienda. "Policy Transparency and College Enrollment: Did the Texas Top Ten Percent Law Broaden Access to the Public

Flagships?" *Annals of the American Academy of Political and Social Science* 627, no. 1 (2010): 82–105.

Loss, Christopher. *Between Citizens and the State: The Politics of American Higher Education in the 20th Century*. Princeton, NJ: Princeton University Press, 2011.

Lucier, Chris. "Using Geodemographics to Achieve Diversity at the University of Michigan." Paper presented at the College Board Regional Forum, February 2006.

Lynch, Frederick. *The Diversity Machine: The Drive to Change the "White Male" Workplace*. New York: Free Press, 1997.

Marimow, Ann. "Brett Kavanaugh Once Predicted 'One Race' in the Eyes of Government. Would he end Affirmative Action?" *Washington Post*, August 7, 2018.

Mays, Joseph J. "School Board Chief Backs Drive to Ax Bohanon Order." *Daily Oklahoman*, February 19, 1968.

McAdam, Doug. *Political Process and the Development of Black Insurgency, 1930–1970*. Chicago: University of Chicago Press, 2010.

McCarthy, Tom. "Bohanon Gives Up City School Reins." *Daily Oklahoman*, January 19, 1977.

McNamara, Kristy. "Race to Stay on This Year's App." *Michigan Daily*, September 12, 2007.

Melnick, R. Shep. *The Crucible of Desegregation: The Uncertain Search for Educational Equality*. Chicago: University of Chicago Press, 2023.

Merle, Renae. "Court Rules against Affirmative Action at UT Law School." *Daily Texan*, March 19, 1996.

Messer-Davidow, Ellen. *The Making of Reverse Discrimination: How DeFunis and Bakke Bleached Racism from Equal Protection*. Lawrence: University Press of Kansas, 2021.

Mettler, Suzanne. *Degrees of Inequality: How the Politics of Higher Education Sabotaged the American Dream*. New York: Basic Books, 2014.

Montejano, David. "Maintaining Diversity at the University of Texas." In *Race and Representation: Affirmative Action*, edited by Robert Post and Michael Rogin, 359–71. New York: Zone Books, 1998.

———. "On Hopwood: The Continuing Challenge." In *Reflexiones 1997*, edited by Neil Foley, 133–56. University of Texas at Austin Center for Mexican American Studies, 1997.

Monts, Lester, and Theresa Sullivan. "University of Michigan Diversity Blueprints Final Report." University of Michigan, March 15, 2007. Bentley Historical Library. https://deepblue.lib.umich.edu.

Morales, Dan. "Hopwood Opens New Era in Pursuit of Diversity." *Austin American-Statesman*, February 7, 1997.

———. "Letter Opinion No. 97-001. Re: Effect of Hopwood v. State of Texas on Various Scholarship Programs of the University of Houston (ID# 39347)." Office of Texas Attorney General, February 5, 1997. www2.texasattorneygeneral.gov.

Munoz, Evangelina. "The Politics of Supporting Diversity in Higher Education: Texas Legislature's Enactment of House Bill 588." University of Texas, 2003. https://repositories.lib.utexas.edu.

Nelson, Gabe. "'U' Gauges Geographic Diversity." *Michigan Daily*, March 28, 2007.

Nissimov, Ron. "UT Austin to Reintroduce Race-Based Criteria." *Houston Chronicle*, June 24, 2003.

Novkov, Julie. "The Conservative Attack on Affirmative Action: Toward a Legal Genealogy of Color Blindness." In *The Politics of Inclusion and Exclusion: Identity Politics in Twenty-First Century America*, edited by David Ericson, 177–206. New York: Routledge, 2011.

O'Connell, Chris. "Kedra Ishop Resigns, Says Unrelated to Admissions Investigation." *Alcalde*, July 2, 2014.

Office of Planning and Analysis, University of California, Berkeley. "UC Berkeley Fall Enrollment Data," 2017. https://opa.berkeley.edu.

Okechukwu, Amaka. *To Fulfill These Rights: Political Struggle over Affirmative Action and Open Admissions*. Columbia University Press, 2019.

Padilla, Alex. "Statement of the Vote: General Election November 3, 2020." Secretary of State, California, December 11, 2020. https://www.sos.ca.gov.

Patterson, Bryce. "Judge Rejects Schools Plans." *Daily Oklahoman*, August 11, 1973.

Perry, John. "Desegregation Suit's Originator Waits." *Oklahoman*, October 8, 1990.

———. "Reactions to Desegregation Ruling Varied." *Oklahoman*, January 16, 1991.

Potter, Halley. "What Can We Learn from States That Ban Affirmative Action?: Education: Our Work: The Century Foundation." *What Can We Learn from States That Ban Affirmative Action?* (blog), June 26, 2014. http://tcf.org.

Price, Eric. "New Admission Policy: Gaining a Fuller Picture." *Berkeleyan*, March 4, 1998. https://publicaffairs.berkeley.edu/berkeleyan.

Reardon, Sean F., Rachel Baker, Matt Kasman, Daniel Klasik, and Joseph B. Townsend. "Can Socioeconomic Status Substitute for Race in Affirmative Action College Admission Policies? Evidence from a Simulation Model." *Educational Testing Service* 18 (2015): 234–45.

Reid, Jim. "City Schools Tackle Job of Carrying Out Court's Racial Plan." *Daily Oklahoman*, June 2, 1967.

———. "Friction Seen; Schools Plan Racial Appeal." *Daily Oklahoman*, July 12, 1963, sec. 1.

———. "'Home Base' School Plan Wins Approval of Board." *Daily Oklahoman*, November 6, 1969.

———. "Integration Appeal Machinery Starts." *Daily Oklahoman*, April 4, 1967.

———. "Judge's School Order Called Unwarranted." *Daily Oklahoman*, October 2, 1965.

———. "Plan Adopted on Integration." *Daily Oklahoman*, May 31, 1969.

———. "Pupils Have Option Not to Shift Schools." *Daily Oklahoman*, August 17, 1970.

———. "School Board, OU Experts Seek Integration Answers." *Daily Oklahoman*, October 21, 1969.

———. "School Board Splits 3 to 2; Reaffirms Integration Plan Turned Down by Boha-non." *Daily Oklahoman*, February 3, 1970.

———. "School Board Urges Judge to Reconsider Integration 'Pairing.'" *Daily Oklaho-man*, February 24, 1968.

———. "School Board Votes to Follow Bohanon's Edict on Integration." *Daily Oklaho-man*, July 30, 1969.

———. "School Pairings Protested Anew." *Daily Oklahoman*, February 16, 1968.

———. "School to Appeal Integration Order." *Daily Oklahoman*, September 15, 1965.

Riley, Jason. "With Justice Barrett, Is the End near for Racial Preferences?" *Washington Post*, October 27, 2020.

Rolland, Megan. "Integration Drastically Reduced Oklahoma City Schools' Popula-tion." *Oklahoman*, April 17, 2011.

Root, Jay. "UT-Austin Pushes Lawmakers to Modify 'Top 10 Percent' Rule." *Houston Chronicle*, January 7, 2009.

Rose, Deondra. *Citizens by Degree: Higher Education Policy and the Changing Gender Dynamics of American Citizenship*. New York: Oxford University Press, 2018.

Rose, Monica. "Proposal 2 and the Ban on Affirmative Action: An Uncertain Future for the University of Michigan in Its Quest for Diversity." *Public Interest Law Journal* 17 (2008): 309–37.

Rosenberg, Gerald N. *The Hollow Hope: Can Courts Bring about Social Change?* Chi-cago: University of Chicago Press, 1991.

Roser, Mary Ann. "Groups Call UT's Efforts Lacking: Civil Rights Groups Want to Intervene in University's Appeal of Hopwood Case." *Austin American-Statesman*, June 9, 1999.

Sanchez, Rene. "Struggling to Maintain Diversity." *Washington Post*, March 11, 1996, sec. A01.

Sander, Richard, and Stuart Taylor. *Mismatch: How Affirmative Action Hurts Students It's Intended to Help, and Why Universities Won't Admit It*. New York: Basic Books, 2012.

Sarat, Austin, and Thomas Kearns. "Editorial Introduction." In *Law in Everyday Life*, 1–20. Ann Arbor: University of Michigan, 1993.

Savage, Charlie. "Leaked Kavanaugh Documents Discuss Abortion and Affirmative Action." *New York Times*, September 6, 2018.

Scalia, Antonin. "The Disease as Cure: 'In Order to Get beyond Racism, We Must First Take Account of Race.'" *Washington University Law Quarterly* 57, no. 1 (1979): 147–57.

Schuck, Peter. *Diversity in America: Keeping Government at a Safe Distance*. Cam-bridge, MA: Belknap Press of Harvard University Press, 2003.

Siegel, Reva. "Constitutional Culture, Social Movement Conflict and the Constitutional Change: The Case of the de Facto ERA." *California Law Review* 94, no. 5 (October 31, 2006): 1323.

Silbey, Susan, and Austin Sarat. "Critical Traditions in Law and Society Research." *Law and Society Review* 21 (1987).

Silverstein, Gordon. *Law's Allure: How Law Shapes, Constrains, Saves and Kills Politics.* New York: Cambridge University Press, 2009.

Singleterry, Wayne. "Angry Moms Balk at Long Bus Rides." *Daily Oklahoman*, October 17, 1984.

———. "City Board Approves School Plan." *Daily Oklahoman*, December 18, 1984.

———. "City School Proposal Draws Large Protest." *Daily Oklahoman*, November 20, 1984.

Skrentny, John. *After Civil Rights: Racial Realism Is the New American Workplace.* Princeton, NJ: Princeton University Press, 2014.

———. *The Ironies of Affirmative Action: Politics, Culture, and Justice in America.* Chicago: University of Chicago Press, 1996.

———. *The Minority Rights Revolution.* Cambridge, MA: Belknap Press, 2002.

Smith, Rogers M. *Civic Ideals: Conflicting Visions of Citizenship in U.S. History.* New Haven, CT: Yale University Press, 1999.

Stevens, Mitchell L., and Josipa Roksa. "The Diversity Imperative in Elite Admissions." In *Diversity in American Higher Education*, edited by Lisa Stulberg and Lawner Weinberg, 63–73. Oxfordshire: Taylor & Francis, 2011.

Stieber, Chris. "University Uses Descriptor Plus Program to Pursue Diversity." *Michigan Review*, April 16, 2007, sec. 3.

Stohler, Stephan. *Reconstructing Rights: Courts, Parties and Equality Rights in India, South Africa, and the United States.* Cambridge, UK: Cambridge University Press, 2019.

Stulberg, Lisa, and Anthony S. Chen. "A Long View on 'Diversity': A Century of American College Admissions Debates." In *Diversity in American Higher Education*, edited by Lisa Stulberg and Lawner Weinberg, 51–62. Oxfordshire: Taylor & Francis, 2011.

———. "The Origins of Race-Conscious Affirmative Action in Undergraduate Admissions: A Comparative Analysis of Institutional Change in Higher Education." *Sociology of Education* 87, no. 1 (2014): 36–52.

Stutz, T. "Senators OK Bill Tracking Colleges' Minority Enrollees." *Dallas Morning News*, May 22, 1997.

Sullivan, Teresa. "College Access, Geography, and Diversity." In *The Future of Diversity*, edited by Daniel Little and Satya Mohanty, 147–57. New York: Palgrave Macmillan, 2010.

Sunstein, Cass. "Gorsuch Paves Way for Attack on Affirmative Action." *Bloomberg Opinion*, June 17, 2020.

Sweet, Martin. *Merely Judgment: Ignoring, Evading and Trumping the Supreme Court.* Charlottesville: University of Virginia, 2010.

Teles, Steven Michael. *The Rise of the Conservative Legal Movement: The Battle for Control of the Law.* Princeton, NJ: Princeton University Press, 2008.

Terbeek, Calvin. "'Clocks Must Always Be Turned Back': Brown v. Board of Education and the Racial Origins of Constitutional Originalism." *American Political Science Review* 115, no. 3 (2021): 821–34.

Texas Higher Education Coordinating Board. "Report on the Effects of the Hopwood Decision on Minority Applications, Offers, and Enrollments at Public Institutions of Higher Education in Texas." Austin: Texas Higher Education Coordinating Board, 1998.

Texas Legislature Online. "SB 1419/HB 588 Legislative History, Session 75(R)," 1997. https://capitol.texas.gov.

The College Board. "Descriptor Plus: Educational Neighborhood Clusters and High School Clusters," 2001. http://secure-media.collegeboard.org.

Thomas, Clarence. "Affirmative Action Goals and Timetables: Too Tough? Not Tough Enough!" *Yale Law & Policy Review* 5, no. 2 (1987): 402–11.

Thompson, J. Phillip, and Sarah Tobias. "The Texas Ten Percent Plan." *American Behavioral Scientist* 43, no. 7 (April, 2000): 1121–38.

Tienda, Marta, Kevin T. Leicht, Teresa Sullivan, Michael Maltese, and Kim Lloyd. "Closing the Gap?: Admissions and Enrollments at the Texas Public Flagships before and after Affirmative Action." Texas Higher Education Opportunity Project, January 21, 2003.

Traub, James. "The Class of Prop. 209." *New York Times Magazine*, May 2, 1999.

University of California Board of Regents. "Policy Ensuring Equal Treatment Admissions (SP-1)," July 20, 1995.

———. "Regents Policy 2102: Policy on Undergraduate Admissions," May 20, 1988.

University of California Office of the President. "Memo to Members of the Committee on Educational Policy: Proposal for Comprehensive Review in Undergraduate Admissions," November 7, 2001.

———. "Undergraduate Access to the University of California After the Elimination of Race-Conscious Policies," March 2003.

University of California Outreach Task Force, Office of the President. "Report to University of California Board of Regents, 'New Directions for Outreach.'" University of California, July 1997.

University of Michigan. "New U-M Undergraduate Admissions Process to Involve More Information, Individual Review." *UMich News*, August 27, 2003.

———. "Preliminary U-M Admissions Figures Report Record-Setting Number of Applications for the Incoming Freshman Class of Fall 2007." *UMich News*, May 25, 2007.

———. "U-M Applications, Projected Freshman Enrollment at All-Time High." *UMich News*, June 30, 2010.

———. "UM Enrollment up in 2007–08." *UMich News*, November 1, 2007.

University of Michigan Office of the Registrar. "Ethnicity Reports/Undergraduate Enrollment by Ethnicity," 2015.

Valelly, Richard M. *The Two Reconstructions: The Struggle for Black Enfranchisement.* 1st ed. University Of Chicago Press, 2004.

Villafranca, Armando. "Bush Extols Hispanic Businesses, Reiterates Opposition to Quotas." *Houston Chronicle*, October 4, 1997.

Wade-Golden, Katrina, and John Matlock. "Working through the Challenge—Critical Lessons Learned for Building and Sustaining a Robust Institutional Diversity Culture." In *Implementing Diversity: Contemporary Challenges and Best Practices at Predominantly White Universities*, edited by Helen Neville, Margaret Browne Huntt, and Jorge Chapa, 1–20. Urbana: University of Illinois Press, 2010.

Walt, K., and R. Hughes. "Minorities Say They Might Ax Funding for UT." *Houston Chronicle*, May 22, 1997.

Warikoo, Natasha. *The Diversity Bargain.* Chicago: University of Chicago Press, 2016.

Watkins, Matthew. "Man behind Fisher Affirmative Action Case Files New Lawsuit against UT-Austin." *Texas Tribune*, June 27, 2017.

Weiss, Kenneth. "UC Proposes Push to Ready Disadvantaged for College." *Los Angeles Times*, May 21, 1997.

Werder, Ryan. "Affirmative Action and Reaction in Michigan." *Nation*, January 25, 2007.

William, Christopher. "Ignoring the Soul of Brown: Board of Education v. Dowell." *North Carolina Law Review* 70, no. 2 (1992): 615–40.

Williamson, Joy Ann. *Black Power on Campus: The University of Illinois, 1965–75.* Urbana: University of Illinois Press, 2013.

Willon, Phil. "Voters Reject Prop. 16, Which Would Have Allowed Affirmative Action Policies in California." *Los Angeles Times*, November 4, 2020.

Wilson, Peter. "Statement to the Regents, University of California Board of Regents Meeting," July 20, 1995.

Woodward, C. Vann. *The Strange Career of Jim Crow.* Oxford University Press, 1955.

Zackin, Emily. *Looking for Rights in All the Wrong Places: Why State Constitutions Contain America's Positive Rights.* Princeton, NJ: Princeton University Press, 2013.

# INDEX

Page numbers in italics indicate figures and tables.

# ABOUT THE AUTHOR

LAUREN S. FOLEY is Assistant Professor in the Department of Political Science at Western Michigan University.

www.ingramcontent.com/pod-product-compliance
Lightning Source LLC
Chambersburg PA
CBHW020539030426
42337CB00013B/914